"Introduction" © Mark Waid

"Mary Batson and the Chimera Society" © Gail Simone

"Summers and Winters, Frost and Fire" © Seanan McGuire

"Tripping Through the Looking Glass, Stepping Into Gotham City: Cosplay, Creation, and Community" © Erica McGillivray

"A Matter of When" © Carla Speed McNeil

"The Other Side of the Desk" © Rachel Edidin

"Nineteen Panels About Me and Comics" © Sara Ryan

"I'm Batman" © Tammy Garrison

"My Secret Identity" © Caroline Pruett

"The Green Lantern Mythos: A Metaphor for My (Comic Book) Life" © Jill Pantozzi

"Vampirella, or: How I Learned to Stop Worrying and Love the Page Turn" © Jen Van Meter

"Confessions of a (Former) Unicorn" © Tara O'Shea

"The Evolution of a Tart" © Sheena McNeil

"Kitty Queer" © Sigrid Ellis

"The Captain in the Capitol: Invoking the Superhero in Daily Life" © Jennifer Margret Smith

"Burn, Baby Burn" © Lloyd Rose

"Tune in Tomorrow" © Sue D

"Comic Book Junkie" © Jill Thompson

"From *Pogo* to *Girl Genius*" © Delia Sherman

"I am Sisyphus, and I am Happy" © Kelly Thompson

"Captain America's Next Top Model" © Anika Dane Milik

"Me vs. Me" © Sarah Kuhn

"A Road That has No Meaning: Revenge in *Sandman*" © Sarah Monette

"Mutants" © Marjorie Liu

"You're on the Global Frequency" © Elizabeth Bear

"Crush on a Superhero" © Colleen Doran

Published by Mad Norwegian Press (www.madnorwegian.com).
Edited by Lynne M. Thomas and Sigrid Ellis.
Editor-in-Chief: Lars Pearson.
Cover art by Katy Shuttleworth.
Jacket & interior design by Christa Dickson.

ISBN: 978-1935234050

Printed in Illinois. First Printing: April 2012.

Also available from Mad Norwegian Press...

*Chicks Dig Time Lords: A Celebration of Doctor Who
by the Women Who Love It,*
edited by Lynne M. Thomas and Tara O'Shea
2011 Hugo Award Winner, Best Related Work

*Chicks Unravel Time: Women Journey Through Every Season
of Doctor Who,* edited by Deborah Stanish and LM Myles (forthcoming)

*Whedonistas: A Celebration of the Worlds of Joss Whedon by the Women
Who Love Them,* edited by Lynne M. Thomas and Deborah Stanish

Redeemed: The Unauthorized Guide to Angel (ebook only)
by Lars Pearson and Christa Dickson

Dusted: The Unauthorized Guide to Buffy the Vampire Slayer
by Lawrence Miles, Lars Pearson and Christa Dickson

Resurrection Code
All-new prequel to the AngeLINK novel series
by Lyda Morehouse

*Wanting to Believe: A Critical Guide to The X-Files, Millennium
and The Lone Gunmen* by Robert Shearman

*Running Through Corridors: Rob and Toby's Marathon Watch
of Doctor Who* (Vol. 1: The 60s) by Robert Shearman and Toby Hadoke

AHistory: An Unauthorized History of the Doctor Who Universe
(3rd Edition forthcoming)
by Lance Parkin and Lars Pearson

The About Time Series
by Tat Wood and Lawrence Miles
About Time 1: The Unauthorized Guide to Doctor Who (Seasons 1 to 3)
About Time 2: The Unauthorized Guide to Doctor Who (Seasons 4 to 6)
About Time 3: The Unauthorized Guide to Doctor Who
(Seasons 7 to 11) [2nd Edition now available]
About Time 4: The Unauthorized Guide to Doctor Who (Seasons 12 to 17)
About Time 5: The Unauthorized Guide to Doctor Who (Seasons 18 to 21)
About Time 6: The Unauthorized Guide to Doctor Who
(Seasons 22 to 26, the TV Movie)
About Time 7 (forthcoming)

For the women who went first, who paved the way for today.
For the women who work in comics now, inspiring the next generation.
For all the women and girls who dig comics.

This is your book.

Table of Contents

Introduction by Mark Waid

To you, Reader, the title of this book might evoke a good, hearty "well, duh." I think it will. I hope it does, given how mainstream comics are today. But as a man fast approaching 50, I have to tell you that had *Chicks Dig Comics* been written when I was growing up, it would have been shelved under Fiction. Shortly after the invention of comic books, during their heyday in the 1940s, chicks definitely dug comics. Boys and girls by the millions devoured these dime pamphlets about superheroes, about cowboys, about science fiction and funnymen and funny animals and all sorts of other things. There was a comic for every taste and every upbringing.

Then came television, and it bulldozed comics.

Cartoons were no longer limited to comic books and rare nights at the movie theater. They were available right in kids' living rooms at the turn of a dial. Same with heroes of the Wild West, spacemen with ray-guns, soap operas, romances, and everything else a young boy or girl might find enthralling. And as long as those urchins had access to a TV, the stories were better than the ones in their comic books; they moved and had sound and, maybe best of all, they were free. Before long there wasn't any money to be made in competing on the newsstand with illustrated adventures of knights and archers and interplanetary swash-bucklers. By the 1970s, when I began my lifelong love affair with comics, the one genre that it did better than television – superheroes – was by far the predominant one. Comics and superheroes had become so synonymous that to this day our parents still assume all comics are about guys in tights and capes. The problem, of course, was that superheroes were designed specifically to entertain boys. Generation upon generation of girls, when given any regard at all by comics publishers, were asked to make do with (shudder) *Archie* or, alternately... well, nothing.

Don't get me wrong. Certainly, girls could enjoy superhero comics. Judging by the fan mail pages published, many did. But if there were any in a 500-mile radius of me when I was an adolescent, they were well-hidden. In the 1970s and '80s, I can promise you that the general public considered comic books (a) as much for boys as Barbies were "for girls," and (b) no kid sister or female schoolmate I ever met had done much more than page through one here and there, probably by accident.

Wait, it gets worse.

As the 1980s and '90s continued to whittle this former mass medium down into a niche market, publishers realized to their horror that once its little-boy audience grew too old for comic books, the industry was doomed. These not-terribly-farsighted publishers doubled down on their existing demographic, "solving" the problem by allowing superheroes to "grow up" with their readers. Stories became more sophisticated and more complex. But they also became more overtly sexualized and pandering, full of busty super-babes and male power fantasies, and even less about anything your average female high school or college student could take even remotely seriously. Comics had become the very definition of nerdboy-Peter Pan culture, and if you think that in the early 1980s when I was in college and eager to get laid that I'd have risked being seen wearing a Flash T-shirt and reading a *Captain America* comic in public by any eligible girl anytime, anywhere, you're insane.

And then Neil Gaiman came along and saved our collective ass.

I overgeneralize. As you'll no doubt read in some of the essays before you here, Gaiman and his legendary and multiple-award-winning *Sandman* series – a beautifully told fantasy/horror myth that had as little to do with capes and spandex as possible (I say to the four of you out there unfamiliar with it) – became comics' unquestioned gateway drug for hundreds of thousands of young female readers worldwide. And those readers, charmed by the magic of the medium, didn't leave once they were done with *Sandman*. They stayed on to create a new audience hungry for comics of all types. Terry Moore's *Strangers in Paradise*. Marjane Satrapi's *Persepolis*. Daniel Clowes's *Ghost World*. Bill Willingham's *Fables*. And, yes... *Batman* and *Spider-Man*, still. (Again, no one's saying that women aren't allowed to dig superhero comics. It's just that, in my experience, they'd appreciate a little more consumer choice.)

It is now 2011 and, yesterday, I accompanied my girlfriend to the Midwestern university at which she teaches so I could sit in on one of her lectures. It was about Gene Luen Yang's *American Born Chinese*, a graphic novel for young adults that placed in the 2006 National Book Awards. My girlfriend, who wears Green Lantern jewelry, a Luke Skywalker jacket, and Dr. Horrible T-shirts, is a full-fledged and unapologetic geek for nerd culture, and the fact that she even exists is not the best part of this story.

It's that, of all those students, two of those students were men. The rest were women. And they could not have been more captivated or come away hungrier to read more comics. I don't know where they were when I was 12, but I don't care. What matters is that they – *you* – are here now.

I'm sorry the comics medium left you for a while, but it's back now, more interesting and diverse than ever. But don't take my word for it. Read on.

Mark Waid
Fortress of Solitude, Indiana Annex, 2011

Mark Waid has been a comics professional for nearly three decades. Though he has served as an editor, a chief creative officer, a publisher, and a production guru, he is best known as a writer, having authored some of the best-selling American graphic novels of all time, including the multiple award-winning *Kingdom Come* from DC Comics. Further biographical information, including his comics "how-to" blog essays, can be found at markwaid.com.

Editors' Foreword

The title of this book describes a phenomenon so manifestly self-evident that we find it difficult to come up with more to say on the topic. Heck, the title isn't even original: The Sequential Tarts' website, Tara O'Shea (Lynne's co-editor for the Hugo Award-winning *Chicks Dig Time Lords*), and Kate Tapley (maker of cute tote bags on Zazzle) all came up with it, as well at different points in time. Clearly, we hit a bit of a zeitgeist. Yet what may be self-evident to us is clearly not so to a portion of the industry.

We decided that the best response was to throw a louder party.

Chicks dig comics.

Women and girls read, buy, collect, love, write, draw, produce, edit, letter, color, dream, and really, *really*, dig comics. Reminding people of this fact is so incredibly easy, we thought we'd make a book about it. As editors, we had no difficulty finding contributors; on the contrary, we had to regretfully turn people away. There are a lot of us out there. We are legion.

If you dig comics, we're here to let you know that you're in good company. Lots and lots of it. If you don't dig comics yet, but you're looking for places to start, this volume has lots of options: fantastic characters and stories to fall in love with, creators to seek out and enjoy. We are not monolithic. There is no one-size-fits-all female comic fan. We've done our best to show not only the diversity of comics as a medium, but of its fans. Some women found their way to comics through *Pogo*, others through *Vampirella*. Some fell in love with Green Lantern, and others with Aquaman. Women express their love of comics through writing or drawing them professionally, through cosplay, through criticism, fan fiction, and the organization of conventions devoted to comics.

Each contributor speaks the comics-based truth as he or she has come to understand it. Some find their own reflection in stories that resonate. Others seek solace in heroes that can be braver than they are. Some of our essayists are having a great time and good-natured discussions with fellow fans. All our contributors, male and female, share with you the fundamental ways in which comic books have molded and changed their lives. Because comics *do* that.

We're here to tell you why we love this medium and the sheer variety of stories that can be told using it.

Turn the page, and join the celebration.

Mary Batson
and the Chimera Society

Gail Simone is a critically acclaimed and multiple award-winning author of comic books and animation, including fan-favorite runs on such titles as *Wonder Woman, Birds of Prey, Deadpool, Secret Six,* and *The Simpsons.* She is also an outspoken voice on social issues.

"It's just comics."

I have lost count of how many times I've heard this expression. Sometimes, it is prefaced with the exhortation to "Relax," or, "Take a chill pill," despite the seeming scarcity of these alleged pills at my local Rite-Aid. Sometimes, the word "comics" is replaced by the archaic and increasingly inaccurate term, "funnybooks."

If you get into an argument on the Internet over whether or not Iron Man's armor should have a nose, be prepared for an endless harangue of discourse from outraged readers, no matter which position you post (I'm pro-noses, as a comfort issue). But if you should dare to post a question about ethics, or about a lack of inclusion in modern comics, then you can fully expect that readers will immediately circle the wagons and go into shutdown mode. Inevitably, you will be told that, yes, "It's just comics."

And it's true, of course. It *is* just comics.

Except when it's more.

I apologize for personalizing this essay, considering the distinguished company I inexplicably find myself in by being invited to participate. But as I lack the remarkable breadth of research that, say, a Trina Robbins has, I have to view the movement of women in comics through my own crack-addled eyes. I'm looking at the role women have played as creators and as characters in the books themselves through three separate points in my life, and I'm now wondering if we somehow won the war when I wasn't looking, and the opposing side just hasn't made it official, yet. It seems women have quietly infiltrated everything to do with comics. The evil plan is working. I happily offer my services as flag waver.

I also humbly offer my flawed and microscopic perspective on the question of "Why aren't there more females in comics?" as witnessed up close and personally. The answer seems to be evolving.

Portrait of the Essayist as a Goofy Fangirl

When I was a little girl, I lived on a farm in rural Oregon. No television, and not much to do. We were poor, so comics, even at the wonderfully low price points they had then, were a bit of a luxury. I would mainly get them in careless heaps at garage sales and the like. To this day, the "careless heap" is still my preferred storage method for comics – no Mylar bagger, *this* reader!

I remember getting a huge stack of reprint comics from somewhere... 100 page DC books and Marvel reprints of their classic Silver Age stuff. The stories just fascinated me, perhaps even more than the current, "real" (read that as "in continuity") stories. It offered a glimpse of history, a feeling that what I was reading was part of something bigger. How wonderful to find this alternate history that was at once bizarre and improbable, but also so much more just and entertaining than the real world. Who wouldn't prefer reading about the Blackhawks to grim reality?

The one problem was, even in my child's mind, I felt like comics had taken a huge step backwards. The Lois Lane in the Golden Age reprints was smarter and funnier and tougher than everyone else at the *Planet*, including Clark Kent. But the Lois of later years had lost that spark almost completely.

Characters like Hawkgirl and Mary Marvel were obviously valuable commodities in the Golden Age. Mary had her own comic filled with adventures that were actually *intended* to be read by young girls, something I felt never entered the minds of the otherwise very talented creators at Marvel, for example.

DC had its shameful parade of oddly unfemale-women, but in particular, those Marvel comics almost seemed to actively promote the message that women are all venal, selfish, boy-crazy, overly emotional, and not particularly bright. As much ground-breaking work as they did, reading the dialogue these guys gave the Wasp, Marvel Girl, and the Invisible Girl was cringe-inducing, even back then.

It didn't help that I didn't know any other girls who had this secret shame, this love of comics, at the time. A female comics fan was a chimera, and there was no evidence to the contrary for a long time to come. Every great once in a while there would be a girl's letter on the letters page, or a girl's name would appear in the credit box. These were extremely rare occurrences and I clung to them like the last life preserver on the *Titanic*.

It can't really be overstated – things were different for comics fans then. We grasped greedily at any real-world acknowledgement that our passion even existed. The idea that you could theoretically go to a theater and have your choice of several big-budget comic book adaptations at one time would have sent our heads into an orbit from which we would be unlikely to recover.

And having the temerity to be *female* and a comics fan, well, that's really simply not to be done. And so I, and I'm sure many others, adopted the early habit of creating my own stories featuring these characters – where once in a while, the girls won, or participated, even. Years later, I would hear a term from the fanfiction community to describe this practice: "headcanon." The mythology you make in your head when the real one doesn't quite include you.

Despite all that, I thought at the time that the problem was *recruitment*.

I thought, if enough women gave comics a try, a fair go, if they let Batman get to first base, things would really start to change. Of course, expecting everyone to love something just because you do is a creative and commercial dead end. But I was a goofy fangirl at the time, and didn't yet know that.

I Begin My Journey of Self-Discovery and Heat Vision

Later in life, comics had taken an ugly side road into a thicket of socio-sexually oddball shock stories. Following the massive and mainstream success of works like Frank Miller's *The Dark Knight Returns* and Alan Moore's *Watchmen*, some marketing genius decided that cruelty sells, and that the circus crowd wanted blood by the buckets. I'm not talking about horror comics, I'm talking about the typical superhero fare, with many titles seeming to go out of their way to present the most gruesome and pointlessly vicious tableaux.

Beloved characters were killed and mutilated *because* they were beloved. Batgirl, a cheerful, independent and optimistic character, blessed with photographic memory and her own agency (and a yellow purse, I think all crimefighters should carry a yellow purse) was shot in the spine in a home invasion story and discarded with all the care of a used tissue. The Joker actually takes her clothes off and takes pictures of her as she's bleeding, her spine ruined.

I was still a comics fan, but this story, and the even stupider ones to follow, shook my faith. I couldn't help feeling that, headcanon be damned, I'd been chumped into buying a product made by people who actively loathed me and my gender. I had made friends online with an executive at one of the big two companies and finally, I asked him flat out what percentage of the readership was female – he had no idea. No one knew, he said. What he didn't add was the obvious follow up – that no one cared. Comics were selling like crazy... who cared if only boys bought them?

So I started a website that became a bit of an unexpected phenomenon. *Women in Refrigerators* listed and discussed the trend, quite popular at the time, of killing and/or depowering longstanding females, often with a creepy and depressing sexual component. The site was covered in newspapers around the world, even in *Harper's Bazaar* (and it still sort of haunts me to this day, people wanting to debate it with me at cons as I'm on my way to the restroom).

The flood of bad PR brought thousands of female readers out of the woodwork. Many creators wrote and said that they too had been dismayed by this trend. And it clicked with people. Creators had to face that female readers existed, and that the Internet allowed them a voice they hadn't previously had.

To their surprising credit, rather than shout me down, the comics industry instead decided to give me a career as a writer. The trusting saps! Er, I mean, those lovable scamps!

I'd become aware through the Internet and the *WiR* website that female creators and readers and commentators did exist, and when I started getting regular work, I was thrilled to meet them. I imagined a sorority of like minds and purpose, and somehow imagined us all sipping lemonade by the Comics Girl Secret Fort immersion pool.

The reality was a bit disappointing. Despite some women having had positions of extreme power, like Publisher Jenette Kahn at DC Comics and Executive Editor Karen Berger at Vertigo, the actual "community" didn't seem to exist. There was a non-profit organization known as Friends of Lulu that seemed to intend on taking that role, to mixed reviews, but my experience was often a bit of a harsh wake-up call. While some female creators, like the aforementioned Trina Robbins and rising star Devin Grayson, could not have been more welcoming, others, even those who had supported my fan commentary, were plainly put out by the idea of another female writer – it was as though there were only room for one or two in the entirety of superhero comics. They had taken on the aspect of prisoners of war, and seemed to regard new inmates with a bit of open hostility.

At conventions I could go a full hour and never see another female. At the first "Females in Comics" panel I attended, there were nine women on the panel and four people in the audience, one of whom was my husband. Powerful talents like Lea Hernandez and Devin were routinely accused of having their work *actually* written by their husbands or boyfriends.

That was a dark time. But hopeful, too. A raft of British writers had brought a different, less exclusive, gender sensibility to comics. Warren Ellis wrote great bastards, but some of those bastards were powerful, fascinating women. And the popularity of *X-Men* and *New Teen Titans* and *Swamp Thing*, and perhaps most especially *Sandman*, said that change was coming... we might have to wait, but it was most definitely coming.

So I began to think the problem wasn't *recruitment*, but *content*.

Surely if the content was there, the women would follow?

And Now I Look and See Mary Batson Everywhere

The world changed and the companies haven't yet figured out how to exploit it, exactly. *Twilight* and *Harry Potter* and manga have shown females will purchase genre books with a vengeance if given the opportunity and an enticing enough read.

The female readership is there, and growing. It's our only growth demo in a tough economy.

I think that battle is over. That snowball isn't going to stop rolling downhill.

Many, if not most, of the best commentators on comics online and in podcasts are now female. The fan community is female in percentages unimaginable just a few years ago. Aspiring female creators come to us for advice in numbers equal to males, a good sign for the future. And most wonderfully, a list of names like Ivory Madison, Nicola Scott, Sara Pichelli, Marjorie M. Liu, Amy Reeder, Kelly Sue DeConnick, Kathryn Immonen, Amanda Conner and many more not only produce topnotch work, but have discovered something lovely... the audience doesn't care what their gender is, even if some publishers still struggle with it on occasion.

And that's just superhero comics. The webcomics, manga, and independent realms have not just female parity, but often dominance.

Comic conventions are run for and by females now. After attending the latest San Diego Comic-Con, I can't even express how *female* it all felt, how so many booths sold products aimed at females, how girls were buying the books and weren't dragged there by their boyfriends. How the LGBTQ community has gained such a powerful voice despite years of being intentionally ignored and sidelined.

It feels a bit like birth.

It's thrilling.

Oh, there are slip-ups. A recent huge initiative to re-launch the DC Universe titles somehow managed to employ only two women out of almost a hundred creators. There are still an awful lot of costumes and covers and poses that seem wholly about the male gaze to the exclusion of all else. And there are still few women being given the opportunity to work on the icon-level titles.

But the war is over. The readers know it. The smart retailers know it. The companies that make the comics are flailing about a little bit, but even they know it. They are going to have to produce product that the female reader enjoys to survive.

I can't tell you how different that is from when I started, or even further back, when I was a little girl and such a thing could only be imagined in the mind of a kid who thought it made perfect sense for Batgirl to wear high heels when fighting.

So, the problem has evolved again. We have a female audience, and it's growing. They are *recruiting* themselves without our help. They are directing the *content* with their dollars.

But now we still have an odd holdout. *Acknowledgement.*

There are still people in power, at every level, who don't see what's directly in front of them. As an example, I recently attended a lovely convention in Calgary, Canada. The audience had a tremendous female contingent, and I was at my booth in Artist's Alley signing hundreds and hundreds of comics for women and girls both.

At one point, my husband struck up a conversation with a young man right in front of my booth. I had 12 women in my signing line. Looking down my row, every single artist, mostly male, had at least one female in line for an autograph or sketch, *every single one*, and many had several. There were also at least two other hugely popular female creators, the gifted Amanda Conner and the wonderful Agnes Garbowska, each with long lines of women ready to buy things from them.

In the very epicenter of that, the young man turned to my husband and said, "I don't care what anyone says, women are never going to read comics."

We won the war. But it may take a while for the opponent to realize he's got a musket ball right through his awareness.

I can wait.

I get to see the female readers and talk to them. And I know that comics mean as much to them as they did to me, as much to them as comics have meant to male readers.

I have spoken with women who were inspired by Wonder Woman to get in shape, or to leave abusive relationships. I've spoken with women who used comics to get through chemo, or to survive the loss of a loved one. I've talked to women who were inspired by female comics creators to make their own art and stories. I've seen the love in the cosplayer's art, and the passion in the female comics retail employees who hand-sell the comics they believe in every day. And yes, I've spoken with several women who felt that comics had helped them through potentially life-ending depressions.

One of those women made something I wrote for *Wonder Woman* into her personal mantra:

Keep Faith.

Trust to Love.

Fight with Honor.

But fight to *win*.

Comics, the good ones, they can inspire, they can fire the imagination, they can please the senses and the heart and feed the soul. They have a healing power, an emotional heft. I'm still crazy about them after all this time. The transformative and creative power they have held over my life can't possibly be overstated, and there are thousands out there who feel the same.

So, yes, absolutely. "It's just comics."

Except when it's more.

Summers and Winters, Frost and Fire

Seanan McGuire is an award-winning urban fantasy and science fiction author from Northern California, where she has learned to love reptiles and fear weather. Her comic collection began when she was nine, with back issues of *ElfQuest*, *X-Men*, and *Amethyst, Princess of Gemworld*. Her fate was sealed, however, when her mother brought home a box of old Warren comics from a yard sale. Since then, she has become a devoted regular at her local comic store (Flying Colors Comics and Other Cool Stuff), acquired more Marvel comics than anyone likes to think about, and memorized the Summers family tree. Her current favorite titles are *Hack/Slash*, *The Boys*, *Fables*, *Girl Genius*, and *X-Men: Legacy*.

If you ever want to start a fight in a room full of female *X-Men* fans, all you have to do is ask the question that makes my comic book store clerks quail with fear: "Who do you think Cyclops should wind up with? Jean Grey or Emma Frost?" It seems like *every* girl who follows the X-Men has an opinion, even the ones whose opinion is "Scott Summers should keep it in his pants and let us worry about Wolverine's love life for a little while." A friend of mine has this whole elaborate theory of predicting personality types based on the Jean/Emma divide (and it works, too, which is the scary part). It's a big deal.

Jean Grey, for the unaware – those DC fans in the audience – was one of the original X-Men, along with Cyclops, Angel, Beast, Iceman, and Professor X. Her role on the team was vital: She was the token girl. That was her purpose, her personality, and her reason for being. Every team needs a girl, right?

Jean had red hair and green eyes and was beautiful and smart and good and basically perfect. So perfect, in fact, that most of the girls I knew either loved her or hated her, because we could never compare. All of the original X-Men fell in love with her at one point or another, including Professor X, as did many of the newer X-Men, but it was Scott Summers who won her heart. This is important.

Moving on to powers: Jean started out as a telekinetic. Later, she developed telepathy, increasing her power level. This was followed by a much larger power jump, one which merged her with the eternal Phoenix Force, creator and destroyer of universes. As Phoenix, Jean could fly, rearrange matter on a subatomic level, read minds, and look good in skintight red spandex. She kept gaining and losing the power of the Phoenix (and dying, or supposedly dying, or whatever) until Grant Morrison's run on *New X-Men* in the early 2000s, where, having been stranded on Asteroid M, Wolverine stabbed her in the gut rather than allow her to burn to death. Jean Grey died for real, re-awoke as the Phoenix, saved the day, was killed again by Magneto, and was buried, allowing her spirit to ascend to the White Hot Room.

You with me so far? Good.

Now, Jean may have been the *first* girl associated with the X-Men, but she didn't stay the only girl for long. By the time she died (for the last time), there were dozens of female mutants running around the various X-titles, including one who was vying for Jean's place in Scott's heart: Emma Frost, the ice-cold former White Queen of the Hellfire Club. Emma, like Jean, was a telepath. And that's about where the similarities end. Rather than being a sweet redheaded All-American girl, Emma Frost was a controlling blonde, born into money and descended from there into depravity. She was practically a cautionary tale for young mutants: Be good, or this will happen to you, too.

Emma was introduced much later than Jean – 1979, as opposed to 1963 – and was originally a villain, which is why she was able to get away with buying all her clothing from Frederick's of Hollywood. Bondage gear is *totally* a costume when you're a bad guy! She never really managed to hold onto a code name, either. She was occasionally called "the White Queen," but that's hard to shout on a battlefield. As her redemption progressed, she became one of the two instructors for the students of Generation X, and started getting called "Headmistress" a lot. After the Gen X kids split up, she moved to Genosha, where she worked for Magneto, teaching young mutants how to handle their powers.

Here's the fast-forward sequence of events from there: Sentinels attack Genosha, oh no! Everybody dies! Except for Emma, whose secondary mutation[1] is triggered by the trauma, giving her the ability to transform into living organic diamond! Lacking anywhere else to go, she turns to the X-Men! Scott and Jean are having marital troubles, on

---

1. Morrison has said that he chose Emma Frost, and gave her the secondary mutation, solely because Colossus was dead at the time and he needed a bruiser. So thanks for dying, Colossus. I owe you one.

account of Jean periodically being an untouchable cosmic force, and him wanting to live a normal-ish life! Emma and Scott start having a telepathic affair! Jean finds out! Jean and Emma have a big fight! Jean dies! Scott and Emma officially become a couple, causing half the female X-fans to go "Yay!" while the other half shriek in anguish! And that brings us, basically, to the present day: Jean is dead, Scott is with Emma, and open war is raging in the margins.

Now, there are a lot of "religious wars" in the comic book world. Marvel vs. DC. Spider-Man vs. Iron Man. The Fantastic Four vs. the X-Men... and yes, I am aware that two of my three schisms are within Marvel Comics. I'm a Marvel girl, and have been since I was eight years old, when the owner of my local comic book store[2] started slipping old issues of *Alpha Flight* into the twenty-five cent comic box. From there, I quickly found my way to the X-Men, the super team that would hold my loyalty for the rest of my life. (Please note that when I say "the X-Men," I mean any and all teams belonging to the extended mutant family. X-Force, X-Factor, the New Mutants, the Exiles, X-Statix, Generation X... I love them all.)

Here were these people who had absolutely no say in whether they became superheroes – they didn't become scientists (the fastest way to get superhuman abilities, at least in the Marvel Universe), or worse, date scientists; they didn't develop strange medical conditions that could only be cured with experimental treatments; they didn't pick up mysterious canes and utter mystic phrases. They were just born, and because they were born different, they could never fit in with the world. So they became heroes, protecting a world that hated and feared them. As a weird little girl who really *empathized* with the plight of the Midwich Cuckoos, this was enormously appealing to me.

The problem, for me, was Jean Grey. She was too perfect. I couldn't find a way to make a connection with her, or to see her as anything other than this impossible ideal I could never live up to. There's a certain degree of "too perfect" that goes on with all comic book characters – how many women that thin do *you* know? And how many of them live on pizza and popcorn, practically the only things comic book women are ever drawn eating? – but Jean had it worse than most. She always had the best hair, the cutest clothes, the sweetest smile. Even

---

2. My local comic book store is Flying Colors Comics and Other Cool Stuff, owned by Joe Fields, the man who created Free Comic Book Day. He's a great guy, and very dedicated to the idea of spreading comics to the next generation. He says that I'm one of his long-term investment plans. He's not wrong.

when she destroyed a planet (yes, a planet), all the boys were willing to stand up for her. I'm sure it was supposed to look like teamwork, but I started asking whether she was using her telepathy to make everyone love her when I was nine. (Seriously. I asked the guys at my comic book store.)

Enter Emma, stage left. Emma Frost was – and is – a genuinely conflicted character, someone motivated more by doing what's right for herself, and for the kids in her care, than by doing what seems like the "heroic" thing to do. After her first group of students, the Hellions, was killed, she became even more committed to keeping the children in her care alive. She's got the perfect face and flawless body of any mutant... but freely admits to using plastic surgery and hair dye to keep herself in that condition. She's shown her willingness, repeatedly, to put herself in danger when her students require it, and the rest of the time, she demonstrates a pragmatism that is appealing because it's so unusual. Save the world? Only after she saves herself, darling, only after she saves herself.

Comparisons between Jean and Emma were, and are, inevitable. Emma may as well have been created as the anti-Jean, at least at first. Jean was modest and innocent; Emma was half-naked and wanton. Jean was heroic; Emma was villainous. The trouble was, when you're starting from Jean's position, there's nowhere to really *go*. There's a reason most perfect fairy tale princesses disappear after the Happily Ever After. Developing Jean's character beyond "the girl, the one everyone loves, you know, the one you wish you could be" would actually have damaged her character, taking away the very core that supposedly made her so appealing.

Emma, on the other hand, was allowed to develop and change. She was allowed to grow as a person – something that's relatively rare in any fictional medium, and almost unheard of in superhero team comics, which are, after all, four-color soap operas full of evil twins and missing babies and everything else my mother used to love about *All My Children*. Our version of Erica Kane might throw fireballs or read your mind, but at the end of the day, she was still a woman in a soap opera universe, playing by soap opera rules. Emma seemed to flaunt those rules almost from day one, going from cardboard villain to sardonic anti-heroine with grace and snide humor. And she did it all while she was wearing three-inch heels.

By now, you should know which side of the divide I come down on. I'm an Emma Frost girl, through and through. I have all the issues of her short-lived solo series, as well as the trade paperback collections. I have a picture of her, framed, on my bedroom wall. I even have the fantastic anime-style statuette of her that was released in January 2011. She sits on the shelf above my workspace, guarding my computer from disk failure. (Before I start sounding like a total obsessive, please note that my bedroom walls also play host to a *Nocturnals* poster, as well as a lot of art people have done for me of my own characters. I even have the cover of *Velveteen vs. Everything* #5, and that's a comic that doesn't exist. Emma shares her shelf with an Allosaurus and a creepy wasp-girl. So I'm not obsessive, I'm just weird.)

Now, I have friends who are on the Jean side of the fence, and we sometimes try to explain things to each other. This sometimes ends with hair-pulling and shouts of "Home-wrecker!" and "Genocidal bitch!", but those are the bad days. Most of the time, we just spend a few hours laughing about all the things we have in common, and agree that our love for different Marvel telepaths is really not a big enough deal to come between us. Besides, they always say, Jean's coming back. Jean always comes back.

They have a point there, I'm afraid. The revolving-door nature of death in the Marvel Universe is well-established enough for the books themselves to make fun of it. When Theresa Cassidy's father was killed, she didn't attend the funeral; wouldn't, in fact, even admit that he was dead. It took several years of Banshee not showing up before she would admit that this time, really and for truly, her father wasn't coming home. Sorry, Theresa. I guess your father was too second-string to rate a resurrection. So why wouldn't a character named "Phoenix" come riding back in to pick things up where she left off?

Do not want. But there are reasons for that, I promise. First off, and most likely to get things thrown at me, I like Scott a lot better with Emma than I do with Jean. Because Jean needed to stay perfect, Scott needed to stay perfect when he was with her. Scott and Jean together are so perfect that they become boring, him the hero with the iron jaw, her the beautiful heroine, both of them striking a pose against an inexplicable sunset. If I thought there was a chance that a resurrected Jean would finally go, "You know what? Screw this. I'm going to Canada," and go bang Wolverine's brains out, I might be more interested in seeing her climb out of her grave again, just because it would be something *new*.

What's more, and this is a bit of me defending Jean – which, believe me, is way weirder for me than it is for anybody else – bringing her back would rob her death of its meaning. Right now, Jean Grey has one of the few truly meaningful deaths in the Marvel Universe. She's been dead for more than six calendar years (Morrison's run on *New X-Men* killed her in 2004), and she died saving New York City, and possibly the world. Upon her death, she was finally able to transcend the flaws enforced upon the Phoenix Force by her mortal state, and became a White Phoenix of the Crown. She now helps to shape reality from her new home in the White Hot Room.

So... meaningful death, followed by confirmed ascension to a higher plane, where she actively works to make the universe run more smoothly? (We have, in fact, already seen Jean manipulate timelines to prevent an apocalyptic future from occurring. Not to worry, this is the X-Men; we'll have a new apocalyptic future in a minute. Ding! One apocalypse for table four.) Why, exactly, are Jean's *fans* the ones clamoring for her return? I'd think that the people who really adored her would want her to stay gone, giving her the sort of happy ending that dozens of senselessly slaughtered characters can only dream about.

And it's not like her impact on Scott's life has been somehow wiped away by his relationship with Emma Frost. For one thing, Scott and Jean's daughter from an alternate timeline, Rachel, is still running around, although she's currently in outer space. Scott's son with Jean's clone was recently killed, but he died defending a girl named Hope who may or may not be the salvation of the mutant race (signs point to yes), and is now remembered as a hero. Scott and Jean Summers changed the world in ways that will last pretty much as long as the X-Men are around. That isn't going to change.

At the same time... I'm going to take a moment here and quote *Uncanny X-Men* writer Matt Fraction: "Jean [Grey] was the great love of Scott's youth. Emma is the love of his life. She brings out the best in him and he brings out the best in her."

For me, that sums up the Jean/Emma divide nicely. Jean was the love of Scott's youth. She was good for him, back when they could both be innocent and young and know that Professor X would always be there to catch them. Jean was what he needed. But when the Scarlet Witch rewrote reality[3] during *House of M*, and everyone got what they wanted most in the world, Scott didn't get Jean back. He got Emma with a ring on her finger. He knew that it was time to let Jean go, and move on.

Okay, so now we've established that I think Jean Grey should stay

---

3. Marvel Comics: Where needing a flowchart to understand what's going on isn't just normal, it's basically the status quo.

dead. Fine. Assuming that Marvel Comics actually allows her to stay gone, why is that an argument in favor of Emma Frost, a woman who never met a pair of thigh-high boots she didn't like? I've actually had people tell me, with great seriousness, that if I were a *true* female comic fan, I would hate Emma, who sets back the cause of women in comics 20 years every time she steps onto the page. If I were a *true* female comic fan, I would find better characters to adore, like Psylocke, whose costume is basically a one-piece leotard that leaves both her buttocks fully exposed, or Husk, whose powers leave her naked half the time.

Um. Thanks, but no thanks. At least Emma practices consistent costume design, however impractical that costume design may happen to be. Besides, I find this particular attitude to be a little disturbing, because it's saying that we want more women in comics, we want more women in positions of authority in comics (Emma is currently the X-Men co leader), but we want them to be the right *kind* of women. Nice girls. Girls who don't wear low cut shirts, or swear, or do naughty things. The phrase "well-behaved women rarely make history" has been bandied about enough to become a cliché, but somehow, this doesn't stop us from only wanting good role models in our comics.

Emma Frost chose the side of the angels of her own free will, because she was so devoted to the idea of training and nurturing the next generation of mutants. How is this not a good role model? She's not perfect – she's miles from perfect – but for me, that makes her all the better. True perfect isn't just boring; it's daunting. I could never be a Jean Grey. I wasn't born with that kind of terrifyingly intrinsic good-girl innocence.[4] But if I work hard enough, and I try to do the right thing for long enough, I might be able to be an Emma Frost.

For women to truly take our place in the comic world, I think we have to allow all types to exist. We need the Jeans *and* the Emmas. Also the Rachels, and the Kittys, the Illyanas and the Clarices and the Meggans. We need telepaths and bruisers, shapeshifters and elementalists, and we need them to have just as much freedom as their male counterparts. When Emma chooses to use her sexuality to her advantage, it shouldn't be any more shocking than it is when Gambit does the same thing – and yet it is. When Jean is swayed by the urge to naughtiness, it shouldn't be any more unforgiveable than it is when Scott feels those same urges – and again, right now, it is.

---

4. Amusingly enough, my best friend was born with that sort of terrifyingly intrinsic innocence. And she's a redhead. It doesn't matter how much I hate Jean Grey. I'm still going to invite her human avatar to my slumber parties.

Do I want Jean Grey to stay dead? Yes. I do. She was the female character we needed when the series began, and Emma Frost is the character we need now. But I do think, and this is one for the Jean fans, I do think that Emma, and all the other female characters of her generation, would not have been created if not for the existence of Jean Grey. Jean Grey and Sue Storm and Janet van Dyne, and all the other early female characters whose purpose was to be the team girl, they made all the wonderful, complex characters we have today possible. Without them, we'd probably be looking at an all-male playground even today.

The X-Men started with just one girl. Since then, they've become one of the best superhero franchises out there in terms of female characters. They have characters with every sort of power set, from the "isn't that girly" light manipulation and phasing to the bone-breaking psychic power armor and absolutely devastating transformation into a living dust storm. There are at least five female characters[5] active at any given time, and usually quite a few more than that. We owe a lot of this richness and depth to Jean Grey. And we owe her the opportunity to rest for a little while. Let Emma take care of things.

Oh, and on the topic of Rachel Summers, Scott and Jean's daughter from that alternate future that I mentioned? She's still out there. So is Ruby Summers, Scott and Emma's daughter from a different alternate future. Our X-Men family tree[6] just keeps getting more complicated, and that may well be the best part of all.

That, and the part where Jean Grey is still dead. Life as an X-girl is pretty good these days.

---

5. Currently active female characters, split between the various books: Emma Frost, the Stepford Cuckoos, Shadowcat, Armor, Dust, Pixie, Dazzler, Mercury, Husk, Domino, X-23, Wolfsbane, Banshee (formerly Siryn), M, Jubilee, Surge, Karma, Psylocke, Rogue, Hope, Layla Miller, Transonic, Ide, Magma, Moonstar, Frenzy, Blink, and I've almost certainly missed a few. These are just the characters currently seeing active duty, in one book or another.

6. I periodically attempt to explain the Summers family tree to people who don't read comics. They usually flee screaming right around the time the clones come into the conversation. And the clones come into the conversation really early on.

Tripping Through the Looking Glass, Stepping Into Gotham City: Cosplay, Creation, and Community

Erica McGillivray is a die-hard geek who spends a ridiculous amount of time being nerdy. She's president and marketing director of GeekGirlCon, a nonprofit that celebrates and supports geeky women with events and conventions. Erica's comic book collection is an earthquake hazard, and she reviews comics on her blog, *6'7" & Green*. In her other life, she's a community attache for SEOmoz, an Internet marketing software company; in lay speak, this means that she gets to tweet, blog, and answer Q&A forums about online marketing and tech for a living. Erica dreams of having a closet full of amazing cosplay costumes. She lives in Seattle.

Just a Normal Fangirl

I am an accidental cosplayer. I tripped over and fell into cosplay head first.

Of course, this is how I do things. This is why, for benefit of comics fandom, I need a T-shirt that says: "My pull list is bigger than yours." And why I spent hours searching for two belts in that perfect shade of sea foam green for a costume, and triumphantly expressed my joy to a confused retail clerk. When I commit to loving something, I want to create and share my love with everyone I know.

Despite this, I'd always been one of those fans that looked down on cosplayers. They were weirdos running around, sometimes in spandex and other poor fabric choices. I stood there judging them... while wearing the dark red shirt I'd bought because it reminded me of *Stargate Atlantis*'s Elizabeth Weir. Oh, I was over there amassing a comic book collection in the thousands and writing epic novels of fanfiction. Cosplay, however, was for weirdos.

So how did this completely normal fangirl end up doing cosplay that changed her fannish life? It began with a quest to better appreciate comic book art.

I write a comic book review blog where I routinely talk about what I'm reading, and pay special attention to women in comics. I've always been one to follow writers, a complete snob when it comes to the plots, characters and themes. Sure, some terrible art could sour a book. But I never threw a comic book at the wall because of the art. Mocked it relentlessly on Twitter, yes. Physical destruction, no.

Don't get me wrong, I love an art gallery; I get lost in them for hours. I minored in studio art and understand the commitment and the talent great art takes. But comic art? From my perspective, it wasn't "real" art, the sort you would hang on the wall next to an O'Keeffe or a Cézanne. It wasn't famous or lush. Often, I seriously wondered why some of these artists were even paid, especially when I'd see yet-another set of balloon breasts or a spine angle that looked like the character's vertebrae were ready to snap.

But occasionally, I'd run across an artist who made me happy, who made me wish for more great art in the books I read. "Amanda Conner," "David Aja" and "Michael Gaydos" were some of the first artist names I would remember – but while they were all very talented and clearly made my reading more enjoyable, if I wasn't sucked in by the story, I wouldn't have picked up a title with their art. I wouldn't add their newest books to my pull list without a good writer, and I *certainly* wasn't going to continue following a poorly written book if the art was pretty.

Then I read Greg Rucka's run on *Detective Comics* – when Batwoman had the lead role – and discovered the art of J.H. Williams III. I loved Williams's art as much as I loved Rucka's writing. I wanted Williams's work in prints hanging in my dining room. I wanted to read every book that Williams had penciled, and to cherish each moment while doing so. *Here* was what the comic medium was supposed to do: Tell a story with *both* words and art. Williams's layouts and pencils spoke just as loudly as Rucka's pen. His art was sharp, painfully beautiful, and engrossing.

If Rucka's writing credit and his having previously developed Kate Kane as Batwoman made me add *Detective Comics* to my pull list, Williams's and Rucka's work together brought it to a level beyond anything else I'd read. They made me fall in love with Batwoman and her world. She is a woman I can relate to: headstrong and a little rockabilly. More to the point, she reminded me of the women I date.

People in love do stupid things, or perhaps they do passionate things of the heart. But in the moment of vulnerability that I was feeling, a seed was planted. That seed grew into an idea, which became a costume. I wanted something more, something I could touch. I wanted to jump into the book and into Batwoman's world.

I thought it would be cool to dress up like Alice, the main villain in the story (now more commonly known as *Batwoman: Elegy*). Alice was a bit of an odd choice for me, as I'm not usually someone who loves villains. In most cases, I'm rooting for the hero – the one seeking justice and fairness in the world, like Wonder Woman or Steve Rogers as Captain America. But occasionally, a villain comes along who's just too fun to pass by: Alice, with her *Through the Looking Glass* quotes and mysterious past, was exactly that! So much about the character was mysterious... what happened to her after she was kidnapped? Who took her and converted her? Will we ever know?

I've talked to a lot of fellow cosplayers about why they chose the characters they did; beyond a sheer love of that character or story, many have expressed the uniqueness behind their translation of the character from page to cosplay. With obscure characters like Alice, it also serves as a way to find fellow fans of your favorite storyline. If another fan shouts out across the room at you, excited about your character, the costume serves as a secret handshake it's instant friendship and a conversation starter. Alice fell right in line as she'd never been cosplayed before, and is an obscure, new character. My costume would stand out, pay tribute, and help me tell people about the wonderful book that inspired me.

Being Alice

Unfortunately, cosplay costumes don't appear out of thin air. They take time and dedication. Most superhero clothing isn't on the rack at Target. Also, while comics can be a very solitary hobby sometimes, with interactions only coming from the computer screen, building a costume – for me anyway – took a community effort.

I emailed my friend Bonita, an engineer and a seamstress, to see if she was interested in this undertaking. With Emerald City Comicon in Seattle only a month away, Bonita and I headed to the fabric store, and later hung out in her sewing and *World of Warcraft* playing room. (I love the dichotomy of that room, which is dedicated to such a traditionally feminine pursuit and also to creating an avatar to go on magical/ mystical/ military quests online.) Bonita harnessed her powers to create a shirt and a cape for my costume. To show my eternal gratitude for her mad skills, I later baked her gluten-free cupcakes.

The day of the convention, Alice wouldn't have come together without my friend Gretchen and my mom. (Yes, my parents chose the weekend of the biggest comic book convention in the area for a visit.) Gretchen fastidiously worked on my makeup for three hours, her arsenal spread all over my dining room table. We kept comparing my face with the source material in the precious comic book, which sat a little too close to my purple eye shadow. My mom curled my hair and made last-minute adjustments on my costume. My stepfather compared the amount of effort to going to the prom, and I quickly informed him that in no way did I spend as much time getting prepared for prom. This was more important.

As we headed downtown to the convention, I kept checking and rechecking my makeup with my Wonder Woman compact. Alice's lips are white and red, and keeping my lips from turning into one pink smear was a struggle. Not to mention worrying about getting lipstick on my teeth. Normally, I don't wear makeup at all, and costume makeup is far fussier than day-to-day makeup. I needed to preserve myself like the panel in a comic book; art come to life.

I wore my costume proudly to the Emerald City convention, where I was more than nervous about the entire outing. Nervous, and lacking peripheral vision due to my cape – they don't tell you that in the super-hero cosplay handbooks. It also goes unsaid that you'll need someone else to carry all your stuff: those all-important con survival items like water bottles, peanut butter and honey sandwiches, and your purse.

Walking through those convention doors truly started my first cosplay experience. There was no going back now, and there was no being shy, as people always ask those in costume to pose for a photo. Though, as a bonus, we were fashionably late due to my taking so long getting ready, and didn't have to wait in long registration lines.

My nerves struck an all-time high as I made my way over to Rucka's and Williams's tables. Would I say something stupid? Would I make an idiot of myself or forget what I wanted to say? At least I knew from past comic conventions that Rucka was a nice guy, and polite to fans of his work.

So I walked up to the back of Rucka's line, waiting for my turn. But in cosplay, you can't hide – and he spotted me, instantly recognizing the costume from his book translated into real life. Rucka's first reaction was, "Oh my god, has Jim seen you?", and then he dragged me over to Williams's table. My Alice was a hit. Both of them really loved my costume, and I was a grinning fangirl.

Then there were photos of the three of us. Many photos. I think when you're in situations like this, everything is a blur. You have to maintain composure and smile, smile a *lot*, for all the cameras in the world are aimed at you. You have to be grateful and thankful – because you *are* – and to show your gratitude in a polite way. You have to think on your feet when Williams wants to know if you're also speaking in riddles, like Alice. (No, speaking in riddles is one step too far for me.) Both Williams and Rucka were extremely nice and very cool to this strange woman dressed like one of their characters.

Of course, I'd brought my comics to be signed. Specifically, the ones with the pages of Alice wearing the exact costume I'd drawn my own inspiration from. Rucka told me that they'd had more stories planned for Alice, but was unsure they'd ever be told, since their *Detective Comics* run had ended. (A couple weeks later, Rucka announced he was no longer working for or with DC Comics, and was leaving Batwoman's fate – and Alice's – in the capable hands of Williams. I still don't know if Alice's planned story will ever see daylight.)

The entire experience was amazing. *Amazing.* I feel like words cannot ever do my emotions justice. I was on top of the world for the rest of the day.

It didn't matter when my head started to hurt from my cape being too heavy, or that I almost fell over when someone stepped on my cape while he rushed toward the front of a panel room. Not many other people recognized me. I certainly didn't have my photo snapped in the same way a Green Lantern or Wolverine would. But most importantly, the creators loved my tribute to their character.

That most important moment still buzzed in my head later, when I met up with my parents. I excitedly showed them the photos from my camera, and told them what happened. We then took the bus home, where my extroverted parents informed everyone about my costume and my experience. It was as though I'd won an award and was 12 again, instead of an adult cosplaying a character from a comic book.

Moments like this will stay with me for my entire life, and I will cherish them. I will always look back at those photos, or put on the costume again, and be happy.

... but that wasn't what changed my life.

Cosplay and Community

Alice was noticed by some local comic book podcasters, who became my friends. They told me about a Ladies Comic Book Night at a comic shop. Yes, a whole night where they kicked the men out, had cookies, and let the women shop. We just hung around making friends with each other – in the way that perhaps we'd always envied fanboys and their ability to make the shop theirs – if just for a couple hours. We could debate over who would win: Jean Grey or Barbara Gordon?

It was at this gathering that I met Jennifer K. Stuller, a pop culture and comic book critic who was selling her book and joining in on the fun. As we gabbed and recommended different books to each other, we started to talk about conventions. Jen told the group of us all about a new, up-and-coming convention she and some women were starting to put together: GeekGirlCon.

Knowing that friendly faces I'd met before would be at the GeekGirlCon planning meeting gave me the spark I needed to attend myself. To check out what these women were trying to do and to see how I could support their effort. I was already thinking about who I'd like to see at GeekGirlCon – and, of course, working out my cosplay.

The organization putting together GeekGirlCon was brand-new, and no one knew what was going to come out of this first meeting. None of women present really knew each other beforehand, but all realized that the geek community needed a convention celebrating women. There was passion, momentum, and lots of geekery. Some of them drove and flew hundreds of miles just to be at this meeting. I came to recognize that same jolt of passion in me, and volunteered to help.

In the ever-growing world of geekdom, there is a rising voice for women. I'd previously gone to comic shows where I was one of two women in a room full of men, but I've watched as the landscape has changed, and there are now more women sitting on the floor beside me, digging through quarter bins for themselves. I do think that cosplay is an area of geekdom which women tend to embrace at a higher participatory level, and can be another way for female fans to connect with each other. We are turning to creation and community as a way to state our presence and celebrate with each other.

Cosplay changed my life. It was more than just dressing up; everything else in my world changed after I donned a costume. In the span of one year, cosplay catalyzed my life from fan to community builder. If I hadn't spent hours carefully sewing on a hair comb to my floor-length cape, I would not be on the path I am today.

The rest, as they say, is "herstory." Here I am, not just volunteering, but leading GeekGirlCon. We are having a convention, and by the time this book hits the shelves, I'll be able to tell you what characters I cosplayed and of all those special moments I had by myself and with others.

See what excellent female characters in comic books do? They make doubters cosplay. Those cosplayers go forth to make friends, connect with creators, and create community and memories. That woman in

2009 reading *Detective Comics* as she watched a friend's rabbits for the weekend would've laughed had you told her that she would dress up like a kooky villain, and that it would change her life. She would've been one of the first in line to buy a pass to a convention celebrating geeky women, but she would have expected to be the only one. The only one standing there in her Alice costume.

An Interview with Amanda Conner

Amanda Conner started out in comics working for Marvel and Archie. She has also worked as a commercial illustrator for Arm & Hammer, Playskool and Nickelodeon. Amanda worked for Marvel on their Barbie line of comics, as well as the *Gargoyles* books. She then moved on to pencil *Vampirella*, working with Grant Morrison, Mark Millar, and Warren Ellis. Amanda has illustrated a number of titles for DC and Marvel, as well as *Painkiller Jane* (for Event Comics, an independent imprint created by Jimmy Palmiotti and Joe Quesada) and *The Pro* (a creator-owned Eisner-nominated book for Image Comics, written by Garth Ennis). She collaborates with artist/inker/ writer and husband Jimmy Palmiotti and writer Justin Grey via Paper Films, a multimedia entertainment studio engaged in screenwriting, art production, and multimedia development.

Q. What can you tell us about your childhood experiences with comics and superheroes?

A. My mother bought me comics when I was sick and staying home from school – it was a good way to keep me from watching TV all day long. The first bunch of comics weren't necessarily superhero comics, they were mostly *Betty and Veronica* and *Archie*, that kind of stuff. My first gift from the Tooth Fairy was a *Mad* magazine and a nickel.

Once I discovered Wonder Woman, that's when it all gelled for me. I wanted to be her. So much so, in fact, that when I was eight or nine years old, when the *Wonder Woman* TV show with Lynda Carter was on, I used to take my mother's silver posterboard – both of my parents were artists, so they had a bunch of art supplies lying around the house – and make it into bullet-deflecting bracelets. My brother had a little pellet gun that would shoot little plastic pellets, and I used to have him shoot at me! More often than not, I would be pelted in the face with little plastic pellets. I'm so glad I can still see. Every once in a while, though, I would deflect the little plastic pellets with the little cardboard bracelets. It actually worked. So that just spurred me on further.

Q. Why Wonder Woman?

A. She was the first female superhero that I was aware of – I didn't even know about Supergirl yet! Wonder Woman was the first one that dropped into my lap, and I was so amazed and happy about that.

Q. Did reading comics influence your choice to become an illustrator?

A. I realized at a certain point – probably later than I should have – that being a superhero isn't actually a paying job. I had a few career choices picked out: I wanted to grow up and be a superhero, or a lion tamer, or a race car driver, because you could go really fast and it was a paying job. I don't know why I didn't get into being a race car driver, it would have been fun. But drawing comics is really fun, too.

I've always known how to draw because both of my parents were artists. Not only that, but my father is a frustrated comic book artist. He wanted to draw comics when he grew up, but got the standard talking-out-of-it from his parents. I think his mom was more into it, but his dad wasn't. My grandfather was in engineering, and wanted my dad to have a manly job that paid lots of money. So instead of being a comic book illustrator, he went into advertising. Now he gets to live vicariously through me. He sees all the comics that I do, which is fun.

I think my mother wanted me to be a painter or artist along the lines of Mary Cassatt or Georgia O'Keeffe, but she's pretty happy that I'm doing comics.

Q. How did you get your professional start in comics?

A. I ended up going to the Joe Kubert School of Art. When I got out of that, I was trying to figure out ways to get closer to comics. I worked at World Color, which was a color separation plant back in the good old days – or the not-quite-good old days when they used to separate color in comics by *hand*. It was nightmarish. But, my godfather owned and ran World Color. He was like, "Yeah, you can work here!" I think I was there for about one or two months before deciding *nope!* This is not the way to get into comics, this is not the way to work *on* comics. It was a dark room with some flickering fluorescent lights and miserable people who were losing their eyesight. I thought, "I need a different job."

So I started working in a new comic book store that had just opened up near my house. It was called Dream Factory, up in Norwalk, Connecticut. While I was working there, I saw an ad in the paper. A professional comic book artist was looking for an assistant, and that turned out to be Bill Sienkiewicz.

I would do backgrounds for him, and sort of clean up the cyclone he would create. He's definitely a man who's all about the process. He's more into doing it than he is into the finished product. Which is amazing, because the finished product always looks gorgeous. But while he was creating a piece, it always looked like a family of raccoons had been brought in by a tornado.

The most fun thing I got to do for Bill was that I got to model for *Elektra: Assassin*. I didn't start modeling for him until, I think, the fourth issue. And you'll notice that at the beginning of the series, Elektra looks like this cold, hard Greek woman in a red bandana – but by the second-to-the-last panel on the second-to-the-last page, it looks like *me* in a red bandana. And I don't look Greek, at all.

It was also really exciting that at the time, Bill had a studio next door to [*The Heart of Juliette Jones* creator] Stan Drake and [*Mary Perkins, On Stage* creator] Leonard Starr! So I got to hang out with those guys. Stan had taken over the drawing chores for *Blondie*, but he was also still doing *The Heart of Juliette Jones* and *Kelly Green* – it was so cool to just watch him draw.

But, getting back to my start in the industry... while I worked for Bill, I would go back and forth into the city with my father, and would hit Marvel and DC with whatever I had in my portfolio. I would call up that day – this was before 9/11, and it was easier to get into places – and say, "Hey, I'm from out of town, and I have a portfolio for review, and I'm leaving today!" Technically, it wasn't a lie, because I'm from Connecticut, which is an hour out of town, and I *was* leaving at the end of the day. So I would corner the editors, make them let me come up, and show them my portfolio. They would always say that my work showed a lot of potential, but it needed polish, or it needed *this* or it needed *that*. I think I went through this routine five or six times.

Finally, Bill said to me, "Marvel is having glasnost, they're letting anybody in," so I went back to Marvel and got my first job with them. It was a Yellowjacket story, and they got Stan Drake to ink me, which I was really, really happy about.

Q. So that took... how long? A couple of years?
A. My first job was in the fall of 1988, for Marvel. I had another small job after that, in which She-Hulk and Wasp are raiding all the hunky guys of the Marvel Universe. I didn't get a lot of comics work after that, so I went into advertising for a while. I got work with Archie Comics,

but I was still doing advertising at the same time. These days, I still do advertising every once in a while, just to keep myself humble and grounded. And to remember why I wanted to work in comics.

Q. You've done commercial illustration for *The New York Times*, *Revolver* magazine, Arm & Hammer and *Nightline*, among others. How did you get into that?

A. A friend of mine was an editor at *Spin* – she had me do some pieces for the magazine that, to this day, I am really proud of. Eventually, this friend went to *Revolver* magazine. They had an advice column written by Vinnie Paul, who used to be in the band Pantera. It was Dear Abby for metalheads; illustrating that was awesome. Lara, my editor, let me get away with doing anything on that. And when you're doing a heavy metal advice column, you get to draw really crazy stuff. I also did some stuff for *Nightline* – they had some really weird concepts they wanted to get across, and had me draw a really, really huge guy that came to Earth and was 24 miles high, or something like that.

I recently finished up a job for Nike, and there's a small company in New York called Kidvertisers that I do work for. They are from way back, from my first ad agency job. On occasion they call me up and ask for something, and I say sure.

Q. Does commercial illustration work differently in your brain than comics?

A. It's more of a pain in the ass. Every once in a while, a job goes smoothly, but it's often full of micromanaging and thousands of little changes. You think you're done and have made the final change... and then the legal department comes in and says everything has to be different, so you do it all over again.

Commercial work also doesn't have a good flow, unlike comics. One of my favorite things to do is to tell a story with pictures – and that's what comics are. I'm given a script, and I get to make finished art from that. I remember something that Joe Kubert told me, and it was worth every penny that I spent on his school – he said, "Make the reader understand the story as if it had no words." That's why I enjoy comics more than commercial work: I get to tell a story. Of course, commercial work pays crazy-money, which is nice to have every once in a while. Mortgage payments come due, and I have to buy toilet paper and cat food. So I do comics for love, commercial for cash.

Q. Let's talk about your comics, then. Some of your work has included Marvel's Barbie line of comics. In an industry that is often critiqued for its unrealistic, sexualized portrayals of women, how did you feel about working on titles that might be assumed to fit that critique, from *Barbie* to *Power Girl* to *Vampirella*?

A. *Barbie* was one of the titles I worked on when I was starting out in comics, but after a while, I got tired of it. I think Mattel handles it differently now, but at the time, Barbie's entire emotional rage ran from "pleasantly satisfied" to "mildly happy." This didn't work for me, because my single most favorite thing on Earth to draw is facial expressions. At one point, I asked my editor to give me all of the stories that focused on [Barbie's younger sister] Skipper, because she was allowed to be a little rambunctious and get into trouble, or have a hissy fit every once in a while. She's much more fun, and much more well-rounded, to draw than Barbie. My editor said yes, and I drew those for a while. But after a couple of issues, Mattel said no, no... they wanted Skipper to be more like Barbie, and that was it for me. I told them that they needed to find another job for me, and my wonderful editor at the time, Hildy Mesnick, put me on *Gargoyles*.

I loved doing *Gargoyles*, even though technically it was a Disney comic and the guys who ran Buena Vista were in charge of it. They didn't have a template for me to work from – instead, I was told to draw in my own style as long as the characters were recognizable as the Gargoyles. *Gargoyles* also had a strong female character – a New York City cop – and I loved drawing her.

I do, occasionally, get criticism for the way I draw female superheroes, but I think the criticism comes from people who don't read superhero comics. They see little snippets, individual images, and assume that the women are nothing but T&A. And then they criticize me for just drawing T&A, and I'm like, no, you have to read it to understand.

Power Girl is a great example of this. People assume she's just a T&A character. One of the things Jimmy [Palmiotti], Justin [Gray] and I wanted to do in *Power Girl* was to make her a strong, lovable person you could know. She could be one of your buddies. I still had people asking me, "Why didn't you shrink [Power Girl's] boobs?", and I said, "Because then it would become an issue." We already know that Power Girl has big boobs, everybody knows it. If I shrank them, it would be pointed out a lot. We wanted to acknowledge that she has big boobs, show her with big boobs, and then move on to the story. I think it worked, for the most part.

Q. Do you ever have difficulty reconciling the need to show T&A for marketing purposes and actual storytelling?

A. You know, I don't think I've ever had someone say to me, "Make this bigger for marketing purposes." Every female superhero character is different, so I try to visualize them that way. Power Girl is around a DDD, while I make Supergirl a very small B-cup. In my head, Supergirl is still a teenager. But I also try to give the male superheroes a lot of different body types. Spider-Man is skinny and can jump and climb walls, but Superman and Batman are really bulky.

Q. How do you decide on the clothes the women you draw are wearing? Power Girl, for instance, always looks sharply dressed in your comics...

A. I kept Power Girl's costume because she's had it for years, and it's become iconic and recognizable. But I added seams to it — personally, I think seams are sexy. The boots that I gave her are actually a pair of boots Jimmy gave me for Christmas. My boots are olive, but I gave Power Girl those in blue. For her street clothes, I tried to think of what I would want to wear. Also, because Power Girl, Karen, is a New York girl now, I would look at what the girls were wearing as I was running around New York. I really do enjoy accessorizing in my art – in real life, I get up, roll out of bed, get a cup of coffee and start working. I never get to dress up for work, so I fantasize about doing it.

As far as superhero clothing for women in general goes, I don't mind sexy stuff. I kind of *like* sexy stuff, I think it's fun, and I think women like to dress sexy every once in a while. The problem is that sometimes you can just tell – I don't know how you can tell, but you can – that the women are made to dress sexy only for the jerk-off factor. But then there's times when the art is drawn really well, and it's still sexy, but it transcends the jerk-off factor.

I have to admit that when I was drawing a few issues of *Birds of Prey*, I put Black Canary back into fishnets because I just love fishnets! Now, fishnets, if you're going to fight crime, are really stupid. But visually in a comic, they are cool looking. I didn't want to give her the strapless leotard, though, I wanted to give her a leather look. I'm dating myself here, but I was thinking of the Fly Girl outfits from the television show *In Living Color*. I was going for those really cute outfits that they used to wear.

The nice thing about that storyarc, which was written by Terry Moore, was that I got to have Black Canary get really pissed about the fishnets, because they are *not* industrial strength, you know? They tend to get holes in them, quickly. If you were a superhero in fishnets, you would get really aggravated. You'd have to go to Macy's and buy them in bulk.

Q. Tell us about Painkiller Jane, another character you're associated with. You worked on her origin story (*Painkiller Jane* #0). Are you happy with how she's been handled in subsequent series?

A. Sometimes I like the way she's been handled, sometimes I'm more *ehh*. She's been written by several people. I think that the person who handles her the best is Jimmy, and I'm not just saying that because he's my husband. I think that Jane is actually what Jimmy thinks of himself if he were a woman. If Jimmy were a girl, he'd be Jane. So I love it when he writes Jane, and he's supposed to be writing a new Jane script for me! There's this story he's been talking about for eight or ten years, and I love it so much, I told him that if he does it with another artist, I'll... I don't know... smother him in his sleep. He's going to write it up for me in a few months, and I can't wait.

Jane is one of my favorite characters to draw because she's such a bad-ass, and because I can draw all of the emotion on her face – it's all showing. Everything is painful and a pain in the ass to her, so I can do some great facial expressions with Jane.

Q. Can you tell us a bit about *The Pro*?

A. That's my other baby. I love that book so much. Every time I see Garth [Ennis], I try to chisel away at him a little more, try to get him to write more *Pro*. Understandably, he says we've told her story already, but I could tell stories like that forever. I really had such fun drawing the Pro herself. She was so disgusted with life – I hate to say it, but the more disgusted a character is with life, the more fun they are to draw.

Q. The story of how that title came about is funny, right?

A. Oh, yeah! I don't remember the year, but Jimmy, Garth, [*Hitman* artist] John McCrea and I got invited to a big convention. It was a gaming, book and comic convention in Essen, Germany. We kept looking for places to eat – it was really hard for poor Johnny McCrea, because he's a vegetarian and Germany is such a meaty place – but at the end of every night we would go to this bar. Of course, the two Irish guys found the only Irish bar in Essen, Germany.

I was sick as a dog, with this awful head-chest-throat cold. So of course, the two Irish guys tell me the remedy for that is a hot port or hot toddy. So I would go and have a hot port and drink myself into a stupor. We're sitting around this big table, and I'm sick and drunk, and we started talking about how funny it would be to have a superhero prostitute. After a minute, we look around and realized, y'know, *we* make *comics*. We could do this.

Q. So it came from a drunken in-joke?

A. Yeah, that's it. I think we were doing foul things with some melted candle wax on the table, that might have had something to do with it. We have pictures of that. Maybe someday, we'll put it in a book if the guys let me. I still love *The Pro* to this day.

Q. And it sold and got nominated for an Eisner...

A. It did! We lost to Mike Mignola for *Amazing Screw-On Head*. I still think of that as my Eisner! But we couldn't have lost to a nicer guy. Actually, I lost it to Mike and his daughter, who is awesome. They won it together. But it was really nice to be nominated for a prostitute book. Who knew that could happen?

Q. What are you working on now?

A. I'm working on that DC project they won't let me talk about yet! It might actually be two DC projects. After that, Jimmy and I and Frank Tieri are doing a creator-owned project called *Captain Brooklyn*. It's about a garbage collector in Brooklyn who gains superpowers, though not in the same way the Pro does. After that, if I'm not working on a second DC story, I'll go straight to the Painkiller Jane project.

Q. Is this through your group film/production studio, too?

A. Paper Films! Yes. It's actually through Paper Films and Image. Image is putting out the *Captain Brooklyn* comic. I'm really looking forward to that. I was trying to figure out my approach for it, and I was going back and forth and looking around for inspiration, when Jimmy called me in to see something on the TV. It was a [famed *Looney Tunes* animator] Chuck Jones marathon, and Chuck Jones is one of my gods. I sat there for however many hours the marathon was going on and I realized, that's it. That's how I want *Captain Brooklyn* to look. I want to unleash my inner Chuck Jones.

Q. Anything else you want to tell us that we didn't think to ask?

A. Probably, but I can't think of it now! If I think of anything I can text it to you, because I'm mentally a 13 year old.

Q. Last question: What would you like to see in the future for women and comics?

A. Here's what I *am* seeing. When I first started going to conventions, I saw mostly guys. I saw 5 to 10% girls, and most of those women were mothers or sisters or girlfriends dragged along as burros to carry all of the comics to be signed. They were there reluctantly, but they were showing love for their man who was into comics. Throughout the years, I kept seeing more and more women, though. Three years ago – I think it was three years because I was working on *Power Girl* – I was at DragonCon and I couldn't believe it. Around 50% of my line was women and girls with stuff for me to sign. It was great!

I used to think that the reason women weren't in comics is that they knew you could make ten times as much money in commercial illustration, and they were simply all smarter than guys. But I think it's gotten to the point where they love comics so much, they don't care. The girls, they've discovered the comics and it turns out, they *love* comics.

I see so many girls and women at comic conventions now. Not only are they getting books signed for themselves, a lot of them come to me with portfolios! And some of the portfolios are fantastic. I think it's inevitable that we'll see more women drawing comics in the next ten years – it's just going to happen. Not because anybody's screaming about it or railing about it, but just because girls love comics. They love comics, they want to get into comics, they don't care that they won't make as much money as if they went into advertising, and they can draw *really well*.

It's inevitable.

A Matter of When

Carla Speed McNeil is author, artist, and head goat-roper of Lightspeed Press. She is a winner of multiple Ignatz and Lulu awards, and won the 2009 Eisner for Best Digital Comic for *Finder*. She is a technophobe in a house that contains seven-plus computers. She's continually amazed at how many stories she gets out of this contrast, and at the fact that her phobia remains firmly in place. She lives with her husband Mike, far too many monitors, not enough movies, some very sharp kitchen knives, and a fish-eagle which insists on stunning itself against the back windows from time to time. She was once compared favorably to Oppenheimer.

Here's what I tell people: When I was eight or nine, I stole a comic book from a cousin (bad girl!). It was "Days of Future Past", the *Uncanny X-Men* time-travel story with the now-iconic "everybody's dead" cover by John Byrne, featuring a grizzled-up Wolverine and Kitty Pryde. There was no comic shop in my town, so I read whatever I could get off the rack at the 7-11 or through mail-order – horror comics, mostly.

I was getting to the point of boredom with *Uncanny X-Men* (Paul Smith had just done his last issue) when I found *Cerebus* #52 and *ElfQuest* #13 in the same waterlogged box at a flea market. The stall-holder was closing up for good that afternoon, and he gave me copy of Pacific Comics's catalogue. I mail-ordered myself half to death with that thing! There weren't very many indies back then, and I think I ordered them all. *Cerebus, Journey, Neil the Horse,* and *Normalman* were a revelation. Although differences in style existed in the superhero comics, they had nothing like the range and freedom found in the black and white books.

The colorless format also made the art seem more possible. The color process of the regular books (in this I include the horrors) put the art at, I felt, a greater remove. When I looked at the crosshatching in *Cerebus*, I could see how it might be done. Later, I started finding original art-work for sale at conventions. That original art *really* made it clear that the work was done by actual humans, with pencils and pens and brushes. At that point, it seemed clear that making comics was a matter of "when" for me, not "if."

Why? Simple. I wanted to write and I wanted to draw. I dearly loved animation, but the eighties were a different landscape for animators compared to what they are now – nearly a different planet. I knew that producing an animated film was slow and expensive, and that almost never did one person's pet project get made. Many other wonderful things might come out of the cumbersome process of making a film, but look at this – with a ream of paper and a copy machine, you can make a story *right now*!

Ah. But comics are not art. Or, at least, not good art. Or, at least, not good enough for anyone to pay you to do them. An art teacher in college told me that figure study was irrelevant to modern art. Another told me that learning perspective drawing was for commercial artists only. There was no illustration major at my college then, and only two watercolor classes – those were taught by the Dean.

I did learn plenty of useful things in college. My professors let me turn in a lot of stuff that wasn't, strictly speaking, what they'd assigned. They did let me graduate. And, along the way, I met a junior professor with a new gallery show. His focus was on "narrative art."

Sounds like the Art World had found a focus I could get into! Unfortunately, what the show turned out to be was a series of large, mud-colored canvases depicting vaguely human shapes. They had titles – *Story of Lilith* and so on. I didn't know the story of Lilith at the time, so I listened to my professor tell it. I concluded that I would never in a million years have figured it out from that immense muddy garage-door-sized rectangle of canvas.

This showed me the limits of telling a story in a single, wordless image. This is not to say that a single image cannot convey a great deal, or that leaving the elements of an image to inspire the viewer to imagine a story can't evoke a profound response. Or, that a great cartoonist can't say everything he or she wants to say with a single image. It just wasn't what I wanted to do. So I didn't stay, free hors d'oeuvres or no.

I wanted to write and I wanted to draw. I didn't know what and I didn't know how. Several years later, I finally threw up my hands and said *fuck it*! I started writing down everything that popped into my head, and drawing everything else. I had a mulch pile in my mind that dated back to early childhood that needed turning. I had reasonable confidence that whatever problems the art might present me, those would work themselves out as I went. I was far less confident about the writing.

Somewhere around 1996, I looked at the two-foot-high stack of notes and drawings and sketchbooks I had amassed, though, and said *fuck it!* again. Nobody wants to read a stack of exhaustive notes, I said, not by itself. There has to be a story. I dug out all the characters who were at the same place at the same time, and only one character connected them, so I started with him. I sat down and drew my first issue of *Finder*, so ignorant of basic pen and ink techniques that I didn't even think to use a straightedge to made the panel borders look nice. Walt Kelly may have freehanded all of *his* panel borders, but I'm noooo Walt Kelly.

For a long time, I did my book as a minicomic. I didn't even know that minis are supposed to be *small*. Like, an 8.5" x 11" sheet of paper folded in half, that size was and is common. Note to hopefuls: Minis are supposed to be small. Photocopiers don't *like* making double-sided copies on big paper. Noooo, they don't. But I went to San Diego Comic-Con with a sackful of minis over my shoulder like a newsboy, stood in that incredibly long line, got a cataclysmic sunburn, and handed out minis to every pro I could find whose work I loved.

Of a couple hundred handed out, I got seven of the best letters ever.

Professional comics creators actually bothered to write to me. Not even 5% of those who got my minis, but so what? Those that did were amazing. Some gave me a thumbs up, some offered useful critique. All of them were okay with my quoting them when I approached a distribution company to go on to the next level, and their names did help me get a foot in the door.

I came from a small business background, so the idea of self-publishing didn't seem odd to me. Get to know a few suppliers, build a relationship with a few distributors, make the rounds with the shops and the trade shows, and you're off. It wasn't easy money. The black-and-white bubble had burst, the distribution implosion had sunk nearly all ships – I was sitting in the lobby of Diamond Comics Distribution the morning that their last viable rival gave up the ghost. I could hear what would be called a Lively Discussion about it in a nearby boardroom.

For 12 years, I self-published under my own imprint, Lightspeed Press. The Internet happened, and I went webcomic. The animation boom gathered strength, and with it a massive turnabout in pop culture. Comics, movies, TV, and gaming are elephantine compared to what they were in my youth. I knew it was coming when I was up early on a Sunday, gagging on paint thinner trying to get my own pointless and forgettable muddy canvas ready for Monday's class critique, when the most bizarre thing I'd ever seen caught my attention from the TV. I called up all my grumpy, hungover friends and made them turn on the TV to watch Ren and Stimpy sing the Log Song. Probably the first and last time I was the first to know about something hip.

It's been cool to see it all flower. Not just flower, but grow into a vast and tangled jungle, full of life. Yes, things are changing, things will change. Digital formats are coming, and who knows what else. Some things we love won't survive. But comics are so different than they were when I got into it. Change has been happening all along, and the field is so much more wide open than it was, so many more people making them. As long as we still have a copy machine and somebody to pedal the bamboo bicycle to power it, we'll have comics. And more and more people to make them.

Anyhow, that's me. I write and draw a comic called *Finder*, now published by Dark Horse, who are proving to be a very good partner. I'm working on a pile of other things, and I hope all of you are as well.

The Other Side of the Desk

Rachel Edidin is currently an editor at Dark Horse Comics. She is also (in no particular order) a semi-professional freelance writer, a lousy but enthusiastic cellist, an amateur wireworker (making things out of it, not walking on it), and a voracious reader. She enjoys good comics, George Orwell's nonfiction, the word "linger," and ugly baby animals.

I edit comics.

I love my work. I love it with a ferocity that surprised me when I first discovered it, and which surprises me still.

It's not that loving my job is a foreign idea to me, nor that I am suspicious of any job that's more than a daily grind, a roof, and an HMO. But I didn't expect to love *this* job, not this much, nor this confidently – not when I handed out my self-consciously awkward cover letter at a convention, and not even when I gave up graduate school and moved four thousand miles from friends and family for the chance to edit comic books.

I came into comics by hook, crook, and sheer dumb luck. I'd spent the two years since college running an undergraduate writing center; my plan, at that point, was to go to graduate school and from there, either to a career in academia or writing or both. Comics wasn't even a Plan B so much as a casual and slightly sheepish flirtation fueled by on-and-off correspondence with an editor I'd met at a convention a few years previously.

When I first came into comics, I saw editing as a means to an end – a means of getting up to my elbows in the publishing process, of accumulating experience and contacts on the way to my long-term goal of writing full time.

And somewhere along the way, the destination less *changed* than became irrelevant. I had fallen for the road. What started a job had become a vocation: At some point, I had stopped just *editing* and become an *editor*.

47

#

Editing floats my boat, rocks my socks, scratches itches I'd never even had the means to reach. In college, I double-majored in literature and writing, and I've spent my professional life torn between analysis and action, theory, and practice. Editing is the first work I've found that seamlessly straddles that divide. I'm a challenge junkie, easily bored by routine; editing is constantly demanding and delightfully varied.

And, more, I'm greedy. There's an old snipe that editorial careers are the fate of frustrated writers. In my case, it's true, but not for the implied reasons: For me, editing feeds an insatiable hunger for *more* that writing alone never could. As a writer, the world of my work is limited to my own stories, and regardless the breadth and volume of that work, *it has never been enough.* As an editor, I am custodian and curator to a body of material whose range extends far beyond the scope of any one writer: a never-ending ocean of voice and thought and idea. In comics, especially, I am witness and catalyst and alchemist to a million revelations, no two quite alike.

The span of books I edit and have edited is wildly, wonderfully eclectic: dark supernatural horror, slice-of-life memoir, high fantasy, satire, science fiction; from the U.S., Australia, Great Britain, Spain, Argentina, Japan, Canada. Many are stand-alone works, original to print; others are series, collections of webcomics, companions to albums, spinoffs from video games. Most are comics; some are prose or art. Their creators are novices and seasoned professionals; rock stars and critics and storytellers. One is a six-year-old boy; another, a woman in her seventies with over 300 books under her belt. Each comes with her own unique strengths, his own unique demands.

More than anything else, it's that multiplicity that keeps me coming back.

#

I am a midwife: I will hold your hand as you labor to produce your life's work, tell you when to push and when to catch your breath.

I am a gardener: What grows here isn't my creation, but I can cultivate it, fertilize and nurture and prune until it reaches heights and takes shapes far beyond what it could have reached wild.

I am a producer: I take your raw sounds, mix, adjust, slide; record and balance and burn.

I am a roadie: My job is to make yours look easy; and if I do it right, the audience will never notice me there at all.

I am a nerve center: I coordinate, cross-reference, translate signals and impulses and needs and wants between brain and body, writers and artists, letterers, colorists, agents, designers and marketers, pre-press techs and public-relations reps.

I am a mechanic: I may not have drawn the blueprints, but I know every inch of these engines, inside and out; and I can tell by the rattle of a bolt or the smell of the smoke what needs to be tightened, oiled, hammered.

In terms of creative engagement, what I am first and foremost is a professional reader: I can take apart an outline, or a set of thumbnails, or a manuscript, see what makes it tick, and anticipate the places where that machinery might catch. I'm far enough from the source to notice what the creators themselves are too entangled with their work to catch; and close enough to communicate it in practically useful terms.

The most common conception of an editor is a fixer. I fix things, sometimes; more often, I point other people towards the right tools and tell them gently but firmly when it's time to let go. I curate and coordinate and integrate and synthesize; manage crises; reconcile necessity and reality.

#

Editing is inherently interstitial. Done right, it's invisible, or nearly so: stitches so subtle as to create the illusion of seamless integrity. Pay no attention to the girl behind the curtain.

If you can hear me, I'm doing it wrong. If you – even you, the writer; you, the artist – can recognize moments where my aesthetic overwrites yours, or my voice wells up between the notes, I'm doing it wrong.

More or less often, a book will call for a direct hand – paragraphs rearranged, entries added to story notes, copy extended. Here, I play mockingbird: Show me two paragraphs of your prose, and I'll be able to call up your cadence, spin so smoothly through your turns of phrase that, looking back, you'll swear those words were yours from the start – and, in the end, they were.

# # #

Regardless what sentences I spend in someone else's shoes, the real price of editing – setting aside might-have-beens – is immersion. To edit well requires a clear eye, and controlled momentum. Getting swept away is a luxury I can't afford, and editing comics I love is always bittersweet: To allow a work I love to catch me up and carry me along is to cheat the story and its creator.

The passion isn't lost, but tempered, from searing blast to steady flame, explosion to illumination; its fuel a future's worth of stories.

# # #

I edit comics.
And I love my work.

An Interview with Terry Moore

Terry Moore has been writing and drawing critically acclaimed comic books since 1993, beginning with his award-winning, seminal comic *Strangers in Paradise (SiP)*. The series is self-published by Moore through his Abstract Studio imprint, and navigates the changing relationship between two women, Francine and Katchoo. Having garnered numerous industry awards and having been published in 14 languages, *Strangers in Paradise* remains a perennial bestseller. Moore recently completed his award-winning SF series *Echo*, and is currently working on two ongoing series published by Abstract Studios: the suspense/horror series *Rachel Rising*, which is already a fan favorite, and the popular *How to Draw* series, which is published quarterly. Moore has also recently worked on Vertigo's *Fables*, and Marvel's *Spider-Man Loves Mary Jane* and *Runaways*.

Q. What led you to a career in comics, and how did you start out?

A. *Strangers in Paradise* #1 was my first published comic book, and was released in September 1993. Before then, I had been working as a musician and TV editor. I was tired of editing, and I noticed the indie comics movement that was so strong in those days. Because I'd been cartooning and writing stories for myself my whole life, I thought I'd give it a try. Once the first issue of *SiP* came out, the next 18 years were a blur.

Q. Knowing what you know now, is there anything about the business of self-publishing your early work that you wish you'd done differently?

A. Actually, no. I think the winding road got me here, and that's what matters. When I was in music and editing, working on other people's projects never got me anywhere. When I made comics, I was determined to stick to my own thing. That made all the difference, I think.

Q. *Strangers in Paradise* is currently your most iconic work, and is a series that many people have very strong positive feelings about. Yet, having finished it, would you write it differently? Now that you can see the end, would you write the beginning some other way?

A. Probably, yes. The thing about comics is you're publishing a chapter at a time, as you write them – so the opportunity to go back and retrofit better ideas later, like a novelist, is not there. Some major plot-lines in *SiP* were developed simply to cover errors I made early on in the story – like giving David, a Japanese-American, a Chinese surname. What was I thinking? So I developed the whole "David Qin" storyline as a way of explanation. That turned out to be a strong storyline, but it wasn't initially planned. In a novel, you never get a chance to see those developments, because they're found and fixed before the book is printed. Silly comics.

Q. Your work is one of the most-frequently recommended works in discussions of women reading comics. How do you feel this has affected your career?

A. It's been good for me. Women are so good at sharing information. I also meet a lot of guys who say they got their wife or girlfriend to try my book, and now they will read other comics. My books are sort of a hybrid gateway for women who don't read comics. If I wasn't making comic books, I would write pop fiction and hope for the same audience. Either way, I'm happy.

Q. Do you have any idea how often you've been told by fans at conventions, "I thought you were a woman"? What does that interaction say to you, and what do you feel it says about your work?

A. It's a compliment, isn't it? It means the writing rang true for them. Maybe, when *Rachel Rising* becomes better known, people will say, "I thought you were dead!"

Q. Your second major creator-owned work, *Echo*, recently concluded. Was there anything with *Echo* that you wanted to do, but hadn't been able to do before?

A. I wanted to question the validity of the great debate between science and religion, and show both sides as having strayed from some sort of third answer. I never say what the third side is, but it operates throughout the story, apart from science or God. Fun, huh?

**Q. We have to ask: What is in Julie Martin's box in the closet in
Echo?**
A. Something she is ashamed of but can't help. I love her for it.
Hopefully, Dillon will, too.

**Q. The first installment of your *How to Draw* series focused on
drawing women. How did that series come about?**
A. There are so many books showing you *how* to draw, but I've found
it also helps to know *why* you draw something. It makes a big difference
in the final work. Several artists can draw the same thing, and each work
will look very different. That has more to do with the *why* in each artist's
head than the how of their skill. So my *How to Draw* series will focus on
what to do with your anatomical expertise. It's the book I always
wished I could find.

**Q. What has your experience been when you've drawn sketches for
fans at conventions? What are some memorable characters and scenarios you've been asked to draw?**
A. Eesh, my experience is that a convention sketch is a lot of hard
work done under highly distracted circumstances, in a fraction of the
time you should devote to it. But you do what you can. It's nice when
someone loves their sketch and you can tell. It's awful when they don't.

I've probably drawn a couple of thousand fan sketches over the years
and the No. 1 request is for Katchoo. After that it's Francine, Tambi
[from *SiP*], Supergirl, Casey [*SiP*], Batgirl, and all the other Marvel and
DC women. I'm actually trying hard to not to do con sketches anymore.
It's no fun when the fan is very specific about what they want and has
strict rules. I'd rather not draw at all than work like that, so I'm trying
to stop altogether. It's hard for me to say no to nice people though. I'm
working on it.

**Q. You've done both creator-owned and work-for-hire – are there
more work-for-hire projects you'd like to do in the future?**
A. Not really. I have my hands full building my own worlds right now.
Besides, no one remembers I drew Batgirl, but everybody knows I drew
Katchoo. Priorities.

**Q. Finally, one of our editors would desperately like to ask you why
Kixie from *Paradise, Too* is obsessed with strawberry cake.**
A. Oh puh-leeease. Because it's just the bestest ever!

Nineteen Panels
about Me and Comics

Sara Ryan is the author of the YA novels *Empress of the World* and *The Rules for Hearts*, the Eisner-nominated short comic "Me and Edith Head," and various comics and short stories. Most recently, she contributed to the anthologies *Welcome to Bordertown* (Random House, 2011), edited by Holly Black and Ellen Kushner, and *Girl Meets Boy* (Chronicle 2012), edited by Kelly Milner Halls. She is working on the graphic novel *Bad Houses* with Carla Speed McNeil, creator of *Finder*.

PANEL ONE

CAPTION: I can't name all the members of the X-Men. I couldn't tell you who killed Superman. Or didn't it happen more than once? Aren't there actually a lot of Supermans? I know there are more than three Robins, and that one of them, notably, is female, but that's as far as it goes.

But I can tell you Mo had a string of unfortunate rebounds after Harriet,[1] Maggie most likely won't get back together with Hopey,[2] Roz and Chicken will never fully succeed in calming Hothead,[3] and Maybonne at any given time is more likely to be riding a bummer than feeling groovy.[4]

The comics you read inevitably inform the comics you write, or to put it slightly differently, you can't separate your fandoms from your creations.

PANEL TWO

1980. I'm nine, curled up on a couch with a magazine.

The first non-newspaper comics I remember reading were in the margins of *Cricket* magazine. At their most minimal, the comics in *Cricket* functioned as footnotes, with Cricket, Ladybug, and the rest of

---

1. *Dykes to Watch Out For*

2. *Love and Rockets*

3. *Hothead Paisan: Homicidal Lesbian Terrorist*

4. *Ernie Pook's Comeek*

the gang explaining hard words and potentially unfamiliar concepts. But the characters were in longer narratives, too. Stories and poems occupied the bulk of the space on each page of the magazine, while the *Cricket* gang's adventures took place in the footers. I always liked the feeling that the division of space created, that the gang were close to the ground like real bugs, sometimes intersecting with the work above them, sometimes not. I didn't know it then, but I was learning something about page layout and storytelling.

PANEL THREE

1985. I'm fourteen, at a sleepover with my best friend. I'm in the top bunk. It's dark.

That's why I can say "I think I kind of have a crush on Skywise,"[5] without actually dying of embarrassment, although I may have giggled. I might also have said that I thought "Separate Ways" by Journey was, like, the perfect song for Rayek[6] to sing to Leetah,[7] because that's what he'd want to tell her in case anything went wrong between her and Cutter,[8] you know?

The *ElfQuest* books were my first graphic novels, and I devoured them the way girls growing up now devour manga. In fact, *ElfQuest's* aesthetic is manga-influenced; Wendy Pini was one of the first American artists to draw in the style. She brought her own spin, of course, and the series's palette and designs are of their time – by which I mean, lose the pointy ears and the elves wouldn't be out of place in a hair-metal video. Why was it engaging? First and most importantly, my friends were reading it, so we could discuss the characters' situations and speculate about future plotlines at delightful, ridiculous length. Also, the elves were totally having sex, in a sort of best-of-both-worlds framework; frolicking pre-battle free-for-alls wherein everybody gets all up in whomever they want in the heat of the moment, and super-meaningful Recognition, wherein the parties involved are not only immediately compelled to mate, they become able to *read each others' minds*. If there's a better-slash-worse combination for an adolescent simultaneously awash in generalized hormones and media-damaged enough to want a One-True-Soulmate, I do not know what it would be.

---

5. One of many instances wherein I favored the wisecracking sidekick.

6. Antihero.

7. Heroine.

8. Hero.

I don't remember thinking about the *ElfQuest* books as comics, per se. They were simply containers for stories about characters I cared about. The fact that they contained pictures and text juxtaposed in deliberate sequence was incidental.

PANEL FOUR

1988. I'm in high school, but I'm hanging out on campus because that's what you do when you grow up in a college town. I'm in a coffee shop reading the alternative newsweekly.

There's that comic again; the one that isn't always funny, with an art style that isn't slick and polished, and I don't really get the title. I mean, who's Ernie Pook, anyway? There's something about it, though, haunting and true. So much is implied in the spaces between the panels.

Still, I was resistant. But ebullient, bossy, showoffy Marlys and her earnest, frequently lovesick big sister Maybonne won me over, and I grew to love *Ernie Pook's Comeek*.

Lynda Barry accomplished so much within the constraints of four panels. One week, the strip would feature a hilariously pitch-perfect school paper by Marlys and Maybonne's cousin Arnold in which he summarized the plot of a kung fu movie with equally accurate kid-style illustrations. Next week, Marlys and Maybonne's mother would be reviling her children, their father and her own life. Barry's ability to swing from goofy humor to bleak, clear-eyed realism, not simply from week to week, but often from panel to panel, was endlessly compelling.

PANEL FIVE

1991. I'm at Common Language LGBT bookstore. I've just gotten up my courage to buy the queer identity accessory of the moment, freedom rings. Can I also handle buying a book with the word *Dykes* on the cover? I can. A dismissive friend says *Yeah, I read those for a while, they're just such a soap opera.* I don't care. I need all those dykes in my house.

Alison Bechdel's *Dykes to Watch Out For* became my field guide to a particular lesbian subculture – based in a college town, with drama unfolding in food co-ops, political protests, group houses, classrooms, vegetarian restaurants, and, of course, the women's bookstore, Madwimmin Books, helmed by the no-nonsense Jezanna. Once again, my way in was through the characters: neurotic self-righteous Mo, calm pragmatic Harriet, blunt libertine Lois, intellectual commitment-phobic Ginger, and the rest of the equally pleasing cast. Despite the art history classes I was taking, I wasn't yet thinking much about the way Bechdel

– or any other comics creator – drew.

PANEL SIX

1993. I'm in the staff office of the Engineering Library. I'm supposed to learn how to be an engineering librarian.

As it turns out, I'm also supposed to learn about comics, as all my close colleagues are hardcore fans. They discuss my reading deficits like doctors trying to come up with the correct prescription for a difficult case.

COLLEAGUE 1: "What do you think, start with the phonebooks?"

COLLEAGUE 2: "I don't know, the phonebooks are pretty dense."

COLLEAGUE 1: "Yeah, but she needs them. She definitely needs *Jaka's Story*. At minimum."

COLLEAGUE 2: "Okay. And she's reading *Sandman* already, right?"

COLLEAGUE 1: "Of course."[9]

They said "the phonebooks" because that's what the compilations of Dave Sim's *Cerebus* comics were called, as they resembled phonebooks in heft and paper quality.

PANEL SEVEN

1993. I'm in the living room of a small apartment, curled into a papasan chair, frowning with concentration as I read.

Jaka's Story was indeed dense. Paragraphs of tiny text next to panels rendered with delicate, precise linework. It was impossible to look at a page without being staggered at the amount of work that had clearly gone into it.

There was a little girl with a looming, fearsome nurse. There was some gorgeous, fiendishly cross-hatched architecture. There was a sad, angry, lovely lady – the little girl grown up – and her feckless-looking but nonetheless handsome man. And then, suddenly, there was a cartoon animal. It had been explained to me that Cerebus was nominally an aardvark, but he was about as much like a real aardvark as Pogo was like a real possum. What was going *on*?

Cerebus was the first comic I read where the artwork engaged me well before the story. I understood that it was a Big Deal, and I knew that reading it and my colleagues' other recommended titles would be a way in to conversations with them about topics beyond the latest loon

---

9. Because it was pretty much a given that if you were an alternatively-inclined lady reading comics at that time, you were reading the work of Mr. Gaiman. See also: clove cigarettes.

who wanted to look things up in our patent and trademark database but refused to tell us what he was looking for.[10]

But sometimes, *Cerebus* felt like homework. I'd be reading along and get the vague sense that Dave Sim was slyly commenting on other creators' work, or satirizing other elements of culture with which I was unfamiliar.[11] I knew the Oscar character was meant to evoke Oscar Wilde, and Julius was modeled on Groucho Marx, but there were a lot of nuances I was missing. It reminded me of trying to read the style of eighteenth-century English poetry that's basically a lot of dudes slagging each other off in verse. I kept at it for some time, although I never loved it, and once Sim revealed his misogyny in all its batshit-crazy glory,[12] I stopped reading.

I don't regret the time I spent in Sim's world. There's value in making it past an intimidating surface; there's value in reading work that isn't to your exact taste. And Sim's undeniably striking layouts taught me that a grid is only one way to think about a page. But I still had a lot to learn.

My colleagues talked knowledgeably about dozens of writers, artists, and editors, regularly weighing the relative merits of different creative teams. Eventually, as I continued to read, listen, and occasionally contribute to the comics conversations in the office, I came to understand just how many contributors could be involved in making a comic, and that you could, potentially, write a comic without also being the person who drew it.

PANEL EIGHT

1994. I'm still in grad school, still at the engineering library. I've just come from Common Language with my latest acquisition. A curious colleague asks to see it, since judging from its size and shape it is clearly a comic.

PANEL NINE

I hand over my copy of *Hothead Paisan, Homicidal Lesbian Terrorist.*

PANEL TEN

He examines it with interest.

---

10. In case we stole his idea.

11. Wikipedia would have been a godsend, but we just barely had a graphical Internet.

12. Issue #186. You can read about it in Wikipedia.

PANEL ELEVEN

He hands it back.

COLLEAGUE: "That was not designed for me!"

That might have been the first time I thought about how many of the other comics I'd recently been reading arguably had been. Designed for him, I mean.

PANEL TWELVE[13]

Various bookstores, comics shops, and conventions, 1994-1996.

I began consciously seeking out the work of female creators of alternative and minicomics. Some, but not nearly all, of the folks I discovered: Phoebe Gloeckner, Aline Kominsky-Crumb, Dori Seda, Julie Doucet, Donna Barr, Roberta Gregory, Erika Lopez, Carla Speed McNeil, Ellen Forney, Leanne Franson, Shary Flenniken, Posy Simmonds.

What was I getting from reading all these women's work? I was becoming increasingly aware of how many kinds of stories could be told in comics,[14] experiencing deeply individual voices and approaches to combining words and pictures, as intimate as the self-published zines I was also reading.

I should note that I didn't totally swear off male creators. I kept right on with books like *Sandman, Concrete,* and *American Splendor,* and minicomics with alternative heroes like Matt Feazell's *Cynicalman* and Sean Bieri's *Cool Jerk and Homo Gal.* I went back in time and caught up with *Pogo* and *Krazy Kat.* I fell into *Love and Rockets* and have yet to re-emerge.

I was learning what I value as a comics reader. Humor. Inventive use of language and layouts. Emotional complexity. Casts of characters who relate to each other in believable ways, even when the tone of the work is broad and exaggerated. My comics reading was less escapism than voyeurism; what I wanted was insight into other lives, worlds seen – or created, as the case may be – through other people's sensibilities.

PANEL THIRTEEN

1997. Living room of a very small apartment. Décor: publisher comps, FedEx boxes full of original art, loose stacks of minicomics and floppies, and graphic novels with cracked spines. I'm sitting on the carpet, which is not entirely free of ink.

---

13. Really this would be a montage-y splash page, but I'm already pushing it with the conceit.

14. Answer: all kinds.

My tipping point as a comics creator came, perhaps unsurprisingly, when I began living with a cartoonist. Suddenly, the process was entirely demystified. Suddenly, I could just read a script and then watch the evolution from thumbnails to pencils to inks. Heck, suddenly I could stand over an artist's shoulder and kibitz, saying, "You need to put her in a different outfit, she wouldn't wear that." From that point on, it was only a matter of time.

PANEL FOURTEEN

1997. Living room of a somewhat larger apartment, with similar décor. I'm slumped on the couch, frowning over my overheating laptop.

All my reading, not to mention all the other writing I'd done, wasn't sufficient to prepare me for writing comics. First, I tried adapting one of my prose stories. There was a passage in it of which I was very fond. It was about the moon. A big yellow summer-moon, shining in the sky. I put the passage in my script, unaltered.

PANEL FIFTEEN

Artist draws a circle on a blank page.
ARTIST: "There's the moon."

PANEL SIXTEEN

He draws some lines emanating from it.
ARTIST: "Now it's shining."

PANEL SEVENTEEN

He looks up from the page.
ARTIST: "Now write me something that advances the plot."

PANEL EIGHTEEN

2011. Living room of a house with similar décor, but fewer FedEx boxes since mostly everyone sends art digitally now. I'm sitting in an Adirondack chair in the corner, staring into the middle distance as I contemplate a script in progress.

I'm a comics creator because I'm a comics fan. And I mean that in the broadest sense; I am a fan of stories told by juxtaposing words and pictures in deliberate sequence, the kind of storytelling that at this time and place is known as comics. Although I love and respect the work of many, many individual creators, what I love the most is the format itself, the way a gap between panels can be a minute or a decade, the way you can destroy a planet, a plant, or a plan in the same amount of space, how the words can be lying while the pictures tell the truth, or vice versa.

PANEL NINETEEN

2012, multiple locations. Girls are sitting cross-legged, perched on tree branches, lying in bed, leaning against lockers. They're looking at screens, zines, phones, small thick volumes of manga, oversized graphic novels.

They're all reading comics. Soon they'll be creating them.

I'm Batman

Like Batman, **Tammy Garrison** has a dual identity. She is a digital preservation librarian by day, and a crazy cat lady, doggie foster-mom, and writer by night. She met her husband (a crazy cat man) on a Nightwing fan forum, and it's been crazy cat-wedded bliss ever since. Her work has been published by LexisNexis and Mad Norwegian Press, and in *Flashshots* and *Luna Station Quarterly*. Her daily micro-fiction can be found at thetinytales. blogspot.com, and she can be found on Twitter and around the 'Net via the username @spastasmagoria. She has been a Batman fan since birth, and has a strong interest in rainbows, cupcakes, those sprinkly heart things, the color purple, and pie.

I'm Batman. Don't let the full-figure, glasses, or breasts fool you; I am Batman.

I can see you saying... *Right. You're Batman.* But why not Batgirl? Certainly, as a librarian and bottle redhead, I have more in common with Silver Age Batgirl, Barbara Gordon, than some elitist playboy with an annoying habit of collecting children to add to his crusade. I have never so much as stood on a rooftop, much less endangered minors in my own private war. Certainly, Barbara Gordon is the safer bet, when choosing a fictional character that I connect with on a spiritual level. Right?

Wrong.

Barbara Gordon is awesome. She saw what she wanted in life and went after it, even when Batman didn't want her around. She encountered adversity when the Joker shot and paralyzed her, and learned how to recreate her life and continue on. You can't knock that. But I never wanted to be Batgirl as a kid. I never understood Batgirl the way I understand Batman.

There are a variety of reasons I identify with Batman. Not because he is dreamy or rich or anything like that. But because he's awesome, and he just... feels right. If I had to choose between all fictional characters in the pantheon of human literature, Batman most closely represents what I am about: punching people, awesome cars, and luring children into danger. Okay, not that part of Batman. Punching people and corrupting minors is bad, ok? (We can all agree to love awesome cars.)

Also, I'm hardly rich, and I really don't have the upper-body strength to hold a guy over a ledge to get him to talk. (Though it would solve a lot of problems if I could.)

Batman is awesome and powerful. He found what he wanted to do in life and pursued it with a vengeance. He follows his instincts and his conscience, even if no one else believes in him or cares what he is doing. Batman is about perseverance, planning, and enduring. He's had screwed-up things happen to him, and isn't unscarred, but continues to go on. And Batman's a big fat jerk.

I actually had a long conversation with one of the editors of this fine book where we discussed why she hates Batman. I couldn't disagree with any of the things she said; he's quite horrible, really. He is emotionally stunted, and he's incapable of telling everyone around him that they matter to him. He uses people, he treats those in his confidence like he's unappreciative of them and their talents, he holds himself and others to unrealistic standards. He's also got plans ready at a moment's notice to take out the entire Justice League – which is just murder on maintaining friendships.

The guy has issues. Dick Grayson is neurotic (a natural product of that trademarked Bat-family upbringing), and he's still more stable and likeable than Bruce Wayne. But, I have to admit... I'm not entirely likeable either. I do things for good reasons that get misunderstood. I'm a bit crap at relating to people. I'm damned near incapable of expressing emotion in a socially acceptable manner.

It's not just readers who don't like Bruce Wayne; loads of characters don't like him either. Guy Gardner's been nursing a grudge since Batman punched him in the face that one time. And that other time. The Justice League never really quite got over that bit where a villain stole Batman's plans for taking out the whole Justice League and implemented it. You'd be sore, too, if your alleged friend and ally thought up plans to kill or neutralize you.

Batman is still in the Justice League. He's still the guy they call when they need a plan, or when they need someone to do something they consider unthinkable.

And, hey, Batman had good reasons for having plans to take out all of his Justice League friends. Can you imagine what would happen to the world if Superman turned evil? The world needs someone like Batman who is capable of making hard decisions. Nobody wants to talk about what happens when their friend Superman goes nuts and starts laser-beaming civilians for jaywalking in Metropolis. (Because they're all hopeful and trusting, but really.) How much egg are you going to have on your face when Superman gets taken over by alien spores and destroys half the planet Earth before you can mount any sort of counter-attack?

It's better to have a plan as to what you're going to do than try to figure it out later, when you're all dead. That's not cuddly, but it sure is practical. However, if a bad guy steals and executes your plans for taking out all your friends, you should at least frickin' apologize to them. At that point, you're just a douche if you don't. So, I try to at least own up when I've screwed up – even if it wasn't entirely my fault. It keeps things polite and cordial. (And keeps your friends from kicking you out of the Justice League.) Sometimes, Batman is an example of what *not* to do, just as much as what to do. See, I'm learning from him all the time!

At the end of the day, I try to get the job done, just like Batman. So often, I find myself asking the question: What Would Batman Do?

I can't remember a point in my childhood when I wasn't consuming and internalizing the lessons (good and bad) of the Batman mythos. That is what they were to me, my mythology. I learned about what was important, how to be a good and contributing member of this world. (And how to punch people. Always pull your thumb back, out of the way, so you don't break it.)

Being a very early reader, I'd sit on the floor of the barbershop where my grandfather got his regular haircuts, reading old comics. Batman was the best of all of them, in my tender, and possibly jaded, four-year-old opinion. The Fantastic Four was just unrealistic. And Iron Man was an "obvious" Batman ripoff (I was four, and was also convinced that K9 from *Doctor Who* worked for the Daleks). And Iron Man drank! Like my grandparents' neighbor, "Intoxicated Mr. Thomas." And yes, I called him "Intoxicated Mr. Thomas."

But heck, everyone knew Batman never did anything bad. He never so much as hit a guy with glasses or used harsh language on the TV show I watched with my grandparents every evening at dinner time. Batman didn't get his super powers from a lantern or a sun, he'd worked for them all. Which is what my grandparents told me you had to do to be successful: work hard. After hard work, according to my grandmother, I could be whatever I wanted when I grew up. Even Batman. (My grand-parents also let me watch R-rated movies and *Delta Force*, so I think that explains everything you need to know about me.)

Another lesson I internalized very early was that bad things happen to everyone. That was courtesy of life itself, as opposed to Batman. But Batman taught me that it's not the bad thing that defines you.

I imagine most people in Gotham think Bruce Wayne is a bit of a burnout. He had potential, but now he's just tabloid fodder. I bet they don't even blame him, much. Who wouldn't waste all his money on fast cars and beautiful women? Shoot, I would, given half the chance.

But, being an only child who saw his parents murdered in front of him at a very young age? That's got to mess someone up, right? Heck, even if he turned out to be a drug user or criminal, I'm not sure anyone would fault him. He'd just be another one of those kids that had too much thrown at him too quickly, and had the monetary resources at his disposal to be the instrument of his own demise.

That isn't the route he took. Sure, it's his façade, the Scarlet Pimpernel idiot's mask that he wears to conceal his true objectives and motives. But, for whatever reason   nature, nurture, whatever   Bruce Wayne became Batman. Other people in Gotham made other choices. Victor Freiz, when faced with the loss of his wife, became a villain – as did countless others.

You decide who you are. You can have something horrible happen to you and become Batman, or you can become the Joker. You *can* get swept up in horrible circumstances and bad choices, but you don't *need* to. *You* can exert force on your own life. *You* can steer your own path.

I did try to follow that, even in those special difficult times known as primary and secondary school. No matter what peers or adults were putting me through, I didn't need to let it make me a certain way. I didn't have to become mean, or bitter or angry.

I employed another lesson from Batman during my young adulthood as I tried to get through college and graduate school while working and paying bills and dealing with what trauma and drama life threw my way: Batman's ability to endure. Did Batman quit when Bane let all the inmates out of Arkham Asylum? Did he rest or stop, until he'd recaptured them all? Did he quit going after the Joker because he was injured and in physical pain? Did he stop fighting Two-Face because of emotional distress? No. No matter what else was going on, what physical and mental limits he had to surpass, Batman endured. Mind over matter.

Bruce Wayne went after his goals. He worked hard, never gave up, and became Batman. Sure, he had advantages like money and time. But hard work can't be discounted.

There aren't any shortcuts in life, but hard work can get you through a lot, including a slightly evil employer, emotional upheaval, and Indexing and Abstracting, as taught by Attila the Hun. I put myself through both undergrad and graduate school. It would have been nice to not have to work and go to school at the same time, but we all can't have Batman's budget. But we *can* have Batman's persistence. I went through on the Batman Education Plan of not letting life keep me from my goals.

Batman is about planning, preparation, and training. He's about detective work, about knowing when to go it alone and when to ask for help. I try to use my time wisely and assess when I have the tools to work through a problem, especially at work, and when it would be better to ask for assistance. Batman knows how to utilize the strengths and weaknesses of those around him. Again, this can cause conflicts if you come off as a "user" of people. But sometimes, you need Superman's heat vision or Zatanna's magic to get the job done. There is no point in wasting other people's time if there is a more efficient way to solve a problem, even if it means reaching out to someone else and letting them be the hero of the day. Pride does not always deliver results.

If your family of origin isn't meeting your needs, make your own. Take in kids and train them to fight crime. Build your own family out of servants, orphaned circus folk, street urchins, the creepy boy next door and his girlfriend, your co-worker's daughter, and the mute daughter of a world-renowned assassin. You *can* choose your family. (And turn them into crime fighters. Maybe.)

Okay, maybe not. Kids are really hard to train, and society frowns on allowing the little tykes to get shot at after bedtime. My point is, you don't have to just accept that your family is dead, or crazy, or criminals. Your family is what you make it to be, or the family you choose it to be.

Batman is always thought of as a lone wolf type character. Even by his allies. They know Batman doesn't play well with others, perhaps even when he needs to. Yet he's constantly surrounded by other people he has let into his cause. The list is long: Dick Grayson, Barbara Gordon, Jason Todd, Tim Drake, Stephanie Brown, Cassandra Cain, Helena Bertinelli, Kate Kane... a group of people in part thrown together by circumstance, but kept together because of their loyalty to a cause, and to one person. It's not bad to have a second family, and it's okay to have a different kind of family. Especially one who understands you at your core level like that.

Another lesson from Batman would be to hug your kids. If Batman's piss-poor at apologizing for things, he's really *super-poor* at showing his loved ones that he cares about them. Really, Batman, would it kill you to hug Nightwing once in a while and tell him you're proud of him? Maybe he wouldn't be that bundle of neuroses he's grown up to be.

I'm not the greatest with expressing my emotions. I have a long history of playing it close to my chest. I can appreciate that Batman really doesn't want show all his cards to everyone. There's a level of vulnerability in even knowing what your own feelings are, that takes a lot of energy to deal with. And sometimes, when you're dealing with the current world-ending crisis on your plate, you just don't have the ability to cope with both at once. I understand that tendency – in fact, I live it. The more the heat is turned up, the less I have time for fluffy stuff. That said, in those quiet moments, I try to tell my friends and loved ones that I care about them and that they matter to me. I might not be the most effective, but, in this instance, Batman has shown me what not to do.

Batman's a lousy human being, a poor friend, and arguably a terrible father, but you can't really argue with his effectiveness. It's perfectly legitimate to ask What Would Batman Do? There is another good reason to ask this question: for all of those situations in life where you know, deep down in your heart of hearts, that Batman wouldn't put up with this shit.

Remember that time I mentioned where Batman totally punched Guy Gardner in the mouth? And Black Canary was sad she wasn't there to see it? It's because, sometimes, even though you *can* endure a great many things (because you're Batman), maybe you shouldn't have to. If your teammate is acting like a big jerkface, and needs to be punched in the mouth – punch him in the mouth.

Sometimes it's OK to just not put up with other people's shit. Batman said so.

Be who you are, especially if it is Batman. It might not be popular, the other superheroes might hate and fear you a little, but be who you are, deep down inside. Be the best you can be at what you do. It's how you maximize your potential. Take it from me, I know. I'm Batman.

An Interview with Alisa Bendis

Alisa Bendis is the president of Jinxworld Inc., and in this role manages the business aspect of the creative efforts of her husband, Brian Michael Bendis. She is a first generation American child of immigrants, has degrees in political science and education, and has sailed around the world. She lives with her husband and three children in Oregon. Some call her the Marvel CFO of Portland.

Q. Can you introduce yourself for our readers? How do you describe or define yourself to others?

A. First and foremost, I am a mother, wife, and friend. However, I think your readers would be more interested in my job as president of Jinxworld Inc., the company my husband [Brian Michael Bendis] and I founded. Jinxworld Inc. is the business side of Brian's career at Marvel Comics, as well as the financial and production side of his co-creations – works such as *Powers*, *Scarlet*, *Takio*, and now *Brilliant*.

Q. It's interesting that you frame it that way, balancing your personal identity with your business role. Do you find that identity is less a matter of rigid definitions, and more a – shall we say – mental lane-changing, often in heavy metaphorical traffic?

A. Yes... I'm a wife, a mother, the daughter of a Rabbi, a sister, a Canadian, a Portlander, a teacher, and a student. Honestly, I enjoy all of the roles equally. They seem to melt together and give me a solid core reason for being, enjoyment, and the satisfaction of a job well done. Feel free to let your imagination run wild figuring out which word matches each role! At the end of the day, I have the pleasure and honor of being able to live a wonderful life.

Q. What sorts of things fall under your purview at Jinxworld?

A. It includes all aspects of the business that are *not* creative. I deal with contracts, agents, managers, lawyers, subcontractors, accountants, payroll, invoices – everything that one would expect goes into running a small business is a part of my everyday life.

Q. Do you have a favorite of the comics you help to produce?

A. My favorite creator-owned book is *Takio*, and my favorite work-for-hire book is *Ultimate Spider-Man*.

Q. What top three Jinxworld projects are you most proud of, and why?

A. *Fortune and Glory*, because I am in it and think it is hilarious. *Jinx*, because I met Brian while he was working on it, and our relationship influenced Brian's creation of certain aspects of the main character – especially her relationship with her family. *Takio*, because it's a collaboration between Mike Oeming, Brian, and our daughter Olivia.

Q. In what directions do you hope to expand Jinxworld?

A. Honestly, I think we'd just like to continue in the same direction. I am so proud of the work that Brian has done, and I like that he writes what he wants to write. Even with work-for-hire, we've always held the policy that he would never take on a project just for a paycheck. He does work that he cares about. I think that's had a lot to do with his success.

Q. What advice do you have for women interested in starting their own comics companies?

A. First and foremost, treat it like a business. Know how to analyze the market, and know what the market saturation is. Establish a corporation or a Doing Business As[1], and take advantage of *all* legitimate business write-offs and expenses.

Educating yourself is also very important. I spent a year working toward my MBA, and have worked in both business and nonprofit areas, but many people thinking about running their own business will need to learn the skills of the trade. I am a *huge* fan of the financial advisor Suze Orman, and would recommend her books and TV show as a way to learn about managing one's personal and business finances. *Rich Dad, Poor Dad* is another amazing book about molding your financial future.

You should also understand your own limits, and recognize when it's necessary to hire experts. I have a business background, for instance, but I don't think I know more than my accountant and lawyer. If you can't – or don't want to – read and understand every word in a contract, get a lawyer. I cannot tell you how many people have signed contracts they haven't read, or been shocked that what they were *told* was in the con-

---

1. An assumed business name or trade name.

tract by those sending it wasn't actually in the *written* document they signed. I am not talking about people trying to be dishonest, by the way. Sometimes, there is a huge difference between what the legal department is told to do and the creative department's understanding of a project.

I would also encourage anyone considering this to be their own advocate – you are your only and *best* advocate in most cases! Invest in yourself and your future. Being creative is fantastic, but if you can't monetize that creativity, what you have is a hobby. And if you can't hold on to what you make, what you have is a lovely memory.

Q. What is the best part of your job?
A. That I get to take part in serious business meetings while wearing my pajamas.

Q. What is the best part of an average day?
A. My day is a routine. I get up and handle business calls and mail, and the accounting for the day. Maybe I make dinner, but most likely we order out. I spend some quality time with my six-month-old baby before the kids come home – Brian picks up our two older kids at school. Dinner and evening time is filled with kids' stuff. At the end of the night, I get to tuck my kids into bed, and I tell them how lucky I am to be their mom. That is the best part of my day.

Q. What did we forget to ask you, that you want to share with the readers of *Chicks Dig Comics*?
A. I am very lucky that my husband and I have so much mutual admiration. We respect the strengths and weaknesses that we both have – he does something I could never do, i.e., writing comics, and I do things he could never do, i.e., handling the business end of his career. We complement each other – support and love each other. It may sound corny, but it is my life. I am very lucky to be able to have found the partner that completes me.

My Secret Identity

When called upon to produce a biographical fact about herself, **Caroline Pruett** will often mention that she once held cards from six different library systems at the same time, or that she spent an entire year listening to nothing but Bruce Springsteen's album *Nebraska*. Besides borrowed books and depressing songs, she likes comics and writes about them at *Fantastic Fangirls* (fantasticfangirls.org). She holds a Master of Fine Arts degree in fiction writing from George Mason University. During the day, she works at a desk; by night, she doesn't fight crime, but she wouldn't mind if you thought so.

Some mornings, dragging my tired ass in to work and waiting for the first cup of coffee to kick in, I like to pretend that I'm Batwoman. Or, rather, I pretend that I'm Batwoman's civilian alter ego, Kate Kane. Specifically, I think about a scene in *Detective Comics* #854, written by Greg Rucka and drawn by J.H. Williams III, where a haggard, sleep-deprived Kate gets dumped by her girlfriend. The girlfriend, a no-nonsense professional who wears beige, collared shirts and carries a briefcase, looks at the dark circles under Kate's eyes, surmises that she's been fooling around with other women, and storms off with the parting admonition: "Call me when you've decided to grow up."

It's not that I have very much in common with Kate. I don't share any of the major traits that comic book creators have used to define her. I'm not a lesbian. I'm not Jewish. I'm not a socialite or an Army veteran, or a pale-skinned redhead, and I certainly couldn't rock a sleeveless, backless tuxedo shirt and a nautical star tattoo with the kind of aplomb that Kate manages to pull off. What she and I have in common is that we are exhausted, and we dearly hope that someone takes a look at us and thinks, "Oh, I bet she was having fun last night."

Here, again, the similarities end. If I show up at the office stumbling around from too little sleep, the most likely reason is that I was playing around on the Internet, or marathoning DVRed episodes of *Masterpiece Theatre* or (all right, honestly, more likely) *The Vampire Diaries*. Possibly, I was doing both at the same time, so that at the end, I had not only killed my chance at a good night's sleep, but had no clear memory of what I just read *or* what I just watched. Just maybe, before getting online, I was out doing something social, like bar trivia night. In the case of a really wild and crazy evening, I might have driven to another city for a Shakespeare play or an Emmylou Harris concert, crashed on someone's couch, and driven straight to work wearing slightly wrinkled clothes.

If Kate Kane rolls in late? She was up all night kicking bad guys in the face.

It shouldn't be surprising that Batwoman is one of "my" superheroes. I'm female, in my thirties, and I've only been reading comics regularly for about five years. The current incarnation of the character has been around for roughly the same amount of time that I've been a reader, and she's implicitly designed for a certain (grown-up, female) demographic that isn't notably catered to by traditional superhero comics. Her story takes the Batman myth of self-created power, channeled through brains and gadgets and steely discipline, and applies it to the life of a mature female character.

She's called Bat*woman* after all, avoiding the problematic "girl" label. Her costume shows no skin, and if it's tight-fitting in a way that would be unforgiving to anything less than a certain conventionally attractive body type, the same could be said of any of her brothers in spandex. The image of other female superheroes has inspired wardrobe controversies involving bare midriffs (Huntress), visible panties (Supergirl), or design features that necessitate the widespread use of the term "boob window" (Power Girl, Invisible Woman, et cetera, et cetera). Batwoman's first appearance in the 2006-2007 DC Comics event *52* inspired a minor controversy about whether her shoes were sensible enough. Once her costume's high-heeled boots were deemed too inconvenient for rooftop vigilante hijinks, the heels were switched out for heavily-tread military grade boots, the better to stomp bad guys with.

Batwoman is, in other words, a comic book character that I, as a progressive feminist woman in my thirties, am supposed to feel comfortable liking. Superheroes (or their unpowered masked-vigilante cousins, the subspecies to which the various Bats of Gotham City technically belong) are widely supposed to represent fantasies of power. The modifiers "adolescent" and "male" are often tacked on to this description, sometimes with the explicit purpose of saying, "What can you, grown-up women, expect from stories that were never meant for you in the first place? Steer clear of that playground and/or go off and find your own, because this place isn't for you." Batwoman exists, it would seem, as an entry point to the power fantasy for people who are a lot like me.

I'm the kind of cultural consumer who can find myself worried about not liking the right things, or liking the right things for the wrong reasons. In theory, I believe that a person should love what they love, and discover that love for themselves. In practice, I spend a lot of time paying attention to the tastes of *The New Yorker*, NPR, my many smart friends, my favorite feminist bloggers, et cetera. I might end up marathoning *The Vampire Diaries*, but something in my head is nagging me about that adaptation of *Little Dorrit* that I really should get around to. If I were looking for a comic to fit that bill, well, the introduction to the *Batwoman: Elegy* hardcover collection was written by talk show host and certified erudite liberal person Rachel Maddow. Funny books don't get much more "supposed to" than that.

I don't want to give the impression that my love for Kate Kane-as-Batwoman comics is anything other than sincere. It's true that if a female peer – an old classmate, say, from my law school days – asked me to show her one of the superhero comics I'd been reading, I might have an ulterior motive for picking the Rucka/Williams *Batwoman* collection. Grown-up women, fully clothed! Beautiful, innovative art! Rachel Maddow likes it! Comics aren't just for kids! At the same time, I'm not faking my love for the book, any more than I'm pretending to like Shakespeare, or Emmylou Harris, or reading long articles in *The New Yorker*. This self-empowered, non-exploitative, adult female character has a strong appeal for me that taps right into a vein of stories that I love.

Here's where it gets complicated. I think it's true that superhero stories have a strong capacity to tap into the fantasy lives of the audience. In the comic book form, particularly, the combination of words, iconic images, and potentially endless iteration on a core of stories that have been kicking around for (at least) 70 years can provide a powerful sense of wish fulfillment. It's not a fantasy that clicks with everyone. There are people who read these comics for other reasons, just as there are people to whom the medium and genre are never going to appeal. Still, I think you could get most superhero junkies (my people!) to admit that on a good day, when it's really working, there is someone on that comic book page with whom they would really like to switch places for a day or two.

Creating and promoting a character like Batwoman, then, interacts with the classic wish-fulfillment mythos in a very simple way. Take the traditional power fantasy and expand the definition of the person who is allowed to live it out. Fans of the genre get a recognizable superhero origin story, while adult women (and lesbians, and Jewish people, and veterans kicked out of the service because of "Don't Ask, Don't Tell"; pale-skinned redheads, too, I suppose, though there's not exactly a dearth of them) have a character to project their fantasies onto.

And yet... fantasy management is a complicated thing. If superhero comics really work on a pure power-fantasy basis, then, when I think about that breakup in the coffee shop, I am projecting myself into the wrong part of Batwoman's life. I should be fantasizing about leaping from rooftop to rooftop, trading quips with Batman, stomping bad guys with those customized boots. The moment when Kate gets dumped should be collateral damage, the sad tradeoff that has to be made in order to keep from sharing her identity with others. Under the classic secret-identity conundrum, if Kate could only reveal her nocturnal activities then, instead of telling her to grow up and storming off in a huff, her girlfriend would be impressed, and a little turned on. Loneliness is part of the responsibility that comes with the power. The panel that ends this scene, where Kate looks forlorn as the other woman stomps out, ought to be a low point.

Instead, this ends up being the moment I most want to *be* Kate. I like her outings as Batwoman; I like the fights and the stomping, and I sure as hell like the costume. The part of the fantasy that grabs me, though, is not the image of physical power, much less some "correct" idea of female empowerment. The particular connection that I want to share with Kate is the power that comes from having a secret.

This aspect of my wish-fulfillment is not, I think, particularly eccentric. Secret identity has been a flipside of the superhero/vigilante's physical power pretty much from the start. Batman had Bruce Wayne, Wonder Woman had Diana Prince, Spider-Man had Peter Parker. Usually there would be at least a token explanation for this plot device – Batman's power thrived on mystery, Peter had to protect his family and girlfriends from supervillains – but the trope took on a life that could sometimes defy logic. Tony Stark used to claim Iron Man was his bodyguard long past the point that anybody could have bought it. More to the point, it's hard to conceive a billionaire/daredevil/narcissist like Tony, having turned himself into a superhero, being able to resist the impulse to brag about it to the world and dare anybody to stop him. The recent film franchise, to its credit, absolutely gets this, and has Tony out himself by the end of the first movie.

Modern superhero comics are still ambivalent on the subject of whether heroes should have secret identities. There are good Watsonian (in-universe) and Doylist (metatextual) arguments on each side, and Marvel's *Civil War* event of a few years back was, as much as anything, an on-the-page squabble about the relevance of genre conventions. Kate Kane/Batwoman still has a double life, and she likely always will. It's not entirely clear, though, that the story she is part of thinks this is a good idea. *Batwoman: Elegy* resonates with the damaging power of secrets. We eventually learn that Kate was kicked out of the military for refusing to lie about her sexuality. In the present day, she openly flirts and dances with other women. She even lets her father in on her superhero identity, and eventually they fall out because she learns he has been keeping secrets about the family's past.

At work here are familiar tropes from many types of fiction: Lying about your identity is bad because it's inauthentic (a golden rule of romance fiction); lying about the past is bad, because deception weaves a tangled web and corruption breeds more corruption (a golden rule of mystery and noir). In either case, the truth will out, and then it will come back to haunt you. Yet superhero stories, which often draw heavily on both romance and mystery, frequently flaunt or ignore these rules when it comes to secret identity. Along with the many logistical and ethical problems, this seems like another argument for dropping the convention altogether.

Yet the secret identity persists and, in the end, I'm glad that it does. If we insist, or accept, that the superhero fantasy is one of raw power, then it's that much easier to let the adolescent males to whom this supposedly speaks chase the rest of us off the playground. Of course, grown women may have as much reason – and as much right – as teenage boys to dream about physical power. In fact, strength and secrecy are closely linked for female heroes. Kate Kane may look like a hungover party girl and thus easy prey for a villain, but in truth she has already looked around the room and found 20 ways to fend off an attack.

Yet, even beyond the allure of hidden physical strength, the fantasy of secret identity has an appeal that transcends demographics. For anybody who knows the experience of getting lost in a make-believe world – for anyone who knows the experience, in other words, of being a geek and being a fan – the secret identity has an appeal that is part of the text itself. It's a dream of meaning, a wish for purpose. Beyond this day-to-day life, beyond what you see of me, I am working on something extraordinary.

Just as soon as I finish up with *The Vampire Diaries*.

The Green Lantern Mythos:
A Metaphor For My (Comic Book) Life

Jill Pantozzi is a pop-culture journalist/host who goes by the moniker "The Nerdy Bird" online. You can find her thoughts on all things geeky including, but not limited to, comic books, movies and video games at her personal blog, *Has Boobs, Reads Comics*. Jill went to school for journalism and spent the first five years after college working as a radio DJ in New Jersey before she made the move back to reporting. She's been a contributor to sites like *MTV Splash Page, Publishers Weekly, Topless Robot*, and more. Along with other work there, Jill contributes the weekly op-ed column "Hey, That's My Cape!" to *Newsarama*. She's currently working full-time as associate editor for the geek girl culture site *The Mary Sue*, and her first comic will be included in the all-female created *Womanthology* from IDW Publishing.

I love *Green Lantern.*

I love the characters, I love the stories, and I especially love how there's something for everyone to be found in the recent "War of Light" storyline because of the *emotions* involved. If you're not familiar with the series, comics superstar Geoff Johns introduced the idea into the Green Lantern books that instead of there being just the one Lantern Corps (green, representing willpower), there are multiple Corps, each with a different color, and each embodying a different part of the "emotional spectrum." Rage, avarice, fear, willpower, hope, compassion, and love are taken to another level entirely by their respective Corps, who each wield special power rings. As a reader, seeing individual characters fueled by just one emotion – instead of the several we experience on a daily basis – spotlights what those emotions mean and can do to an individual.

Humans are emotional creatures, and in my experience, comic fans are especially emotional because of our deep passion for these four-color marvels. When you care about something that much, no matter its impact on the world at large, it becomes serious business. If you've ever visited a comic book forum or comment section online, you know what I mean.

To me, comics are a form of entertainment, but they've managed to make me *feel* more than anything else ever has, and that's likely one of the major reasons I keep coming back for more. Although I've only been reading comics for about seven years, and am still considered a newcomer by most, these colorful books have led me through that emotional spectrum and back.

Red Lanterns: Rage

The Red Lanterns, embodying rage, are my favorite Corps of the spectrum. I mean, come on! They vomit napalm blood, and one of their members is a cat.

The Red Lanterns get angry at just about everything – which, coincidentally, is often how comic fans are perceived. Kill off a character? Fans get angry. Bring a character back from the dead? Fans get angry. Change a character's costume? Fans get *really* angry. You see what I'm getting at.

I am certainly not immune to this. I experienced an intense personal comic book rage when DC announced they were relaunching their entire line (and much of their continuity) as "The New 52" in 2011. As much as I know about the ins-and-outs of the comic industry, and no matter how much I realize that I do not own these characters, some of the changes made got me pretty upset. The worst was when I learned that Barbara Gordon, who had spent the last 20 years in a wheelchair after the Joker shot and paralyzed her from the waist down (Alan Moore's *The Killing Joke*, 1988), would regain the use of her legs. Barbara had been fighting crime as the computer genius/ information broker Oracle, but now DC was telling us that she would return to her former Batgirl identity.

I really saw red over this. I'm a redhead who spends most of her time in a wheelchair thanks to my being born with a type of Muscular Dystrophy, so it's safe to say that Oracle was someone I admired. I expressed my anger and disappointment at DC swapping one of their most prominent disabled characters for one who was able-bodied in an op-ed piece titled "Oracle is Stronger Than Batgirl Will Ever be" for *Newsarama*. Luckily, I wrote that piece after taking some time to digest the news, but it didn't change the fact that I was angry. I look up to Batman, I look up to Wonder Woman, but I could relate to Oracle like no one else. Barbara Gordon is fantastic no matter what, but her Oracle persona was something special. I'm less angry about it now, but I still wish that DC had seen the continuing potential in Oracle, and marketed her the way she deserved.

Orange Lanterns: Avarice

The Orange Lanterns – or should I say the *only* Orange Lantern, Larfleeze – are not known for sharing. The gist of Larfleeze? He's so greedy that he wants everything. No matter what (or whom) it is. If he knows what it is, he wants it. If he *doesn't* know what it is, he wants it. Other characters can wield an orange power ring, but the rings tend to control their wearers. As a result, Larfleeze is so full of avarice that he doesn't allow anyone else to join his corps voluntarily.

Larfleeze is absolutely a reflection of our own materialism. I'm not a greedy person naturally (except maybe when it comes to spending time with those I love), but I freely admit I am deeply attached to the action figures sitting on my shelf right now. They're not at all important in the grand scheme of things – yet if anyone tried to take the figures away from me, or tell me they weren't worthy of my devotion, I'd be a very grumpy fan indeed. Larfleeze may desire a broken toilet seat the rest of us see as trash, but someone could potentially see the need for a few garbage bags in my room, too. Would I let them get within ten feet of my precious collectables? Never.

I keep pretty much all of the comics I buy every week, but I don't consider myself a comic collector. No, where my *real* greed comes into play is with toys and action figures. Whether they come from Toys R Us or Etsy, I gotta have them all. It's honestly a good thing I don't have money to burn, or else I would probably need an intervention for all the comic book memorabilia I'd be purchasing.

I'm greedy in one other big way: I feel like the comic book characters closest to my heart are *my* characters. I didn't create them, I don't own them, but I'm so invested in them they truly feel like *mine*. I know I'm not alone in this, and the long history that comes along with DC and Marvel properties are at least partially to blame. The characters are embedded in our culture. Everyone has an opinion on them. Tell me your neighbor didn't have something to say when they took away Superman's red underpants.

Sinestro Corps: Fear

The Sinestro Corps, as the name suggests, is led by Sinestro – an ex-Green Lantern who was a scary dude even when he was on the side of the heroes. The Sinestro Corps seek to instill fear in others; Sinestro himself is a master at doing so, but seems to be mostly immune to fear himself. I wish I were that lucky.

Unfortunately, fear plays a rather large role in my comic book life.

My first attempt at cosplay was extremely daunting, and I was scared out of my mind. I chose to dress up as Poison Ivy, a member of Batman's Rogue Gallery. Her costume (depending on who's drawing her) is basically a one-piece bathing suit made out of leaves. I can't say how I come across to others, but I'm not the most extroverted person, so when it came time to take off my coat and actually reveal the costume on a convention floor, I really wanted to get back in my car and hide.

Did I mention this was the middle of winter in New York? Granted, I was indoors for the show, but it still felt odd to be wearing that modest amount of clothing. Not only was I frightened to be cosplaying at all, but I was also incredibly worried about a wardrobe malfunction that thankfully never happened. I found comfort after tons of strangers told me I did a fantastic job on my costume, but there was nothing quite like that initial terror.

While I was *angry* at the characters and storylines that DC was changing in its "New 52" relaunch, it was really a fear of the unknown that bothered me. Comics are not only a source of entertainment, they're a big comfort for me as well. What if I didn't like the new stories? What if the changes were so drastic I stopped reading them all together? Since the majority of my reading list is DC comics, this could have potentially meant a major change for my routine. Not going to the comic shop every week to pick up the newest DCs would just be... weird.

There was also that tiny chance that it would derail my career path. (You know, nothing to panic about.) Writing about comics was not what I set out to do when I decided to be a journalist at age 13, but I've come to truly love it. Sure, I can write on just about anything, but could I find something to write about that was also a hobby I enjoyed? Neither of these scenarios have come to pass, but for a time, they put a fear in me worse than any character death ever could.

Green Lanterns: Willpower

Willpower is something I have to search for a lot while doing my job, so it's a good thing the Green Lanterns are a constant source of inspiration. Wielding their green energy constructs takes incredible willpower; without it, they'd fail in their mission – or worse, die.

Fortunately, in my line of work, things aren't so life or death. However, it's sometimes a challenge to give your opinion on a particular topic – because, well, everyone has strong opinions in comics. It's one thing to talk about something you're enjoying, that's easy. It's far more challenging to go into critical territory – to review a comic that perhaps wasn't so great, or to criticize a publisher for their actions or inactions. It's especially challenging if your thoughts don't follow public opinion – or anger those specifically involved.

As a writer, you put yourself out there for public scrutiny – in the comic community, that scrutiny can be brutal. Folks are really attached to their comics, and the Internet breeds a *special* kind of emotional outpouring – such as calling a writer insulting names, or being otherwise rude or offensive. I've gotten my fair share of "critical" comments on my opinion articles, which seems weird because it's an *opinion*, my personal viewpoint. You'd think I'd be entitled to that, but some people still find a way to tell me I'm wrong.

The feedback I'd receive on opinion pieces used to really upset me, but after seeing the ebb and flow of Internet commentary and speaking with others in the industry, I came to realize a few things. No. 1: Not everyone commenting online is in his or her right mind. No. 2: Anonymity breeds terrible behavior from human beings. The things these people have the nerve to say online would never come out of their mouths if they saw you face to face. And No. 3: Continuing on after receiving harsh criticism can take a lot of effort (especially if the critics have hit a nerve), but for the most part it's better – and a lot more fun – to just laugh them off. The willpower it takes to not fall into their traps can be phenomenal, but it's totally rewarding when you see someone getting angry (particularly those pesky trolls) *because you're not reacting.*

Blue Lanterns: Hope

The Blue Lanterns are all about hope. From what we've seen so far, they're a pretty serene and peaceful bunch. I'd like to think I'm a hopeful person. My ability to stay optimistic in comics can run low in the midst of what sometimes feels like constant negativity, but there are some hopeful things happening, too.

I started my own blog as a means of getting back into writing after I'd worked as a radio DJ for a few years. I used my blog to cover my first convention, and then sent the post off to a few comic book websites. Comic Book Resources sent back an extremely positive response, and it wasn't too long before I was working for them. Yes! I was getting paid to write about comics! It made me hopeful that the choice I had made to stray back into writing was the right one.

Something else that really fills me with hope? Creators that "get it" – they depict a wide range of characters in realistic and respectful ways. There are tons of fantastic indie creators who do a remarkable job at this, but the same cannot always be said for the two biggest comic book publishers. Time and again, Marvel and DC publish stories and hire creators that promote stereotypes and demean women, which is a disservice to both new and established readers. At times the publishers don't seem to recognize that the comic book readership has evolved, and there's a need for their stories and marketing to change along with it.

Fortunately, many people working in the industry *do* understand this. Creators such as Greg Rucka, Cully Hamner, Gail Simone, Francis Manapul, Marcus To, Dan Slott, Cliff Chiang, Jamal Igle, Jesus Saiz, and Paul Cornell give me hope. Hope that comics will continue to evolve into an inclusive rather than exclusive form of entertainment. Hope that we'll see a wider range of body types illustrated on comic pages. Hope for storylines that include characters who are minorities, of all sexualities and gender identities, or who have disabilities – and treat them not just with respect, but as characters who can be equally if not more successful than those already out there.

Some of these creators purposefully crusade for these things in the industry, while others find it comes naturally to their work. Whatever the case, they are part of the reason I look forward to the future of comics with a sense of optimism.

Indigo Tribe: Compassion

Comic readers still don't know a great deal about the Indigo Tribe, who represent compassion (something sorely lacking in this world), are completely selfless, and shun all individualism. While that last part isn't for me, their apparent goals in the Green Lantern universe are probably the closest to my heart. A lot of people don't understand compassion – which isn't pity or feeling sorry for someone. It's sympathy and empathy, it's goodwill towards others. It's putting yourself in their shoes and attempting to understand what they're going through.

I have a great deal of compassion for women working in comics – and yes, I'm technically a woman working in comics myself, but I'm talking specifically about those who are really in the thick of things, working for comic publishers, or self-publishing their own properties. There are women who write and draw comics, who edit comics, who promote comics, and who are making such strides at giving the comic book industry more gender balance. We can all appreciate their successes, but I feel for them because they chose to work in this male-dominated industry for a simple reason: They love comics and the art form as a whole. They want to be here, and they want to make it better for the next wave of women who yearn to do what they're doing.

Comics is a tough and intimidating industry to break into, with men still holding the majority of the decision-making positions. A lot of women are self-publishing (a hard road for anyone, even if they're successful) and showing other women out there that they can do it too.

While it may surprise some, I also have compassion for the comic companies themselves. While they often deserve the flack they get for certain aspects of their marketing or business practices, comic publishing has been struggling in recent years, and that's a difficult situation for anyone to face as they go to work each morning. Not to mention how they're on the receiving end of constant complaints from fans about the tiniest changes to comic titles and their characters.

Ah yes, the fans. I feel for them most of all, especially those who have loved comics their whole lives. They have experienced so many more ups and downs through the decades than I have, and from even the little slice of the industry and comic book storytelling that I have witnessed so far, it makes me truly sympathetic to their woes.

Star Sapphires: Love

Love can make you do crazy things, but – despite the purity of their motives – Star Sapphires sometimes take their core emotion to a violent, unhealthy place. They represent the opposite extreme of the emotional spectrum as the Red Lanterns, after all. Thinking in those terms, the love I've experienced through comics is often equal to the rage I've felt.

I love my blog – without it, I wouldn't be where I am today, and it's a comforting outlet to have. Through my site, I've been able to show a large segment of male readers that there were also women who read comics and have the same strong feelings about them. Some have viewed it differently, but my blog title – *Has Boobs, Reads Comics* – is a satire that says, "yeah, and?" My content showed who I was, my love for comics, and that I was a serious part of the reading audience.

Thanks to my blog, I have met and become friends with industry creators, and formed communities and long-lasting friendships with other bloggers. This happened simply because I was being myself, and sharing my love for comics. A lot of us found our way to Twitter, where even more friendships were made. Of all the things the comics industry has done for me, I'm the most thankful for this – it's amazing how my love of reading comics (an activity meant to be enjoyed alone) wound up granting me a new, wonderful social group. And introducing people to comics, who may be into other geeky activities but never made the jump, is such a rewarding experience.

I love every minute of this. It's really a good time to be a comic fan, because right now, Hollywood is scrambling to produce TV shows and motion pictures that are based on comic books. Of course, those shows and movies can be hit or miss, but the public's enjoyment of superhero and non-superhero comic characters alike has evolved into the wonderful gift of their coming to life on the big and small screen.

All These Feelings Are Exhausting, But Worth It

With every new movie/television show announcement, a funny thing happens. Comic fans go through the entire emotional spectrum. And so do I.

Some people prefer certain genres – horror, drama, comedy, romance, etc. To me, superhero books are the complete package, and *Green Lantern* is the most all-encompassing package of them all. It has horror, drama, comedy, romance, and more in spades, and it's always a pleasant surprise to find out which emotions I'm going to feel when I sit down and open up an issue. It's the anticipation, and the ability to make me feel, that makes me keep coming back for more. Although I wish DC had thought to make smaller replica power rings for tiny lady fingers like my own, I can still imagine playing a part in saving the universe – or destroying it as the case may be – with whatever emotion I feel most connected to.

Green Lantern – and the world of comics as a whole – may be an emotional rollercoaster for me at times, but I wouldn't have it any other way.

Jen Van Meter has been writing comics for 15 years. She is best known for her series of Hopeless Savages comics from Oni Press, who jump-started her career by hiring her to write the comic book tie-in material for *The Blair Witch Project*. She has also written superhero and adventure comics, including *Black Lightning: Year One* (DC), a Black Cat mini-series collected as *Spider-Man: Black Cat*, and *Avengers: Solo* (Marvel).

Welcome, dearies! Your old fiend Auntie Jen's here to bring you a gruesome tale of surprise, terror, ambivalent social politics, literacy, and suspense! Our story begins long ago, when the Vietnam War was barely over and the President had been caught – as we kids understood it – burglarizing a hotel. People were talking about something called "Women's Lib" while the Dallas Cowboy Cheerleaders roamed the earth communicating by CB radio with Burt Reynolds. ABBA and Saturday Night Live *were new.*

Back then, my little gremlins, grocery stores and gas stations sold comic books on spin racks, the pause button had yet to be invented, and school bullies were accepted as an inconvenient fact of life rather than a problem, in much the way we now regard other people using mobile phones impolitely and ATM surcharges. Also, no mobile phones or ATMs. Strange times these were – marked by wondrous technological advances, international terrorism, an energy crisis, social upheaval over race, class, gender, and sexuality – and the setting for a little story I like to call…

OR: HOW I LEARNED TO STOP WORRYING AND LOVE THE PAGE TURN

Read on, ghouls and goonies, IF YOU DARE…

Brent King[1] was my first monster.

When we were in kindergarten, Brent figured out how to fold his eyelids up and roll back his eyes; the pink, raw-looking tissue and blood-shot whites may not have hurt him, but the effect was unsettling and he could hold it for a good 30 seconds. He would do this at the lunch table and dare the other boys to look; if they did anything but grin, Brent would point at them and shout, "You're a baby! A *girl* baby!"

Later, he figured out how to stick straight pins through the top layer of skin on his fingertips and wave the painful-looking result in our faces. First grade, if I remember correctly, was all about eating disgusting food combinations open-mouthed, letting the results spill down his chin. Eventually, he graduated to showing off insects he had tortured and other things – worse things – but I'm going to stop there. Suffice to say, Brent had a lot of bits like this and they always came with a dare and a threat, issued only to the boys: Look away and you are a *girl baby* or a *sissy*, and, by the end of third grade, a *pussy*.

I remember feeling grateful that my girlhood let me off the hook as far as Brent was concerned; if I didn't admire his wet belches and zombie stares, it didn't change my status in his eyes one bit. At the time, we girls felt we had it easy compared to some of the boys because they suffered so much more immediately under that measuring gaze. But there was also a tension I don't think we were then able to articulate, a constant hum of threat; whenever a new girl joined the class, the first thing we told her was to stay near a teacher or a group at recess, to never ever get left alone with Brent.

Almost all the kids were scared of him, certain further torments awaited anyone he deemed deserving. Without ever laying a hand on another kid or directly threatening to, he had us all ducking, and we didn't question his right to behave as he did any more than krill question a whale's right to eat them. That's the thing that pains me most when I recall those first couple years of school: It never once occurred to me to ask a teacher or parent for help, because I saw no indication that they didn't think behavior like Brent's was perfectly normal.

I don't mean to suggest that I was bullied at home – I wasn't – but the tone of the times was "nobody likes a tattletale," not "it gets better." The bully-as-villain characters showed up in kids' books and television, but usually with a humor beat; we were encouraged to view them as ignorant buffoons to be avoided, bested, or won over, and involving

---

1. Brent King is a pseudonym very far afield from the real name of anyone I knew or know.

adults was represented as an embarrassment to the whole kid community. When the fictional bullies were truly threatening, the solution was usually a noble bigger kid with bigger fists; no good at all against someone like Brent. I remember once saying something about him to a teen-aged boy who lived on my block; he got very grave and asked, "Is he hurting you?" It was comforting to know in that moment that if I'd said yes, this kid would have gladly gone to bat for me, but instead I had to shake my head and watch him frown, uncertain what he could offer. I didn't have words for what I felt, that Brent was hurting our *spirit*.

It was a rigged game – a bully's dare always is. I set the terms, you ante up your reputation, your self-esteem; whether you meet the terms or not, I retain my power position as the arbiter of success or failure, so the house always wins. That contract, such as it is, poisons our positive sense of challenge and risk, our *daring*, by externalizing its source and changing the stakes. Rather than doing something nervy or new because we want to see if we can, because we're curious, because we think we should or because taking the risk is kind of thrilling, we start to bully ourselves, thinking instead in terms of the *pussies* we'll be – in others' eyes or our own – if we don't. Our moxie becomes something more toxic, a losing bet we can keep enacting all by ourselves, even when it drains the delight out of achievement, the thrill out of risk.

What I needed in my life right then was an adult who would confirm that my fear of Brent – of his sadistic need to terrorize us, not his inside-out eyelids and half-chewed food – was reasonable. I needed an adult perspective that could armor me against his assault on my confidence. And in June 1975, I found it in the bottom drawer of a dresser in my great-grandparents' cabin: three copies of *Vampirella*, two each of *Creepy* and *Eerie*, and one *House of Mystery*.

It was an old place, and every kid who had ever stayed there had probably left a couple comics behind. Dig to the bottom, and you might find romance and crime comics left there in the '40s, and layered on top of those an archeological survey of superheroes, *Archie*, war comics, westerns, *Little Lulu*, and *Richie Rich*. Even before I could read, I had enjoyed it as a rainy-day option, but that day I opened the drawer and found these gorgeously lurid painted covers by the likes of Frank Frazetta, Jack Davis, and Tom Sutton, all emblazoned with copy promising outright that the terrifying contents would curdle my blood, tingle my spine, and chill my bones: I opened them and read them. Over and over. Every single one. Later that summer, I would spend all my tooth fairy and bottle-deposit money on more.

But why? Until I encountered those comics, I would have sworn to you that Brent was right about me, that I couldn't *handle* being scared, grossed out or surprised. I accepted as facts that I was chicken, that it was because I was a girl, and that it was at once shameful and perfectly normal that this was the case. And believe me, I'm not suggesting that these notions came to me solely from Brent; I'm well aware that he was only parroting something the rest of the mainstream culture was dishing out to us both. So *why* did I read those comics? Why did I *dare*?

Because they *wanted* me to. Right there on the covers: "Come with us, into a world of ghosts, vampires... creatures of shadow!" "Join Us... Beneath the Werewolf's Moon!" The comics neither knew nor cared that I was a girl, that I was seven, that I hid behind the couch when the winged monkeys appeared in *The Wizard of Oz*; these books wanted me to read them and admitted it. And inside? A friendly lady vampire, a ghoulish pair of comedians dropping truly terrible puns, and a Bible figure in a mod suit cracking wise about crime and punishment – all addressing me not with a sneer about how I probably couldn't handle the stories they introduced, but with a promise that I could, and that the payoff would be worth any scares I encountered. As unlikely as it might seem, Vampirella, Cousin Eerie, Uncle Creepy, and Cain – the hosts of these anthology comics – came to form for me a kind of bizarre league of anti-bullies, inverting the oppressive gambit Brent had worked on me and challenging its persistent underlying premise that as a girl I was somehow not up to the task of *looking*, of confronting whatever might be there to be seen.

In the wake of the Vietnam War and the Civil Rights and Women's Movements, the horror and suspense genres were having a kind of renaissance; the stuff was everywhere. Here's how it looked to me, a child at the time: A local TV channel (one of only four) ran five horror movies in a row every Saturday, *Dark Shadows* came on just after the game shows and before my babysitter's soap operas, the movie theaters were full of everything from grindhouse to sophisticated suspense, *The Exorcist* had just won an Oscar, and *Carrie* was a bestseller. If I came out at night for a drink of water, grownups were watching things like *Night Gallery* and *Kolchack: The Night Stalker*.

Maybe it was that sense of *zeitgeist*, maybe it was just Brent's setting the terms for what bravery meant, but despite feeling resigned to my scaredy-cat status, I had already been drawn to the horror genre; I suspected there was something in there I wanted, but had come to accept that I did not deserve nor would I find a way in. I had tried some creepy movies and television shows and they hadn't worked for me; without the now-ubiquitous pause button, they were all or nothing, like roller coaster rides. Once the bar came down and the story started moving, I was stuck, with no opportunity to control the experience short of walking away entirely. They were also humiliatingly social; if it got to be too much, everyone heard me yelp, saw me cover my eyes or leave the theater. Without the freedom to negotiate the terms of the encounter, scary movies and television were, for me, just like Brent: something to be endured, never enjoyed.

I had looked to prose as well, but R.L. Stine and the *Goosebumps* books were over a decade away, and my reading skills could not yet keep up with the Lovecraft I would one day adore. I had asked our librarian for "something scary," but the ghost story and folk tale collections she'd found for me were all plot, no suspense. Looking back, I realize the "age appropriate" books she was handing me were written precisely so as to *not* scare children, but I can't bear Mrs. Arthur a grudge on that account. I was a little kid, after all. (And bless her heart, it was she who would just a couple years later hand me *A Wrinkle in Time, Frankenstein,* and *The Haunting of Hill House* with a sly remark about the sort of literature "nice girls ought to read and write.")

Not everyone wants or needs what horror has to offer, and I freely admit that there's much within the genre that is as bullying, sadistic, and misogynistic as anything a hundred Brents could have imagined (though the same can be said of other genres). Beyond the invitational cover copy and non-threatening host personalities, though, those comics and the adults responsible for them gave me information no other *accessible* source was providing, information I needed:

1. Children can be evil too. And grownups know it. In these anthology comics, easily every fifth or sixth story featured some sort of "bad seed" kid: sometimes possessed, sometimes the product of abuse or neglect, sometimes an alien, and sometimes just a nasty, horrible person. I found it enormously comforting to realize that the adults listed as writers and editors in the mastheads – Archie Goodwin, Bruce Jones, Nicola Cuti, Louise Jones, Bill DuBay – knew that kids like Brent were possible. The more I read, the more it sank in that if these stories were in a scary comic meant for adults, then perhaps the adults were as frightened of a kid like Brent as I was. Their looking away made a lot more sense in that light, and recast my own fears as reasonable, the product of neither my age nor my gender.

2. You will never see anything as terrifying as what you don't see.
The event between the panels, the contents of the old lady's basket, the object that everyone is recoiling from, the thing that casts that shadow; all of it is scarier than what's right there to be looked at, and there's nothing there at all if you don't imagine it. I learned this from some people whose names – Alex Toth, Al Williamson, Jeff Jones, Bernie Wrightson, Carmine Infantino, Dick Giordano – weren't meaningful to me for a decade or more, but whose talent as artists showed me the power of my own imagination as well as the ways in which it could be manipulated by others. They didn't have to draw the guy getting his head torn off by a werewolf for me to know it was happening; the artists' slight-of-hand – and, I eventually saw, Brent's main intimidation technique – was to get me to tell the worst part of the story myself. Making this association didn't mean I wrote off the possibility that one day Brent would escalate his attacks in dangerous ways, but it did arm me with the knowledge that his power was largely derived from our accepting his terms.

3. Mean people get that way somehow. A lot of the stories in these anthologies were pretty simple morality tales and revenge fantasies – terrible people getting punished for their crimes in ironic and horrible ways – and that came with its own satisfaction. I didn't necessarily conclude that Brent would one day be bullied by a bigger (or undead, or alien) bully, but I admit it was vindicating to see that the adults responsible for these stories agreed that there would be some justice in it if he were. What was more challenging, but probably healthier for me, was the vast number of stories in which the horror was seated in what was done to *create* the monster. The bigotry of the extended community in "My Monster... My Dad" (Jan Strnad and Martin Salvador, *Creepy* #76) turns the child of a loving, warmly portrayed interracial couple into a little psycho who murders his stepfather. Another that had a big effect on me was "Brain Food" (Maxene Fabe and Fred Carillo, *House of Mystery* #215), in which a boy teased by classmates for struggling in school takes, in essence, a smart drug which in turn makes him the addicted agent of aliens intent on eating his peers.

The empathy lesson was stark and unavoidable to me: Kids like Brent got that way somehow, and might themselves need pity and help. I wish I could say that absorbing this notion helped me work some kind of empathy-magic reversal in Brent's life, but I can't; he was persistent at making himself unapproachable. But I did stop *hating* him, and I tried to be nice, and if it didn't change who he was, it at least changed who I would be the next time I met someone like him.

4. The page is there for anyone to turn it. The choice to turn the page is yours, no matter who you are. The structure of a comic, any comic, teaches the reader the importance of one's own agency and engagement, but I place my learning it squarely at the feet of Vampirella. There she was, all adult and sexy in a Playboy-bunny-like costume that had been co-designed by a woman (Trina Robbins, as I'd learned from the letter-column in #13), asking me to read her stories. Her tone was like my big sister's on the days when she felt more protective than annoyed toward me, welcoming and warm.

Unlike the host characters in the other comics, she was also the lead in her own serial narrative, which ran alongside the other one-shot stories she introduced; fighting monsters wherever she met them, Vampi struggled to maintain her sunny disposition and integrity despite being hunted by the father of her true love, Adam Van Helsing. That the art was often sexually exploitative didn't register with me at the time; what did stay with me was her strength, her determination to do good in the world, her confidence that her actions mattered, her agency. She gave me what Sarah Connor would offer a decade later in the *Terminator* films and what Buffy Summers would offer another decade after that: a role model that placed all the traditional heroic traits in a woman's body with little in the way of apology or compromise.

One of fiction's services to the young, I'm convinced, is to resist the Brent Kings of the world for us and with us. Engaged by a story, we get to reclaim and revive our moxie, not only by identifying with characters who call tyranny by its name and model a range of ways to defy intimidation, but also, in the case of suspense and horror, by *practicing* against the stories themselves. Where meeting a bully's dare in real life usually produces little more than a hollow feeling of temporary respite, meeting a story's dare – moving past a cringe or a quickened pulse to get to the end – can bring catharsis, laughter, pity, enlightenment, a sense of validation, any number of emotional and intellectual satisfactions. A *good* scary story offers us something *useful* in return for engaging, rewards us for pushing past fear, helps us to recognize the external dare for the empty-handed long con that it is, teaches us to turn the page with confidence.

Confessions of a (Former) Unicorn

Tara O'Shea is a Chicago-area writer and web developer. In addition to co-editing the Hugo-Award winning anthology *Chicks Dig Time Lords* (with Lynne M. Thomas), she also designs and maintains websites for authors such as Seanan McGuire, Claudia Gray, RJ Anderson, and Paul Cornell. As a journalist, her articles, reviews, interviews, and essays have appeared in such publications as *Tor.com*, *Firefox News*, Titan's officially licensed *Angel* magazine, *Yahoo! Internet Life*, *The 11th Hour*, *Audio Revolution*, *MediaSharx/ZENtertainment*, and other online and print publications. For more information about the author, please visit her website at fringe-element.net.

Comics For Heroes was a classic hole-in-the-wall comics shop. It was tiny, with a table of back-issue boxes that took up 80% of the main room. It smelled sweetly of old paper, a smell that gets under your skin and makes me think of childhood. The walls were lined with displays and, up high where kids couldn't potentially break them, action figures, toys, art books, statues, and T-shirts. The front door and windows were covered by posters and standees, faded to black and white by the sun. My mother was convinced it was an opium den, and insisted on accompanying me the first time I went, to ensure that I would emerge from this cave of wonders alive and (mostly) sane.

What made Comics For Heroes so special was its owner – Linda Schein.

Linda was younger than my mom, with black hair and a gold-capped tooth. She was a full-blooded Native American from the Choctaw Nation, and had served in the Marines as a radio operator. What I remembered most was that she always wore a faded blue *Chicago Tribune* apron, the pockets of which held all her cash to make change. There was no cash register; Linda would write down what you bought on a pad of paper in pencil or pen, and give you free handouts of *DC Direct* and other promotions with your books.

It took me almost a year before I figured out new comics arrived on Wednesdays, and specific titles shipped on certain weeks. Linda would let me hang out and talk for hours at the shop, paging through *Previews* to see what was coming, and she would special order anything in its pages and allow patrons to pay in installments over time. I still remember buying a George Perez Wonder Woman T-shirt, $3 at a time, until I'd finally paid it off. I wore it until it was faded and stained and no longer fit, and didn't care if my classmates teased me.

You might think that being a comics geek would mean I was "just one of the guys." But boys my own age weren't looking for girls to pal around with and talk capes. They wanted girls in Laura Ashley dresses with Swatch watches with whom they could go to school dances. Not weirdos who sat beneath the metal fire escape stairs reading *The Flash* and *New Teen Titans*.

I didn't care. When I looked at the DC Comics masthead, I saw Publisher Jenette Kahn, Editor Karen Berger, artists Jill Thompson and Colleen Doran, and writers Mindy Newman, Kim Yale, and Barbara Randall. I saw women working in comics and knew that I could grow up to be like them. It was an amazing feeling. I could be *exactly* who I was, yet stand up and be proud. I could be a fan of *Batman*, because Jenette Kahn read *Batman*. She was my hero and my inspiration, as each month I read her *Publishorial* columns printed on the inside front cover of every Deluxe Format title. There she talked about everything from her childhood love of *Batman* to the day-to-day operations of publishing comics. She provided a peek into the mysterious world of how comics were made, and while it didn't answer all my questions, it did give me a foothold on understanding not just the stories I was reading, but the industry that generated them.

When I was 15, Linda let me work part time in the store, pulling back issues to prep for Chicago Comic-Con, which was held every July 4th weekend. I had heard about it, but never gone, and dreamt one day of actually going and meeting the writers, artists, and editors who fed my imagination monthly with their stories.

I used to show up for work early, sitting on the metal stoop in the broiling summer sun in jeans and a button-down oxford cloth shirt, waiting for Linda or her daughters Nibe and Angie to arrive and unlock the shop. Once inside, I'd be handed a list of title names and issue numbers, and spend a few hours combing through the books on metal shelves in the back room, checking them off as I found them and put the bagged, boarded, and priced comics into the back issues boxes out front.

Linda let me read whatever I wanted, and I sampled everything from *Uncanny X-Men* to *Captain Carrot* and *Howard the Duck*. I sneaked peeks at the forbidden "adult" comics like *Omaha the Cat Dancer*, and Milo

Manera art books. Looking back, it would probably horrify collectors to know a grubby, sweaty girl had read the back issues they bagged and boarded and sealed in a vault, with dreams of going to college on the secondary-market sales of a title that would – in about a year – end up in quarter bins.

What was amazing about that summer wasn't just that I had my dream job. It was seeing with my own eyes the world of other comics readers from the opposite side of the counter.

There were kids and adults, men and boys. A few fellow female unicorns. Casual readers and folks who made the weekly Wednesday afternoon trek like me. I still remember the businessman in his thirties who wore a shiny gold Batman tie-clip. It opened up a door in my head with an idea. Anyone could read comics, and everyone did.

No-one who came into the store thought it was odd that it was run by a woman and her daughters. People came to Comics For Heroes – instead of going to the relatively new, flashy, brightly-lit stores modeled after record shops like Gary Colabuono's Moondog's Comicland – because of Linda. Because of the family atmosphere of the store. Girls and women in particular came to the store as an alternative to Larry Charet's Larry's Comic Book Store on Devon Avenue, precisely because it was run by women. If you ever wondered about the existence of Comic Book Guy on *The Simpsons*, wonder no more. Those shops definitely *did* exist. But Comics For Heroes was never one of them. At Linda's, no judgments would be made the second someone with two X chromosomes stepped beyond the threshold.

Linda knew all of her regulars – by face, if not by name. She always had a smile for everyone, and would take the time to point out what books were hot, look up prices for back issues in the Bible-like fine print of the *Overstreet's Comic Book Price Guide*, and chat with people.

Every penny I made went right back into the store. The truth was, I'd have worked there for free.

But I didn't work at Comics For Heroes again after that first blissful summer in the late 1980s. Life got in the way, and after I graduated high school, I went away to Spain for a year when my father got a job there. I bemoaned the fact that I couldn't get my monthly fix overseas, and so Linda had a pull-box for me back home. I came back in November 1991 to buy its contents, catch up, and pick up a few more items to sustain me over the following six comicless months in Madrid.

When I came back from Spain, in July 1992, the first thing I did was make that familiar trek to the store. I had money in my pocket, stories to share, and when I arrived, Nibe and Angie were there, but no Linda. I hugged them, and asked where their mother was.

Nibe solemnly told me she had passed away two weeks earlier, having been in a coma following a car accident. She was only 44 years old.

I couldn't wrap my mind around it. I stumbled out of the store with a few comics in a bag and walked home in shock. I was only 18 years old, and I had never lost a friend before. I didn't know how to process it. I felt so horrible for her children, and was angry with myself for my initial reaction, because their having to constantly deliver the news to every new patron who walked in expecting to see a familiar smile and dark head behind the counter must have been a special kind of torture.

The store remained open for a few more years, but it wasn't the same without Linda. Her sister-in-law helped run it, but the clientele who had come there for years had come specifically for Linda. That, combined with the bubble of the speculator market bursting in the mid-1990s, made the store's close another example of the failing direct sales market.[1]

Two days after I came home from Spain and found out Linda was gone, I finally went to my very first Chicago Comic-Con at the Ramada O'Hare.

# # #

For most people, San Diego Comic-Con is their Mecca, their geek prom, the highlight of their year. But as a kid, the idea of flying out of state for a convention was tantamount to hopping on the space shuttle for a quick trip to the moon. I set my sights on an attainable goal: the second-largest comics show in America, which happened to be in my own backyard.

There I was, an 18-year-old geek girl in a tank top, jeans, and flannel shirt, wandering the labyrinthine halls of the Ramada O'Hare, the last year the Chicago Comic-Con was held there before it moved to the Rosemont Convention Center.

It was a strange first convention. Image Comics had launched, and rather than having their panels and signings in the meeting rooms, they had erected giant circus tents outside in the parking lot. It felt like at least half – if not more – of the attendees had forsaken the con itself to

---

1. There had been over 7000 direct sales stores during the 1980s. Today, there are barely 3000. Chicago's original comics retailer giants like Larry's and Moondog's were gone by the turn of the millennium.

stand in mile-long queues for Erik Larsen and Todd McFarlane's signatures. It certainly seemed that way, as Peter David actually purchased pizza for those brave souls who attended his panel, as a thank you for actually showing up. That pizza, along with chocolate from one of the colorist's tables in an Artists' Alley that stretched along the winding corridors of the crumbling hotel, was the only food I ate that Saturday.

I wandered the con, spending a lot of time down in "Underground Hell" where the indie publishers had set up, getting anyone and everyone to gleefully deface the "I'm an Image Comics Fan" cardboard fans that we'd been given along with our programs and swag-bags.

I still have those two fans, decorated with sketches by Ben Edlund of *The Tick*, Mike O'Barr who created *The Crow*, and *Girl Genius*'s Phil Foglio. One unsigned message reads, "We have the freedom to do anything we want and raise the standards of comic book art – we just chose to copy Marvel," and that summed up how I felt about Image, despite the fact that they outsold DC Comics that year while having only six titles, which published (on average) one issue each.

I went to the obligatory "Women in Comics" panel and was surprised to see a token male writer sitting next to the female panelists. His name was Gregory Wright and he was writing *Silver Sable* for Marvel. After the panel, he stopped me in the hallway to ask me in all sincerity what comics girls read, because he thought they were only interested in comics about Barbie.

"Dude," I replied, "I read *Batman*, *Suicide Squad*, and *Lobo*."

It was that moment when I realized something I had been in denial about my entire life: As a female reader of mainstream superhero comics, I *was* a unicorn. There were perhaps 20,000 attendees at that show, and you could probably count the women who weren't "booth babes" or comics professionals on one hand.

It was a wake-up call.

Here was a professional comics writer at the most popular comics company in the world, looking to me to speak for my entire gender. So I did. We talked about how some girls only read indie books like Peter Bagge's *Hate* and Daniel Clowes's *Eightball*. Others were given issues of *Sandman* or *Swamp Thing* by their boyfriends, and would be part of the target audience for DC's Vertigo imprint which would launch the following year. We talked about the appeal of story and characters over the name of the artist on the book, and how "Bad Girl" art – where the characters were posing like Playboy centerfolds – was a turn-off. But mostly, we just talked about *comics*.

To Wright, and probably to most of the men in that building, I was a mythical creature so rare he had *never even met one before*. Someone who could discuss the history of Batman with as much seriousness and geek cred as any guy, who happened to have breasts.

Interestingly, I found out almost two decades later that Wright had taken what I'd said back to Marvel, letting them know that what female readers wanted was more intellectually challenging material and less cheesecake. According to Wright, they thought he was crazy.

Every summer that I lived in Chicago, I attended Chicago Comic-Con. In 1993, still living with my parents, my mother gave me a lift to and from the show. Neil Gaiman was the Guest of Honor that year, and programming included a midnight reading and free copies of *Sandman* #50. It was the first year in Rosemont's ginormous Convention Center, and I remember sitting on the marble floor reading comics, only to almost be run over by rock star Steven Tyler as he and his entourage swept past like a tornado, scattering fans in his wake.

In many ways, comic book conventions were industry trade shows that the fans were invited to attend. But back then, the show was still about *comics*. Panels were more than just a slide show of what books each publisher was bringing out that year. There were fantastic panel discussions, arguments, fireworks, and hilarity. There was a chance for fans to finally ask the questions interviewers never asked, and get answers from the top talent in the industry ten feet away on a dais.

It was *magic*.

When Chicago Comic-Con 1996 came around, I was back in Chicago and came by the Hyatt Regency on Thursday night to hang out in the sports bar, Knuckles. It became the hub of convention activity for a solid decade, and I became a dedicated Chicago Comic-Con barfly.

There were years where I never even purchased a membership to the show (or, more specifically, didn't get a press badge for the show, as by then I was freelancing as a journalist). I would take off work early and go to the hotel to hang out with whoever was there. They were good years, full of great times, and friendships that began in Knuckles that would last a lifetime. But all that time – all those years of drinking until they kicked us out and then moving the party to the lobby or a friend's room – I was aware that I was still considered a unicorn. I was still a girl who just happened to be "one of the guys."

Then, around the turn of the millennium, I noticed something. *I was no longer alone*. I was starting to see the gender balance of the convention floor tip ever so slightly towards gender parity.

At MegaCon 2003 in Florida, I got my first taste of a comic book convention with a strong anime and cosplay attendance. Having never attended DragonCon – which was (and is) arguably the premiere costume convention of the comics and media con circuit – the influx of young girls on the convention floor who had grown up with comics, animation, and imported Japanese manga in chain bookstores fascinated me. They weren't mythical creatures. They were just kids – as I had been – attending a comics show to have a good time.

I was no longer just seeing a handful of goth girls, cosplayers, and mothers with their children. I was seeing women and girls of all ages wearing Wolverine and Flash T-shirts, there to meet their heroes. Women were no longer in the minority – there was gender parity out there on the floor. They weren't just fans, either. There were loads of women in Artist's Alley, and the Indie Publishers' rows, hawking their wares alongside the boys. The women whose names I'd read on DC's masthead as a child hadn't faded away – they had been joined by more female artists, writers, inkers, colorists, and editors. Comics may still be a male-dominated industry, but comics fandom had changed in ways I couldn't have imagined as a 14-year-old girl getting teased by her classmates.

The culmination for me of this remarkable sea change was the Wizard World 2008 "Women in Comics" panel. It was headed up by Johnny DC editor Jann Jones, and featured Gail Simone and artist Katie Cook. But sitting on the panel was a young colorist named Carly Spade. She was about 20 years old, and was wearing a Supergirl costume.

Something I never once thought I'd see in my lifetime: a comics geek girl just like the one I had been at her age, on a panel. A comics professional. Dressed as Supergirl.

I may have teared up, I was so overcome with joy. Because *no-one batted an eye*.

Summer 2011 marks my 20th anniversary of attending comic book conventions. I'm not a cute 18-year-old comics geek anymore. I'm a woman in her late thirties, who picks up the odd floppy or trade now and then, but for the most part has left comics behind. Too many changes to beloved characters. Too much continuity to keep track of. Too expensive a habit for someone who now has a mortgage to pay.

But in my heart, I'm still the little girl in Wonder Woman Underoos. I'm still the gawky teen who found refuge, place and purpose in Linda Schein's Comics For Heroes.

And, I'm proud to say, a *former* unicorn.

The Evolution of a Tart

Sheena McNeil has a deep-seated love of reading and writing, as well as an interest in all things Japanese. This combination led her to manga, which in turn led her to write for Sequential Tart (sequentialtart.com). There she found a deeper appreciation for all sequential art, and eventually became the webzine's editrix-in-chief. She expresses her own art mainly through customizing My Little Ponies, an area she helped pioneer in the Pony-collecting community over a decade ago. She is also a modern-day samurai, learning and instructing the Japanese martial arts of swordsmanship in Satori Ryu Iaido and short staff in Shindo Muso Jodo.

I'm a Tart and proud of it! *Sequential Tart (ST)* is a webzine created entirely by women, with a focus on women in the comics industry and sequential art in general. Our writers are from many different countries, cultures, and tastes, so our coverage is quite dynamic. The comics we cover are also global. For more than a decade, we have been proclaiming and proving that "chicks dig comics," and we're not slowing down.

I was in high school when *Sequential Tart* found me. Or, rather, when Tart Jen Contino found my website, and sent me an email asking if I would like to write reviews for this all-women, comics-based webzine. It sounded awesome! I have always loved to write, and at the time was becoming heavily immersed in all that is anime and manga.

This happened in Fall 2000, when *Sequential Tart* was about two years old. The website came about because, in the mid-to-late '90s, a wonderful and talented group of women found each other through a Garth Ennis fan website run by Steff Osborne. She was also running a private email list – the Garth Ennis Estrogen Brigade – for the women who came to that site. The topic of comics journalism eventually came up in their discussions, at least in part due to a *Wizard* poll which asked questions such as (and here I'm paraphrasing a bit), "What are the top ten comics pickup lines to use on girls?"

The comics pros and fans who comprised the Ennis mailing list were frustrated by such things, because they enjoyed "non-girly" comics like *Johnny the Homicidal Maniac* and *Preacher*. They loved the sequential art medium, but felt ostracized by the "boys only" mentality. They were tired of seeing a continual bombardment of large-breasted women in comics, and were over being told what, as women, they should or shouldn't like to read. They knew they couldn't be alone in this; after all, they had found each other.

As a magazine didn't exist that catered to their tastes or ways of thinking, they decided to make their own. In 1998, after creating the building blocks for a website, they conducted their first interviews at San Diego Comic-Con. The first issue of ST was launched in September.

Creating *Sequential Tart* has always been a labor of love – so many of the women who have written for the webzine have done so because they have something to say and very much want to contribute. We give of our time, money, and energy – sometimes to the point of causing struggles in our personal lives – to bring new articles, interviews, and reviews to our readers, and to show the world that women are an important force in and around the comics industry.

At first ST was published every two months, but it quickly progressed to being monthly. I joined at this point – everything that was produced would go live on the first day of the month, which made for a lot of content all at once. It was a little daunting at first, and I'm sure if I looked back on my earliest reviews, I would wish they had never seen print. However, I quickly fell into the camaraderie, support, and loving friendship these women provided.

Before long, working on *Sequential Tart* expanded my horizons where comics were concerned – I had already been engrossed in manga, but slowly became reacquainted with American comics, both mainstream and indie. I found myself hunting down copies of *Poison Elves* and *Tank Girl*, and digging through the dollar bins at the only comic book store I was able to visit. I gained an appreciation for comics such as *Spawn* and *Vampirella*, and also fell in love with darker, yet humorous stories from two very talented comic creators: Jhonen Vasquez and Roman Dirge. Vasquez's *Johnny the Homicidal Maniac* and *I Feel Sick* were instant favorites that I would read over and over. Dirge's *The Monsters in My Tummy* led me to *Lenore*, which made me laugh harder than I had since the first time I played "Frog in a Blender" by Joe Cartoon (it never gets old). *Lenore* became one of the first comics I later shared with the man who became my husband – he loves it just as much as I do, so it continues to be a special comic in my life.

Sequential Tart as it exists today is broken up into sections such as Features (which focuses on comics), Culture Vultures (pop culture), and

Report Card (reviews). Other sections have come and gone – during the height of the anime and manga craze in America, we had a section called Atsukamashii Onna (which roughly translates to "tarty woman") that focused entirely on these art forms from Japan. I was, of course, heavily involved with this section.

Then, the summer of 2002 brought an exciting opportunity for me... the current editor of Atsukamashii Onna, Dani Fletcher, was moving to Japan and would be unable to continue her work with *ST*. When Dani and the other editors approached me to take on her role as editor of the section, I was ecstatic! I had a couple months of working hand-in-hand with Dani to learn the ropes before she left me in charge though I would have loved to have been in her shoes as well, going to Japan. It was around this time that the Friends of Lulu (a non-profit organization promoting women reading comics and female participation in the industry) presented *Sequential Tart* with a Lulu of the Year Award. We were all excited by the recognition of our work.

The Atsukamashii Onna section lasted through the end of 2003 – the American manga market was changing by then, and the slow descent from its peak had begun. We as a group decided to simplify and stream-line the webzine, which included doing away with the Atsukamashii Onna section. Coverage on manga (along with comics from anywhere else in the world) was incorporated into Features, and anime was rolled into Culture Vultures.

Meanwhile, *ST* helped me to become acquainted with – and even a fan of – the more adult forms of sequential art. Two artists in particular captured my interest: Toshio Maeda and Sen'no Knife. Both of them worked in the horror genre, which is a favorite of mine, so it's really no wonder why I would be drawn to their works. Maeda's titles include *Urotsukidoji: Legend of the Overfiend*, *La Blue Girl*, *Demon Beast Invasion*, and *Adventure Kid*. (The last title is one of my personal favorites, because there's some great humor here as well; it's more fun and light-hearted than Maeda's other works.) Maeda is known as the master and creator of the "erotic-grotesque" style, while Knife is at the other end of the spectrum – with beautiful art, and sex scenes that aren't depicted in the same stark and graphic way as Maeda's work. Knife does cover a myriad of fetishes, and that makes his stunning artwork even more erotic.

Another genre I've been able to indulge in is yaoi (and boys' love). It all started with *Kizuna* – one of the most well-done yaoi, a classic. It's not too hard or soft, so it's a perfect introduction to see if you like this type of comic.

I'm not the only Tart that loves adult reading material – every February, we have a "pr0n" issue. Everything from romance to hardcore sex is covered – there's homo and heterosexual material, and even mixed species love or love with robots and androids. You name it! You have no idea how awesome it feels to not only say we read *and* enjoy these works, but to converse intelligently on them and even provide suggestions for would-be readers. Guys are typically shocked to discover that women like porn too, but they generally accept the fact pretty quickly. It brought a smile to my face when I got an email from a male *ST* reader about my review of *Cool Devices*, and asking if I had any reading suggestions along those lines.

When the Atsukamashii Onna section was dissolved, I took over the editing of the Culture Vultures section. From there, I switched to being the senior Editrix for Report Card, a job that entailed my handling all review copies, being the liaison with company reps, etc. – most of which I was doing already.

My association with *ST* continued pretty well in those days, even as I finished college and began vet school (though I soon learned it wasn't the path for me) – it required some crazy organization of my time, but through it all, I wasn't willing to give up my involvement with *ST*. I adored the webzine, even when it seemed almost overwhelming to be spending *that* much time and energy on something that was entirely on a volunteer basis. However, the more I did with/for *ST*, the more I learned about and came to appreciate the comics (and manga) industry.

In 2006, I had the perfect trifecta: enough frequent flier miles to warrant a free flight, fellow Tarts I could room with, and time off from my summer job to travel. I was going to my first convention: the behemoth that is the San Diego Comic-Con! It was one of my best experiences in life, as well as with *ST*. I met and got signatures from some of my favorite creators, including Peter S. Beagle (*The Last Unicorn*), fantasy illustrator Brian Froud, and John Lustig (*Last Kiss*). I was also able to find some new favorites, such as Michel Gagné (*Insanely Twisted Rabbits*) and David Peterson (*Mouse Guard*). I even met up with a husband and wife comics duo I'd interviewed – Tavisha Wolfgarth Simons and Rikki Simons – which was exciting on both a personal and professional level. Plus, they surprised me with a signed print of an art piece they did for *Sequential Tart*, from a time when we used virtual "cover" images.

I went to an amazing assortment of panels at the con, spent hours wandering the aisles in the dealers' room, and basked in the wonder that is comic nerdom at its finest. My cousin Tara Platt and her husband

Yuri Lowenthal were there as guests, as they're voice actors on *Naruto* and other anime. It's always exciting to see family – *especially* when they're being trailed by rabid *Naruto* fans who scream at them from halfway across the dealers' room – but the icing on the cake was being introduced to, and getting an impromptu interview with, voice actor Dan Woren. One of the characters he voiced was Roy Fokker, veritech pilot from *Robotech* – and yes, I wanted a veritech of my very own. *Robotech*, among other foreign and domestic cartoons, was a huge part of my childhood, and while I didn't know the names of voice actors at that time (who did?), I was bubbling over with fangirlish glee that I somehow kept restrained inside.

And yet, all of that *paled* next to the shining grail of my Press Pass experience: Thanks to the aforementioned Jen Contino and the wonderful guys of Boom! Studios, I conducted an in-person interview with the legendary Yoshitaka Amano (*Vampire Hunter D, Final Fantasy, Sandman: The Dream Hunters*, etc.). I planned for this meeting for weeks – I borrowed a hand-held recorder, created a set of questions, and *dreamed* about what it would be like. I was even willing to be a stand-in "booth babe" for Boom! for a couple hours, if it guaranteed this once-in-a-lifetime experience. Both Amano and his translator liked my unusual questions, some of which Amano had never been asked before. Some pictures and two signed books later, and I was the happiest person on the planet. I did not want to leave that booth – but sadly everyone, including me, had a schedule to keep.

Sequential Tart continued to grow and change over the next year, and in 2007, we revamped the webzine with a major facelift. Our internal deadlines functioned largely the same, but content was no longer released as one big hurrah on the first of the month. Instead, content began going live every Monday, to keep readers coming back more often. Reviews went live once a week as well, and were written, submitted, edited, and published weekly rather than monthly. But if the deadlines were more frequent, I was pleased that – as the senior editor of Report Card – I got to learn about new potential reads every week. There are *so* many comics and manga that I've tried out – or gotten hooked on and had to track down every volume of – simply because a Tart did an interesting review of them, or I read a random issue or volume from a pile of comics that we bought, borrowed, or were given as press copies. Part of my job for the majority of the time I've been with *ST*, in fact, has been to liaison with companies and creators so we could acquire review copies. It's been interesting to interact with the comics industry on that level – I've seen whole companies come and go, and I've helped to support new hopefuls as they brandished their first published comic. It's literally been an eye-opening experience, introducing me to so many things I would never have picked up in a bookstore.

Sequential Tart celebrated its tenth anniversary in 2008. In Summer 2010, talks began concerning change for *ST* – which included me becoming the new editrix-in-chief. While this has been in addition to my still being the senior editrix for Report Card, and so has meant even more work, I'm loving my new role – which shortly preceded my own tenth anniversary with *ST*.

As I write this, another face-lift for the webzine is in progress. *Sequential Tart* and the group of women that work on it is always evolving – even the core group that's been involved with the zine for years continues to grow. As we learn and share with each other and the readers, our love and knowledge of comics also expands.

One thing's for certain: With amazing women like these continuing to spread the word about a medium they love, more chicks will begin to dig comics, and the industry will continue to acknowledge the importance of women in all aspects of comics. I look forward to what new story I'll enjoy next, but I also look forward to more time spent sharing my love and knowledge for this powerful medium with women who feel the same.

Kitty Queer

Sigrid Ellis is a writer of fiction, non-fiction, and comics; an editor; a parent of two homeschooled children; and an air traffic controller. She lives in Saint Paul, Minnesota, with her partner, their kids, her partner's other partner, and a host of pets both vertebrate and invertebrate. Her work can be found in the online speculative fiction magazine *Strange Horizons* and in Mad Norwegian's *Whedonistas: A Celebration of the Worlds of Joss Whedon by the Women Who Love Them*.

I was sitting on the top bunk when I told Rogue I was gay. This was in the spring of my sophomore year of college, so that meant the bunk bed was in Bigelow Hall on the Macalester College campus. I was in the dorm room by myself, it was nighttime, and the fluorescent gleam of the overhead light reflected off of the Jim Lee *X-Men* triptych poster stuck to the opposite wall with duct tape. I was crying in horrified humiliation, but the look in Rogue's eye told me I was going to be okay.

To say I probably ought to have figured out my complete lack of heterosexuality a little bit sooner in life is... a vast understatement. I blame Chris Claremont. Chris Claremont – writer of the various *X-Men* comic book titles during my impressionable adolescence – and the editorial policies of Marvel Comics at the time. You see, I was raised by liberal parents in a middle-class household, and in my household we did not subscribe to stereotypes. One could not judge a character by their looks or mannerisms or skin color or speech. This meant that I got into a fight with a classmate in sixth grade over the sexuality of pop star Boy George. Just because he *looked* gay and *sounded* gay and *dressed* gay didn't mean he *was* gay, I said. When presented with the cases that justified and reinforced cultural stereotypes, I insisted that the presumption could not be true.

I had the Boy George conversation in 1985. By 1992, I went to a college where people wore Act-Up T-shirts, sported Queer Nation pins and buttons, and the GLBU quarterly dances were the best party around. In Marvel Comics, Northstar had just come out as gay. Being queer, in real life and comics, was an act imbued with anger and frustration. Even

Northstar was angry. But whatever concern I had for social justice issues was abstract and impersonal. I still didn't connect gayness, or queerness, with my life. I didn't want to protest the President or march for reproductive rights; I wanted to spend all of my time in moon-eyed devotion to my best friends and/or dorm-mates. In the same way that Kitty Pryde was devoted to Rachel Summers and Illyana Rasputin.

Some of you reading this essay might not be as all-consumingly familiar with Kitty Pryde's life in the '80s as I am. She was a teenager, a member of the X-Men, living in the mansion-school-headquarters of the team. She had two best friends during this time frame: Illyana from the New Mutants team, and Rachel. Both were teenage girls, for a value of "teenage" that includes time travel, dimension-hopping, demonic aging, and alternate universes. This is, after all, superhero comics. Kitty was passionately devoted to each of them.

This devotion took a variety of forms. In *New Mutants* #35, the New Mutants are all killed by the Beyonder. Kitty is not merely the only person who remembers the team ever existed; we find out in *Uncanny X-Men* #202 that she is also the inheritor of Illyana's soul-sword and armor. This is due to the special bond the two girls share. The nature of said bond is never explained. One might think that Peter, Illyana's fanatically protective older brother, might be the person who gets the sword and the memory. Nope. Those go to Kitty, the roommate.

In *New Mutants* #36, Kitty gets injured, kidnapped, and strung up by a demon. To save her friend, Illyana reclaims her demon heritage and the soul-sword. Much teary cradling of each other while declaiming affection ensues.

In all scenes of Rachel and Kitty – *X-Men/Alpha Flight* #1-2, *Uncanny X-Men* #188-207, most issues of *Excalibur* – the two young women touch each other. A lot. They stand closely, they link arms, they hold hands. When Kitty's life is threatened in *Uncanny X-Men* #196, Rachel knows it through a hitherto-unmentioned psychic bond she has with Kitty. Rachel goes berserk and nearly murders a man for Kitty's sake. The running gag in early issues of *Excalibur* is that any time Kitty gets injured in a fight, Rachel goes nuts, sacrificing everything to save her friend.

These scenes were written under the Comics Code Authority. Structured to be much like the Hays and Breen codes governing movies, the CCA prohibited depictions of sexuality in comics:

2. Illicit sex relations are neither to be hinted at or portrayed. Violent love scenes as well as sexual abnormalities are unaccept-

able.

[...]

5. Passion or romantic interest shall never be treated in such a way as to stimulate the lower and baser emotions.

6. Seduction and rape shall never be shown or suggested.

7. Sex perversion or any inference to same is strictly forbidden.[1]

At the same time that Kitty and her roommates were declaring their soulbonds with each other, Scott Summers of the X-Men was married to Madeline Pryor. They were *married*, and their relationship was shown through hugging and the occasional kiss. Their most risqué moment, before it was revealed that Madeline was an evil clone programmed to steal Scott's sperm to make a superchild, was on their honeymoon, where they cuddled while she was wearing a nightie and he was wearing shorts. Let it be made clear: Marvel treated all sexuality as something to be hidden away.

As is so common in queer history, though, an ostensibly fair and even-handed treatment of sexuality in comics makes gay and lesbian relations invisible. The heterosexual pairings among the X-Men could kiss or hug, could call their time together a date. The queers could not. Moreover, there's that "perversion" clause. Ego-dystonic homosexuality was removed from the American Psychiatric Association's Diagnostic and Statistical Manual of Mental Disorders in 1986.[2] *New Mutants* #36 was published in February 1986. When it was written, lesbianism was legally and medically a perversion. Chris Claremont and Bill Sienkiewicz, the writer and artist of *New Mutants* at the time, could not say that Illyana came to the rescue of her some-time girlfriend Kitty who had been defeated by a demon with a penchant for classic bondage porn. But they could write it, and draw it, without ever acknowledging that is what they were doing. The relationship, the subtext, the highly sexualized imagery, all these things were presented not as queer kink but as friendship and heroism. The kind of relationship *any* high school girl might have with her best friends.

I cannot in any way speak towards the intentions of Chris Claremont, the artists, editors, or anyone involved in the making of X-Men comics during the late 1980s. I don't know what they meant to tell me. But I know what I saw. I saw romantic love presented as simple friendship. I

1. Comics Code Authority 1954 – www.comicartville.com/comicscode.htm

2. psychology.ucdavis.edu/rainbow/html/facts_mental_health.html

saw heroism, a kind of knighthood and self-sacrifice, to be what any friendship should expect.

In early 1992, I was re-reading my *Excalibur* comics, specifically *Excalibur* #24. Reading these pages again, in the new climate of the GLB-Union, my almost entirely not-heterosexual friends, and constant political awareness, something went "click" in my head. In this issue, Kitty has been separated from her Excalibur teammates. She is staying with a woman named Courtney Ross, an old friend of Captain Britain's. (This is not actually Courtney, it is a villain, Sat-Yr-9, but Kitty doesn't know that.) Courtney wakes Kitty with an offer to take Kitty out for her birthday, to cheer her up since all of her friends might be dead. Kitty initially declines, sulkily, until Courtney... well, until she seduces Kitty into saying yes.

Panel 1: Kitty is facing Courtney over the cake as they both sit on the bed. Kitty is wearing pajamas, Courtney is wearing a white dress with a high flared collar and puffy sleeves. Courtney has some pink frosting on her finger. Her finger is in her mouth and she is sucking the frosting off.
COURTNEY: So, there's no need for lies between us, okay?
KITTY: Okay.
KITTY: But I'm afraid I haven't a clue about what to do with today.

Panel 2: Two-shot of Kitty and Courtney. On the left of the panel Kitty is sitting cross-legged in her pajamas, looking at Courtney. On the right, Courtney is leaning forward, her hand extended towards Kitty. She has frosting on her finger, still, the same finger she was just sucking. The frosting-laden finger is nearly touching Kitty's mouth.
COURTNEY: Actually, I have a few ideas.
COURTNEY: If you're willing.

Panel 3: Kitty holds Courtney's hand gently by the wrist. She is sucking on Courtney's finger, her chin tilted slightly down, eyes looking up and over their hands at Courtney's face.
KITTY: Lead on, Courtney, I'm all yours.

Panel 4: Both women lean towards each other, their foreheads nearly touching, identical smiles on their faces. In this panel, we cannot see their eyes, just the smiles.
COURTNEY: I'm so glad.

The two proceed to then spend the day together, with Courtney buying Kitty a sports car, exotic dinners in foreign locales, and expensive sexy clothes. Every scene they share speaks of excess, seduction, hinted debauchery, and the possibility of corruption.[3]

I re-read this scene over and over again. I knew, now, in 1992, what this looked like. This looked like Spin-the-Bottle or Truth-or-Dare, it looked like the drunk and stoned random kissing games people played in the dorms on a weekend night. It looked like a challenge thrown down and accepted. I stared at the art. Courtney or Sat-Yr-9 or whoever was *seducing* Kitty Pryde. And Kitty was saying *yes*.

I went through my back issues, flushed and slightly sick, my heart racing. There in the pages of the comics I loved, the characters I loved were... were very possibly loving each other. Every year, Macalester held GLB visibility week, when students chalked the sidewalks with the names of famous queers. My first year I had blinked at some of the names in astonishment, confused. Eleanor Roosevelt? Seriously? And I'd gone to look up some of the evidence. I'd learned, as a consequence, about GLBT invisibility, how queer relationships are unacknowledged in history. I read up on Hollywood's part in the conspiracy, about the Celluloid Closet. I'd done, in short, what the GLBUnion *wanted* people to do during queer visibility week – I learned about gay history.

My comics had invisible queers.

What did this mean for me?

I went on a walk around the campus, chain smoking cigarettes in the light spring rain. I could feel something happening inside my head, and I didn't like it one little bit. I got back to my dorm room and sat on my bunk and stared at the posters lining my walls. The thing unfolding in my mind was taking shape. Kitty and Rachel, Kitty and 'Yana, they were best friends. I tried to mold my best friendships on their model. The love they felt for each other, the passion, this was how I felt towards my closest female friends. If Kitty Pryde wasn't straight, if her love for her friends was instead sexual, then... then what did that make me?

A dozen half-remembered conversations floated through my thoughts, mixed with images of comics, images of my life, whirling around. Tears started to form in my eyes, and I flushed bright red in the privacy of my dorm room. Kitty Pryde wasn't straight. She likely never had been. I... was not straight. I likely never had been. Moreover, it was probably perfectly obvious to dozens of people in my life that I was a

---

3. scans-daily.dreamwidth.org/ 411719.html

complete idiot. A complete, closeted, idiot.

I looked across the room at Rogue, smiling at me from the Jim Lee poster. She looked so cocky, so confident. She also looked really hot, goofy hair notwithstanding. I wiped my eyes and said it. I looked Rogue in the eye and managed a whisper. "I think I'm gay." She kept smiling.

How was it I had missed this? I looked at the X-Men poster again and tried to examine the admiration I held for the figures on it. When I looked at Rogue, what did I imagine? What thoughts crossed my mind? What did I want to say or do? Do with, or for, or to... Oh. Okay, yes, Sigrid, you really, really ought to have realized your sexual orientation before this point. Why didn't I? What had stopped me?

The artist for *Excalibur* #24, Alan Davis, said in his online forum that, "although I knew Chris had some plan for Sat-Yr-9 to corrupt Kitty and that the various Cross-time versions of Saturnyne were attracted to Kitty, I had no idea what, if any, the goal of this relationship was to be. I just played it as a lesbian affair."[4] Davis knew something about Claremont's intentions that I did not know, and drew what he thought a lesbian relationship, with willing participation from both parties, would look like. Kudos to him, it looked rather a lot like the same-sex flirting I saw monthly at the GLBUnion dances licking of the fingers, et cetera. What I did not know is that Claremont included this sort of girl-on-girl sensuality in all of his comics, hiding it from the CCA as heterosexual female friendship. It wasn't until 1992 and Davis's fairly blatant art that I got the hint; actual straight women maybe don't feel this way about their friends. It was entirely possible, I realized slowly, that finger sucking and licking was not a strictly heterosexual activity among friends.

Rogue didn't judge me. Neither did my friend Scott, who I called in a not entirely coherent manner to come get me. Scott drove around for hours while we talked about comic books, and Northstar, and whether Nightcrawler (an X-Man who was also a devout Catholic) was also gay, and the gay Catholic monks that Scott had slept with. When I finally managed to squeak out that I might not be straight, Scott lit a cigarette and suggested we go get coffee at a local family restaurant. He politely ignored me, singing along with the radio, while I lit my own cigarette and finished crying.

From December 2002 to May 2003, Marvel published a mini-series called *Mekanix*. In this series, Kitty Pryde comes out. Claremont finally

---

4. www.alandavis-forum.com/ viewtopic.php?f=3&t=59#wrap

has her almost kissing Xi'an Coy Manh, a fellow former X-Man who is an out lesbian. Kitty's bisexuality seems to only exist in Claremont's mind – no other writer of her since has done anything with this. But I'm okay with that.

I could wish that Kitty talked about it more, or occasionally ogled a woman. But it's fine with me that she dated Peter Rasputin. It's fine with me that she put all romance on the back burner to focus on saving planets, riding through space in bullets, snarking with Emma Frost, and trying to not die. I have my *Mekanix* and my *Excalibur*. I know that Kitty was struggling with her identity and her sexual orientation all through her high school years as she and her roommates fell in and out of love with each other. I know she came out in college, and that the coming out was a surprise to her. I know in my heart that she told Rogue, and that Rogue shrugged and didn't care.

I can blame Claremont – and I do – for my not coming out earlier than I did. But I also have to credit him for slipping queers into my comics when the CCA forbade it. When I did finally come out to myself, the X-Men didn't judge me. They accepted this new form of oddball difference the same way they'd always accepted me with open hands and an invitation to be a hero once more.

The Captain in the Capitol: Invoking the Superhero in Daily Life

Jennifer Margret Smith is a graduate student in Media and Cultural Studies at the University of Wisconsin-Madison, where she studies superhero comics alongside a host of other media. She has written comic reviews for *Best Shots* at *Newsarama* and interned at Marvel Comics in the *X-Men* editorial department, and she blogs at fantasticfangirls.org. She may be the only Princeton alumnus with fond memories of the thesis-writing process. Captain America remains her inspiration.

On March 9, 2011, Wisconsin governor Scott Walker rammed through a controversial piece of anti-union legislation in the absence of Democratic senators who had crossed state lines to prevent that very thing from happening. Wisconsin union members and their allies, who had been protesting the bill for weeks, stormed the Capitol building in Madison once more, pounding on the doors when they were denied access and slipping in whenever a door was opened for even a moment. Once inside, they made their way up several flights of stairs with their chants and their signs to stage a sit-in, hoping that their distance from the doors would prevent their removal should the police attempt to clear the building. "Tell me what democracy looks like!", they yelled, stomping on the floor to keep the beat. "This is what democracy looks like!"

I was among the multitude who stormed the Capitol that night. As a first year graduate student at the University of Wisconsin-Madison, I'd become moderately involved in the protests – more involved than some, though not nearly as involved as those who slept on the cold marble floors of the Capitol for days on end. When I heard the news of the bill passing, I didn't even hesitate to board the next bus and make my way down to the Capitol to join the protestors. I had no sign, no friends to join me, no real plans except to follow the crowd. But March 9th was a Wednesday, and as a result there were two things I *did* have: a Captain America T-shirt on my back, and a pile of brand new comic books in my backpack. Sitting in solidarity with my fellow union members on the second floor of the Capitol rotunda, my back against a stately pillar, I flipped through my comics and drew strength, as I had for weeks, from the crusaders for justice who populated those panels and pages.

I was not a comic book fan growing up. I never tied a towel around my neck and jumped off a table in simulated flight, and I never deflected imaginary bullets with my mother's costume bracelets. The closest I came to an interest in superheroes as a child was a fixation on the 1990s *X-Men* cartoon, and I do vividly remember standing in front of electric fans, letting my hair blow around me and pretending to command the winds and rains like Storm. But for the most part, I didn't participate in the time-honored childhood practice of pretending to be the heroes of the page or screen, saving lives and possessing more strength than a frail, youthful form could ever in reality hold.

But I did, eventually, discover comics. In the summer of 2006, the summer after my sophomore year of college, I borrowed hundreds of comic books from a friend and began my trek down the path of comic book fandom, a path that would quite literally change my life. I started with the X-Men, my old childhood pals, and moved on from there to the Avengers, the Marvel Universe, and eventually the DC Universe. I fell in love with the medium, with the shared universes, and with the talent of the hundreds of creators whose work I was absorbing. But most of all, I fell in love with the characters.

College was not an easy time for me. I was shy and awkward, and I wasn't sure how to make friends. Everyone I felt close to was back in my home town, and my classmates were strangers who stayed up late into the night drinking and blasting music while I diligently read the novels for that week's English lectures. I'd always been a good student, studious and conscientious, and I was happy with the progress of my college education, but the college social world left something to be desired.

It was during one of these fits of malaise during my junior year of college that I discovered Dan Slott's *She-Hulk*. On the first page of the first issue, protagonist Jennifer Walters – a heroine who shares my first name – sits in her law school dorm room amid piles of books, studying with earplugs as the sounds of a raucous party and Chumbawamba's "Tubthumping" pound through her walls. On the next page, we see her law school graduation, and the lonely picture her father takes of her, diploma in hand, while her classmates gather in large, celebratory groups for their own photos.

Reading that comic represented a moment of painful recognition for the lonely college student I was. Yet this was merely the introduction, the flashback to a time in Jennifer Walters's past. Soon enough, she would receive a blood transfusion from her cousin Bruce Banner and become the She-Hulk, a beautiful 6'7" green superhero with an immensity of physical strength matched only by her outgoing, confident personality. She'd still be a lawyer, but she'd be a lawyer with friends and a sense of purpose – a lawyer who could beat up bad guys, party with celebrities, and face down any criticisms that came her way. During one storyline, she would even go undercover using the name "Jennifer Smith" – my own (albeit very common) first and last name. She was, the comic quickly revealed, the wish-fulfillment I'd been waiting for, the equivalent of Spider-Man for the awkward girl nerd.

I joked at the time that all I needed was for one of my cousins to offer me some Gamma-irradiated blood, and everything would be perfect. But I didn't need to be green to be She-Hulk, no more than she needed to change herself to pretend to be Jennifer Smith. All I needed to do was summon up her confidence and her strength in my own toughest moments, to invoke her name when a situation threatened to drown me in law student Jennifer Walters-esque despair. One summer night, several years later, after playing pool at a bar with my high school friends, I saw a girl who had tormented me from kindergarten through twelfth grade enter the room. Immediately, I felt the signs of a panic attack rising within me, could feel myself slipping back into the meekness of my 18-year-old self, quaking with fear, changing my route in the hallway between classes to avoid her notice. *But no,* I told myself in the bar that night. *You're She-Hulk. You're better than this. You're better than her.* Head held high, I imagined a green hue sweeping across my skin and marched out of the bar with my friends to a more desirable locale.

But if Jennifer Walters had become my alter ego, my avatar, another comic book character would become something else entirely: an inspiration. In that same semester that I discovered She-Hulk, I also discovered Captain America. Unlike most fans, I had no preconceptions about the character, no false impressions of a right-wing jingoistic patriot that some new Cap readers seem to possess. And what I found on the page was a man whose views largely reflected my own: a sense of patriotism that doesn't ignore America's flaws, and a faith in the country's capacity to someday live up to its ideals. I also found a hero who was a genuinely good man – a purely heroic, if imperfect, figure to combat the glut of antiheroes and misunderstood villains who capture the imaginations of so many other fannish folk. I'd always been a fan of the good guys, and Steve Rogers was the best guy there was.

It didn't take long for Captain America to become my favorite super-hero. I began reading every comic in which he appeared, amassed a small collection of Captain America toys and T-shirts, and even brought a tiny stuffed Captain America with me when I went with a friend in Philadelphia to visit the Liberty Bell. Captain America tapped into my love for American history (particularly of the twentieth century), my interest in World War II stories, and my interest in good guy superheroes punching Nazis in the face. But more important than my fandom was my identification. If Jennifer Walters was wish-fulfillment, an outward expression of inner desires, Steve Rogers was an ideal I wanted to live up to. I saw in myself parts of Captain America, good and bad: his sense of justice, his stubbornness, his desire to please everyone, his awkwardness in certain social situations that his decades-long sleep hadn't prepared him for. But in Steve Rogers, unlike in myself, those traits were all mag-nified. I sought justice, but sometimes didn't have the determination to carry through with it. I strove to be good and kind to all people at all times, but I frequently faltered. Steve Rogers was given the Super-Soldier Serum to transform him into the peak of human perfection, but it wasn't his body or his fighting skills I admired. It was his equally-perfect soul – a soul that was pure without crossing the line into the unrealistic and superhuman – that attracted me to the character and made me ask myself, without embarrassment, "What would Captain America do?"

When Marvel killed off Steve Rogers in March 2007, I didn't fret. I'd already learned, less than a year into my comic book reading tenure, that death is rarely permanent in comics. But what followed was a spate of comics that ruminated at length on the role of Steve Rogers in the Marvel Universe, meditations on his meaning as a character and as a symbol in the wake of his death. I read all of these comics, and by the end of the summer of 2007, I realized just how much time I'd been spending thinking about Captain America. Suddenly, all the pieces fell into place. I was about to become a senior in college, and with senior year would come the expectation of writing a 100-page senior thesis. As an English major, I was free to look to any medium to apply my skills in textual analysis, within reason. So I chose *Captain America* comics, and their relation over time to changes in American culture, politics, and history. What had started as a private symbol and obsession, a personal inspiration, became my academic calling card, and it was a chapter from that thesis that ultimately earned me entrance, two years later, into the

Media and Cultural Studies graduate program at the University of Wisconsin-Madison, where I would begin a serious, focused, scholarly study of superhero comic books.

Three weeks after I turned in my senior thesis, however, my paternal grandfather passed away. He was just shy of his 82nd birthday and had long been waging a battle against increasingly failing health. John Wesley Smith was a World War II veteran, a man who'd lived through decades of a changing America. He was a stubborn, reserved, but intensely likable blue collar guy who worked on the brickyards that built my hometown and saw three children and eight grandchildren grow to adulthood. He lived ten minutes away from my family's house, and for a few months during my freshman year of high school, he stayed in our home after suffering a heart attack. He was, by far, my closest family member outside of my parents and my younger brother, and I loved him dearly.

I'd compared him to superheroes before – when I discovered he'd once worked on a shrimp boat, the connections to X-Man Cyclops were inescapable. But though my grandfather didn't live to read my thesis, didn't even live to see my cousin and me become the first in our family to graduate college a few weeks later, I began to realize in the wake of his death who he'd become in my mind: Captain America. Here was my Cap, my heroic veteran full of kindness and generosity who never quite did get the hang of newfound technology.

During the thesis-writing process, I'd borrowed some of my grandfather's compilations of the music of his youth – big band and swing – to play as I worked, getting me into the mindset of a character that came to adulthood in the 1940s. When my grandfather died, I played those same CDs again, and cried, and imagined that if Captain America were real, he'd certainly find a way to come to the funerals of as many World War II veterans as he could. I imagined Steve Rogers showing up in disguise at my grandfather's funeral and striking up conversations with the mourners, giving me the chance to talk about the man my grandfather had been and how he'd very much been my own private Captain America. It was my most visceral fantasy, and possibly the most self-indulgent, but in a time of grief it was exactly what I needed. Even in this dark hour, I looked to this fictional superhero for the guidance and support that I needed but couldn't possibly articulate.

All of this brings me back to the Capitol rotunda of Madison, Wisconsin, and the union protests of 2011. I had very personal reasons to support the protests: Not only was I a member of UW-Madison's teaching assistants' union, I was also the daughter and granddaughter of men who had worked their whole lives in union jobs, relying on those organizations to protect them and allow them to put food on their families' tables. As a new Wisconsin resident, I was shocked to find a state that had seemed so liberal and progressive at first transform after election day into an autocracy with a man on top who refused to compromise or even listen to the opposite side, who claimed the destruction of half-century-old collective bargaining rights for state employee unions was a "budget" issue, and who showed no respect for the pre-existing laws of the state he now ran.

But what fueled my fire, what bolstered my righteous rage, was the thought that Captain America, and all the other heroes of my comic book fantasies, would not let this stand. These crusaders for justice had proven time and again that the mark of true patriotism was dissent, that peaceful protest and standing up for one's rights was a valid and worthy goal, and that a group of like-minded souls might form to fight the foes no single hero could withstand. I fantasized about Captain America, Superman, Green Arrow, and a dozen other superheroes descending on the Capitol with speeches and defiance. I even imagined Bernie Rosenthal, Steve Rogers's 1980s civilian girlfriend, bringing her legal expertise to the same college where she had, in the comics, earned her law degree. But more than that, I imagined that we, the protestors, *were* the superheroes, that we were invoking their ideals and their passion and channeling it into our chants and phone campaigns and signs and marches and drum circles.

In drawing my inspiration from superheroes at these protests, I was far from alone. In the first week of the protests, I saw a man in a makeshift Captain America outfit standing outside the Capitol with a sign raised above his head that read "Unions Assemble!" Protest signs compared Governor Walker to everything from Darth Vader to the Joker, drawing on popular culture representations of evil to attempt to explain actions that seemed otherwise incomprehensibly mean-spirited. As the protests wore on, and the people of Wisconsin held the Capitol day and night for days on end, a "dance for democracy" corner was set up with music blasting, giving protestors a chance to dance and let off some excess energy. When I made my way over to the corner, I found a girl dancing her heart out while wearing Batman's cowl. "Batman doesn't dance" was my first thought, but then again, this was a girl. Maybe it was actually Stephanie Brown, the then-current Batgirl, fighting for justice and bouncing around through the night all at the same time.

While being a superhero comic book fan does not mean that a person resides in a childish fantasy world with no hint of maturity, it often means, in the absolute best sense, that we retain a childlike sense of wonder and empowerment. We're all still that little girl twirling an invisible Lasso of Truth, gaining strength from the icons whose adventures we follow month after month. Like Catholic saints or Pagan gods and goddesses, superheroes represent a pantheon of figures that any fan can invoke at just the right moment. Whether we're pretending we're Pepper Potts to alleviate the pain of a boss's ridiculous demands or channeling the confidence of the Black Cat while getting dressed up for a night on the town, we rely on these fictional icons as personal touchstones, constellations of traits and experiences from which we can draw strength. It doesn't matter that Captain America isn't real – my grandfather and Scott Walker are, and Cap's spirit, his symbolic resonance, allowed me to mourn the former and fight against the latter. Every day I carry with me the confidence of Jennifer Walters, the principles of Steve Rogers, the wit of Hank McCoy, and the personal discipline of Scott Summers, prepared to deploy each at the most opportune time. Comic books have helped me to internalize heroism while recognizing my own, and for that I couldn't be more grateful.

Burn, Baby, Burn

Lloyd Rose was, for ten years, the theater critic of *The Washington Post*. Prior to that, she was the Literary Manager at Arena Stage. She has written for *The New Yorker* and *The Atlantic*. She wrote an episode of *Homicide: Life on the Street*, and is the author of three *Doctor Who* novels and the Big Finish *Doctor Who* audio *Caerdroia*.

Like Botticelli's Venus, she's born from water. But Phoenix doesn't gently drift to shore on a shell, tresses draped to conceal her charms. She erupts from an ocean crash like a rocket, her hair flying around her head, her body aggressively exposed by a skin-tight outfit. Her emergence is phallic, her presence overwhelmingly female, and few women who read comics have failed to love her.

As every fan knows, the original Phoenix – a new incarnation of X-Man Jean Grey, drably known up to that point as Marvel Girl – came to a bad end. Believing her friends dead, she fell under the spell (literally) of Mastermind, who with mental manipulation urged her most forbidden desires to emerge. They sure did. Among other side effects, a planet died, and so, soon after, did Jean / Phoenix.

The phrase "female empowerment" fits Phoenix like a ballet shoe fits a panther. She was *way* beyond that, a goddess of destruction unleashing days of wrath. Yet her beginnings are humble, even sleazy – some stirrings in the teen-aged libido of her co-creator (along with artist Dave Cockrum) Chris Claremont, stoked by a particularly memorable episode of *The Avengers* in which Diana Rigg appeared in a corset-and-boots ensemble accessorized with boa constrictor. He borrowed from the show the Hellfire Club (itself based on a real English organization that once hosted Benjamin Franklin as a guest), in which the villains dressed in eighteenth century finery and the women like dominatrixes. This is the company Mastermind introduces the mesmerized Jean into: a perverse, if stylish, gang who hope to control Phoenix for their own ends. Before they get their comeuppance, she shows a lot of leg.

Claremont was mocked at the time by some (male) comics fans and writers as having done nothing more than write up a personal sexual fantasy. But if lust can legitimately fuel major artists like Picasso and

Joyce, why should it be banned from pulp? Yeah, there's something a little snicker-worthy about Jean's strutting around in an S&M outfit while the plot proceeds with an absolutely straight face. But then, realizing what's been done to her, she more-or-less rips out Mastermind's brain, leaving him a drooling husk. Joke's over.

Phoenix owes more to Rigg's Mrs. Peel than that one *Avengers* episode. John Steed's first partner in the series had been blond, leather-clad Honor Blackman, a Tough Broad who could be as physically dangerous as a man. (Blackman also played the tough lesbian gang leader Pussy Galore in *Goldfinger*, whom only the supermale James Bond was studly enough to seduce.) She too has her descendents, notably Sigourney Weaver's Ripley in the *Alien* movies. But these characters, however talented the actresses, were basically conceived as guys with breasts. Rigg's style was different – witty, sophisticated, and sleekly feminine without being vampish or girly. Her most famous avatar is Buffy, who could pound a vampire into dust then regret that she broke a nail in the process. (Though it turned out to be the quiet Willow who, in Joss Whedon's description, "went all Dark Phoenix.")

Comic book heroines prior to Phoenix didn't have this sort of poise and self-sufficiency. In the Marvel Universe, they tended to have secondary powers – witchery, prehensile hair, becoming invisible (known in real life as fading demurely into the background). Jean Grey was an example of the type: She had a telekinetic power that moved things around and she left the heavy lifting to the boys. Phoenix is on a whole different level, yet she doesn't simply borrow the fighting style and strength of a superhero. She's a whirlwind rather than a missile. In spite of her explosive birth, Phoenix's force isn't phallic. It's a spreading force-*field*, a cosmic tsunami.

When Jean-as-Phoenix visits her frightened parents, she tells them, "I am what I am." A goddess, then, at the very least. But where in Western mythology is there a goddess like this? The Greeks relegated small aggressions to minor goddesses of spite, discord, etc.; petty, girly stuff. The Norse had Hel, but she was more spooky than raging. You have to go to India, to Kali's precursor/aspect Durga, to find Wrath in its exaltation of power and terror. According to one source, when Durga first confronted the demon Mahishasura he, "underestimated her, thinking 'How can a woman kill me, Mahishasur [sic] – the one who defeated the trinity of gods?' However, Durga roared with laughter, which caused an earthquake." She burns him to a crisp.

Unlike the monstrous Kali, Durga is beautiful. So is Phoenix, magnificently so in the way only a comic-book heroine can be – like a super-charged Pre-Raphaelite woman, all voluptuousness and masses of hair, but with a force even the Pre-Raphaelite paintings of sorceresses don't have. Nor is it just her impossibly gorgeous body. John Byrne (who took over from Cockrum) may have at one point lovingly sketched her left buttock as she steps into the frame to confront the White Queen, but he also made her elegant and glorious, the curves of her body and hair like lines of force. Her joy in her power is the rapture of an athlete. If on one level she's no more than a pin-up, on another she's an illustration of male love for women, of awe, wonder, and appreciation. (And this in spite of the fact that Byrne didn't like the character; he thought she was too powerful and disrupted the X-Men as a team.)

Byrne had drawn at least one Cosmic Woman prior to Phoenix: the Scarlet Witch, as possessed by an earth entity called Chthon. She lost that silly headdress and her wildly floating hair looked *dangerous*, like something that might electrocute you if you touched it. But she was only a warm-up for Phoenix, just as the pre-Mastermind Phoenix was only a warm-up for Dark Phoenix, the monster from Jean's id. The corrupted Phoenix's outfit mutated, in that handy comic-book way, from green to red, and the light around her (courtesy of colorist Glynis Wein) from yellows and golds to deep purple-black and a sickly-looking mauve, feverish and diseased colors. Frenzied with appetite, she became Death, the Destroyer of Worlds. Sure, it's all a bit overwrought, even ridiculous. But some of the tale's dark chords have a Wagnerian resonance.

There's another resonance in the story too, at least for women. Claremont stuck to the letter of the comics-for-kids code in his story details. But any reader past puberty knew that Mastermind's mental penetration and deception of Jean was a rape of her mind, and no one believed that, with such power over such a stunning woman, he wasn't enjoying her body as well. When Jean briefly recovers her sanity before mutating into Dark Phoenix, she accuses Mastermind of using his powers to unleash her "darkest fantasies." The twist is that, in spite of the set-up, those fantasies aren't sexual.

Dark Phoenix attacks, torments, hates. She barely stops herself from harming her family, and when she takes on her former friends the X-Men, she's out for blood. This isn't lust, it's scorched-earth rage. We're looking at Hell-hath-no-fury, and it's no longer a cute put-down. It's the fury of the raped woman, the violence of rape turned outward – savage, merciless, beyond reason, all the male clichés about "crazy women" in full scalding flow. Obviously, she had to go.

But how? In thinking about what to do with their near-omnipotent villainess, whose mere presence threw ordinary action stories off-kilter, Claremont and Byrne had considered several options. Dark Phoenix was going to fly off into interstellar space to be an occasionally returning bad guy like Galactus. Or she was going to be stripped of her powers and turned into a nice little human, Scott's wife, a secondary character. Or she'd have the "bad" Phoenix Force removed and have to live with what she'd done. Jim Shooter, Marvel's editor-in-chief at the time, thought that the last idea was morally ludicrous, to say the least, and demanded her death. So she committed suicide with some huge blasty raygun-thing on the moon. It was a lousy end to the story, but so were all the others. Diminished, she was dead anyway.

Comics being what they are, she was reborn several times, coming to several more bad ends. No one could figure out what to do with her. She had the power of a nova and could eat stars and was a redhead to boot: too hot for the Marvel Universe to handle, really. Jean Grey was finally killed off, and though the Phoenix Force is still drifting around occasionally possessing someone, when that someone isn't Jean the effect's just not the same. The real Phoenix is the woman who burst defiantly from her drowning grave, shouting the corny and epic lines, "Hear me, X-Men. No longer am I the woman you knew. I am life and fire forever. I am Phoenix!" Yes she was. And then some.

Tune in Tomorrow

Sue D runs the blog *DC Women Kicking Ass*, which celebrates female comic book characters. She also appears in the *3 Chicks Review Comics* podcast feature on *Comic Book Resources*. Her lifelong love of comics began after seeing Batgirl on TV, and she may have been influenced to go to journalism school because of Lois Lane. She was probably wooed by her future spouse, in part, through gifts of Catwoman comics. And her bedroom is definitely overrun with an extremely large collection of Batgirl memorabilia. She is happily creating a new generation of comic book fans and her children consider "Free Comic Book Day" to be only behind Christmas, Halloween, Easter, and their birthdays as "the best day of the year."

The words are simple and straightforward. They promise nothing, yet create a sense of anticipation. They signify a conclusion and the start of something new.

"Same Bat-time, same Bat-channel!"

"Tune in tomorrow!"

These words end episodes of the 1960s Batman television show and episodes of the long-running soap opera *Days of Our Lives*, respectively. They represent the two fandoms I've belonged to for more than two-thirds of my life: superhero comics and soap operas.

Beginning to watch a soap opera is a challenge, very much like picking up an issue of an unfamiliar comic book series. You don't know who all the characters are, you're not sure what it means, and your reaction may be driven by others already in the fandom. My mother watched a number of them but her favorite story (as she would call her soaps) was *Another World*, a program that appeared on NBC for 35 years. Her favorite character is, she tells me as I watch for the first time, Iris Carrington. Within moments, I see Iris is impetuous, manipulative, and haughty. She is the show's villain. But I will soon learn that Iris Carrington makes things happen.

After a few minutes of recounting the back history, my mother tells me that Iris is about to get payback for an unpardonable sin: not passing along a phone call from the show's heroine, Rachel, to Iris's father Mac (who is married to Rachel – this is a soap, after all), which resulted in Rachel losing her baby. This moment is a huge payoff for months and months of teasing. The moment is so intense and welcome that my mother jumps out of her chair and claps her hands as Mac storms into Iris's home. It is mesmerizing. I was hooked. Iris would become one of my favorite characters.

Comics and soap operas are incredibly similar. Both offer stories that never end. Characters have the same names, but wear different faces and possess tweaked histories. There are villains so evil they cause the heart to palpitate, heroes so complex they fuel tales that go on for years. Each has a cast of characters that require flow-charts to figure out who is related to whom. So why aren't more soap opera fans also superhero comics fans? And why aren't more fans of superhero comics fans of soap operas?

Soap operas were a phenomenon, even appearing on the cover of *Time* magazine. At one point, there were 16 daytime soaps on the air, each of them attracting millions of viewers. Like superhero comics, they reflected social changes. In the 1960s, soap operas were primarily produced by soap companies such as Proctor and Gamble. Their shows had a common look and style – and their stories and characters reflected white, middle-class, Midwestern values.

DC was the king of comic books at this time, but it would soon find itself competing with Marvel. Marvel was the younger, hipper publisher who changed comics with new, younger characters like Spider-Man. These characters had real-life problems and their stories took place in more realistic settings. Similarly, new soaps appeared reflecting the real world. *One Life to Live* and *All My Children* contained the classic tropes of soaps, but included contemporary aspects such as classism, drug addiction, and conflicts about both the Vietnam War and the emerging women's movement. The shows now featured black actors as stars; simultaneously, the first black superheroes began appearing in comics. The real world had permeated both daytime and comics, and they began to attract a new audience with shows like *The Young and the Restless* – in which the cast spent their time hopping in and out of bed.

Here, from the mid-1970s until the late 1980s, the confluence of soaps and comics is most apparent. In 1975, Chris Claremont was charged by Marvel to take on the X-Men. Claremont made *Uncanny X-Men* into the longest running soap opera in comics. Under Claremont, the characters still fought evil and saved the world, but they spent pages upon pages talking about their feelings, their desires, and their loves, both fulfilled and unrequited.

I recently read some of the Chris Claremont/John Byrne runs on

Uncanny X-Men and was amazed at the way the stories emulated the soaps. Let's look at *Uncanny X-Men* #183 from July 1984. On the cover you have a typical superhero battle, but when you flip open the comic, you see a young man and woman sitting on cliff. The looks on their faces show this is an uncomfortable conversation. Beside them we see the title of the issue in a typeface that looks like draped ribbons: "He'll never make me cry."

The two star-crossed lovers, Peter Rasputin and Kitty Pryde, could easily be any of the soap "super couples" that reigned during the 1980s – Luke and Laura of *General Hospital* or Bo and Hope of *Days of Our Lives.*

And the dialogue in this scene? He's given his heart to someone else. She listens, eyes like saucers brimming with tears as her internal monologue rumbles with angst while he betrays her.

This is classic soap opera moment. Kitty has plenty of moments of pure heroism in *Uncanny X-Men*, but in this issue, she will go off to her room to cry into a pillow.

Just as the soulful angst of Luke Spencer and Laura Baldwin topped the television charts and become a pop phenomenon, so the trials and tribulations of Kitty and Peter, and Jean Grey and Scott Summers, climbed to the top of superhero comics. (Coincidentally, when soap operas adopted the outrageous plots of superhero comics, as *General Hospital* did with its "Ice Princess" storyline in the 1980s, the shows had their greatest success even attracting a large male audience as well.)

DC Comics responded with its own youth-centered team book: *The New Teen Titans*, which was filled with stories of young male and female superheroes who spend as much time in moments of romantic angst as fighting evil.

I'm a DC girl, so my preference is *NTT* over *Uncanny X-Men*. The character I focused on was Donna Troy, a.k.a. Wonder Girl. Except for her ability to fly and super strength, Donna resembles the typical soap ingénue – upbeat, in love with life, a friend to all, and a woman in love. She wasn't just a superhero; she had a successful career as a fashion photographer. She also had great hair, easily the equal of any soap actress. She wasn't a pushover; she was both strong and resolute. She made things happen.

The leading characters in soap operas are mainly women. While there are many popular male characters, the stories really aren't about them. They are about Viki Buchanan, Carly Corinthos, and Erica Kane. *The New Teen Titans* and *Uncanny X-Men* both made women leads as well. *Uncanny X-Men* was as much about Storm and Jean Grey and Kitty Pryde as it was about Scott Summers and Wolverine. *The New Teen Titans* was as much about Donna Troy, Starfire, and Raven as it was about Robin, Changeling, and Cyborg.

Some say that soap operas are pure plot. I disagree. Soap operas reuse the same plots over and over. It is the characters that make me tune in tomorrow.

Characters keep me reading superhero comics. While I enjoy and admire Batman, I identify with Barbara Gordon. I respect Superman, but identify with Lois Lane, the hard-driving reporter who combines a great career with a great marriage. When I pick up a comic, I enjoy the idea that there is more than just a story on a page. I love that the actions of a character are driven by years of history just as in the soaps. Yes, I also enjoy when each of them go off to vanquish evil and kick ass, but these moments of connection are just as important.

The comic market has changed dramatically. The market that once sold half a million copies per month of *Uncanny X-Men* is lucky today to get maybe a couple dozen books each month selling 10% of that number. Soap operas have also suffered a slow decline. Now soap operas and superhero comics are trying desperately to survive. Two of the remaining soap operas, *All My Children* and *One Life to Live*, were cancelled in the last year. DC Comics recently underwent a massive makeover while also adding digital distribution.

Traditional soap operas are close to dead. Comics, for now, live on. But I think there is still the potential to bring more female readers into the fold of superhero comics. Not every woman wants to read a superhero comic with the dramatic beats of a soap. But I think many women want to read female characters that are strong protagonists who, like the characters I enjoyed growing up, "make things happen." When the big two – Marvel and DC – create books like DC Comics's *Birds of Prey*, female readers respond.

Who knows? If the stories are there and marketed properly, readers may – as the soap operas once instructed – tune in tomorrow for another episode. Or, as I do, download the next 20 pages the following month.

An Interview with Greg Rucka

Greg Rucka is the award-winning author of over 16 novels and countless comic books. He's been privileged to write some of the greatest pop-culture icons in modern history, including Batman, Superman, Wolverine, and Wonder Woman, and is currently the author of *The Punisher* for Marvel Comics. He is renowned for having written a number of series that have greatly advanced the profile and development of female characters in comics, including *Gotham Central*, *52*, *Detective Comics* (featuring the acclaimed *Batwoman: Elegy* storyarc), *Whiteout*, and *Queen & Country*. Rucka lives in Portland, Oregon, with his wife, writer Jen Van Meter, and their two children. When not parenting, writing, or sleeping, he is most often thinking about parenting, writing, or sleeping.

Q. How did you first become interested in comic books?

A. I found them young. I remember being in the checkout line at the Nob Hill Market in Salinas, California – I couldn't have been more than eight – and getting one of the little, digest-sized, Lee/Kirby reprints that had re-tellings of the original Hulk stuff in black and white. I also remember picking up *Archie* and *Jughead*. I think that was sort of the natural entry point into comics for a lot of people in my generation: The comics were around, they were in front of us, we read them, we liked them.

I had a bonus impetus in that I have an older sister, Brandy, who has Down's Syndrome. When we were growing up, we watched *The Incredible Hulk* TV show with Bill Bixby and Lou Ferrigno, and she developed the craziest crush on the Hulk. And she didn't differentiate between the two – she got that Bixby and Ferrigno were supposed to be aspects of the same person.

I've spent a lot of time thinking about it – and I used to say this was a little glib, but I think it may be accurate – but in large part the appeal was here was this guy, David Banner as played by Bill Bixby, who is really the gentlest, kindest soul you could ever encounter. Yet, when people around him were threatened and he became enraged, he would turn into this incredibly powerful – yet very gentle – protector who would deliver a smack-down to the bad guys, but never, ever, *ever* do wrong to an innocent. I think that spoke to Brandy, very loudly.

Later, when I was ten or 11, I went into my first comic book store – it was in Monterey, California – specifically to buy *The Incredible Hulk* magazine, which had these stories by Doug Moench. I bought a particular issue that was essentially the Incredible Hulk vs. Three Mile Island – it was exactly what you would expect, but when I presented it to my sister, she had *no* interest in it at all. And, of course, she wouldn't have done – it was a completely different animal than what had appealed to her. But *I* was fascinated by it. I remember taking it to school, and trying to copy the panels – I can't draw, and that was pretty much when I learned from the attempt, that I couldn't draw! I would literally trace it and it still came out bad!

Q. Was there something about the comic stories being a literary experience that appealed to you, made you more engaged with the characters than their TV personas did?
A. Like many writers, I had a very isolated childhood spent mostly reading. About the time I entered eighth grade, I changed schools and fell in with a group of like-minded geeks. They all collected comics, and in particular they collected *Uncanny X-Men*. That was what all my peers were doing, so that was what I did – and it was the last straw, the final act that turned me into a passionate lover of the medium. And this was, you know, later in Claremont's run. I think the first issue I got was *Uncanny X-Men* #160, and I fell in love with Kitty Pryde immediately. Because on top of everything else, she was Jewish, and I was seeing representation!

That soon led to my going to comic book stores and finding stuff all by my lonesome, such as the Miller/Mazzucchelli *Daredevil: Born Again* storyarc. And that was another turning point for me: I'd found this material on my own, I had recognized it as very special in the context of everything else going on in the medium. It was the first book that I actively hunted down and collected on my own.

When I left for college, I sold my comic collection, thinking, "I'm not going to be able to do this in college." But, lo and behold, somebody very wise in Poughkeepsie, New York, had opened a comic book store a block and a half from the Vassar campus. So I went right back in. At that point, we're talking post-*The Dark Knight Returns*, post-*Green Arrow: The Longbow Hunters*, and in particular when Denny O'Neil and Denys Cowan started on *The Question*.

Q. You've become very associated with that character. Is it fair to say that the O'Neil/Cowan run was a seminal experience for you?

A. It was another one of these comics that elevated the form for me. I was a freshman in college, and my best friend in the world – Nunzio DiFilippis, who's another comics writer – was a psych major, and he was reading *The Question* with me. And he turned to me one day and said, "You know, [Thomas] Szasz is this very famous guy in psychology, known for this book called *The Myth of Mental Illness*, and it's very deliberate that Denny O'Neil is doing this..." All of a sudden, I realized, *I'm reading something else than I thought I was*. It was a great series all along, a really beautifully executed comic – but when you look at that run *now*, it's an examination of what sanity is and how we judge it. So many of the people that [the Question] encounters in the first 24 issues are people who are doing things that look insane. They are doing things for reasons that make perfect sense to those characters.

Q. Did this re-ignite your love for comics?

A. Absolutely. From that point on, I was buying comics consistently, unless economically I couldn't. I went to grad school after Vassar. Jen [Van Meter] and I had just gotten married, and we were *desperately* poor. I'm fond of saying we were so poor, we were gaining weight; we were eating pasta all the time. But once every two weeks or so, we scraped together enough money and – although I was going to U.S.C. and *hated* driving in Los Angeles – we'd grit our teeth, climb in the car, drive out to Santa Monica to Hi De Ho Comics, and preciously buy ten dollars' worth of comic books. And we'd take them back and *love* them until we could go out again.

Q. At what point did you progress from being an avid comic book reader to someone who wanted to *write* comic stories?

A. I tried to write a comic with a friend of mine when I was at Vassar, and that didn't quite work out. It was my first attempt at writing in the form, but the desire was there the whole time. Even when I was looking at my graduate work – which was, "Well, I am writing a novel, I want to be a novelist" – I was reading comics. I got started in the industry directly as a result of that.

Q. How so?

I had two novels [*Keeper* and *Finder*] published, and a friend of mine who was working at DC started showing my novels around. Patty Jeres, who at that time was in marketing at DC, took an interest and eventually put me in touch with Bob Schreck when he and Joe Nozemack were starting Oni Press. That's how I ended up writing *Whiteout* for them.

Patty also introduced me to Denny O'Neil, after she brought my novels into Denny's office. The story goes that Denny had read the first one and didn't know that the second one had come out. Patty said, "Well, it just so happens he's here in town right now, would you be willing to meet him?" Denny said sure, and so he and I went to lunch. The result of that lunch was Denny saying, "Okay, why don't you try to write me something?" I said all right, and that was the start of the *Cataclysm* storyarc running through the Batman titles. Jen and I were living in Eugene, Oregon, at that point, and I spent the flight back drafting what ultimately became the first of the Renee Montoya/Two-Face stories.

Q. You are known for creating or developing a number of iconic female characters – Tara Chase in *Queen & Country*, Carrie Stetko in *Whiteout*, the Kate Kane Batwoman, etc. Is there any particular reason why you tend to write so many series with women in the lead role?

A. I wish I had an easy, simple answer for that, and I'm not sure that I do. It's true that I was raised in a feminist household – I never grew up in an environment where it was permissible to apply a gender standard to what men could do or what women could do.

Second, I like women. I genuinely like them. I say this as an ostensibly straight guy, who can say that I *like* women and I don't necessarily want to *sleep* with every one I meet. So, there's that.

But, I think, in all honesty? In all sincerity? I female-identify. I like writing about female characters. I can even go back through my writing – and here I'm talking about the stuff I wrote when I was in my teens, stuff that should never, ever in a million years see print – and those stories almost universally have female leads. Now that I think about it, the very first thing I wrote of merit – and I say "merit" only in that it won a short story contest and got me out of school for a day – had Mrs. Claus as the lead character.

I can cite these various reasons, but I honestly can't tell you *exactly* why I've gravitated toward female leads. There are, certainly, points where my writing evolved and I gained what, for me, were pretty crucial understandings of how to write women as my point-of-view characters. But I wish I could say, you know, "Well, I nearly drowned and was saved by a squad of nuns." It's nothing like that, it's just that I like women, and I like writing female leads.

Q. Your writing has also demonstrated an affinity for lesbian, bisexual or otherwise queer-gendered female characters. Is a portrayal of non-hetero orientations important to you?

A. I think there are two things going on there. The first is I don't like – and in particular I don't like *comics* – that have been so tragically misrepresentative of the world. Maybe it goes back to my interest in Kitty Pryde. It mattered a great deal to me that she was Jewish, and although Marvel may not have realized it, it really did buy me as a faithful reader for the next four years.

Also, inasmuch as I have always been aware of feminism and interested in feminist politics, I've been very aware of sexual politics and issues of sexuality. And, not to be glib about it, but if I female-identify and I'm in a heterosexual relationship, what does that make me? I've always been comfortable in my own body, enough that I'm pretty content being biologically male. But certainly intellectually, and emotionally, I'd say that I've always identified far more as female than male.

Part of it, again, is really just wanting to hold up the mirror in such a way that more accurately reflects the world. We write these very fantastic stories where the Batmobile never gets caught in traffic, and yet, we don't see guys kissing guys. That's problematic! The more we fail to represent the world, the easier it becomes to say *this* doesn't matter, or *this* isn't normal, or *this* isn't right. Instead, we should be putting it out there and saying, "This is part of life, this is what happens."

Q. Can you give us an example of your efforts to better reflect the non-heterosexuality in the world in which we live?

A. When I wrote *Whiteout*, I very deliberately wanted to play with female homoeroticism. I'd been watching a lot of John Woo, and one of my favorite films is *Hard Boiled*. There's that moment when Chow Yunfat and Tony Leung – I think it's Tony Leung – are in the morgue, right? And there's that speech about:

"When this is over, I want to go someplace. I want to go to Antarctica."

"Antarctica. Is it not always cold there?"

"Yes, but it is also always light, and that would be nice after so much darkness..."

... and then there's this poignant moment when they're looking at each other, and you just scream at the screen, *Kiss him!!* You know?

I came out of that film thinking that we have all these buddy cop stories, and they're always two guys, so I thought about doing a buddy cop story with two women and playing with that homoerotic subtext. It wasn't until I was working with [*Whiteout* artist] Steve Lieber that the subtext actually became text, with him adding in things like the *Dykes to Watch Out For* mug – which, in retrospect, I kinda wish we hadn't done, because it turned into something far more overt. Carrie Stetko isn't supposed to enter that story queer – she *may* be bi-curious, but she doesn't know it in *Whiteout*. After all, she's come out of a marriage with a husband who's died, so she's entering the story believing she is hetero.

Q. Was that the case with Renee Montoya, whom you featured prominently in *Gotham Central* and later made into the new Question?

A. I knew from the start that Renee was queer. I really don't know why. She always read to me as queer and in the closet, so I always wrote her that way. I finished my first story with her knowing that at some point down the road, eventually Two-Face would say to her, "I love you," and she would be like, "Good luck with that!"

Q. What about Bridget Logan in the Atticus Kodiak novels?

A. I knew she was bi, but I also knew that her bisexuality was somewhat insincere. Bridget does a lot of stuff in the early novels for effect and appearance, because that's the character. It was her statement of rejecting everything from this working-class Bronx, Roman Catholic cop family background. The best situation for her, if she could have gotten away with it, would have been finding herself a nice African-American lesbian to bring home to dad.

In the same series, Dale is gay. And it mattered a great deal to me that Dale's relationship with his partner Ethan is stable from the moment Ethan enters the series. They don't share a lot of screen time, but I really wanted to make it clear that, of all the dysfunction that's going on in the Kodiak series, Dale and Ethan are not part of that. In fact, they have the healthiest relationship.

Q. At this point, we have to finish off the list... what about Kate Kane as Batwoman?

A. I was given Kate – she was gay when she started. And God bless DC Comics for that. I mean, there are many things you can perhaps lay a torch at that building for, but DC said from the start that they were bringing Batwoman back, and she was going to be gay. She's going to be *gay*. We're not going to say *maybe* she's gay, we're not going to do a Very Special Episode of *Batwoman* where she comes out. She's queer from the start, and she's perfectly fine with it. Any other trauma in her life not-withstanding, she is not at all troubled by her orientation.

At the time, I was writing the Renee-and-Charlie storyline in *52*, and the story dealt with Kate, so I ended up with the character as a result. And I'm very glad and proud, I hasten to add, of what [editor] Michael Siglain and [artist] J.H. Williams III and I did with the character. When all is said and done, there will be a short list of my works for which I will be remembered, and I hope *Batwoman: Elegy* will be one of them. I'm very proud of that one.

Q. About three years passed between Kate's introduction as Batwoman in *52*, and her becoming the star of *Detective Comics*, in the *Elegy* storyline. Were there any unexpected stumbling blocks once it came time to give Kate her own series? Did DC's support for the title come and go in the interim?

A. I have two things to say on that particular subject. The first is, I wrote the first issue of *Elegy* at 22 pages of script; it was really tightly done. But as I was reading it over, I went, "Oh my god, nowhere in here do we know she's queer!" I'd written an issue No. 1 for this character that needs to introduce all these things, and this fairly crucial detail is nowhere evident! Never mind the fact that this issue was going to get some attention from the queer community, because they were going to want to *see* how Kate was represented. It would have been a *horrible* mistake to release the issue and not make that clear.

But it was tightly scripted. I was scripting specifically for [J.H. Williams III], and if you've seen *Elegy*, you *know* how those pages are laid out. There is not a lot of wiggle-room. I called my editor – it wasn't Michael Siglain at the time, it was somebody else – and said, "Look, I need two more pages. I never ask for extra pages, I never do. But it's a first issue, I think it's justified, here's why." And the editor in question said, "No way, we can't do it, you're just going to have to make it work or leave it out." I said, "No, you don't understand. This has to be in there, and I don't have any room, you've gotta give me two more pages." And he said, "Well, I'll talk to [then-executive editor] Dan DiDio."

So I got off the phone and called Dan, right away, and said that I needed two extra pages and here's *why*. Dan sort of laughed and said, "I'll do you a deal, you can have your two extra pages if you get me the script for the second issue of *Final Crisis: Revelations* by next week. And I said, "Hah! It's already in!" To which he said, "Well, then you've got your two pages."

The editor in question emails me half an hour later with, "I talked to Dan, and there's no way we can get you those extra two pages." I wrote him back and said, "That's really funny, because I just got off the phone with him."

I know there are people who will throw really big stones at Dan DiDio – but when I explained the situation to Dan, there wasn't a moment's hesitation. He was like, "Hell yes, take the two pages and let me know if you're going to need two more."

The other thing worth mentioning is that Jim and I would have these conversations while we were working on *Elegy*, and wonder exactly how much we could get away with. The big one that worried us was the scene when Kate and Renee have been in bed together, and Renee's coming out of the bathroom. And they're having what, to me, was a very honest sort of new-in-love-giddy-moment – Kate was saying, "Don't go to work today, stay with me." Jim drew the kiss on that page, and it is without a doubt the best kiss I have ever seen in a comic book. But when I saw that page, I did wonder if we'd get flack for it.

So the editor, Michael Siglain, submitted the page to DC and we didn't hear anything and we didn't hear anything and we didn't hear *anything*. Finally, I called up Mike and asked, "What's going on with the book?", to which he replied, "Oh yeah, it's fine. Why, were you worried?" I was like, "Yeah, kinda," and he was like, "Nah, nah, nah, we are past that benchmark, *miles* past. You guys are good to go."

So. There was support at DC for *Elegy*, and I will always grant them credit for that.

Q. Did you have any thoughts on what might have come next for Kate and her cast of characters?

A. My initial plan, if I'd stayed on the book, would've gone the better part of a year with Kate and Maggie Sawyer circling each other and getting closer and closer to trying a relationship. At which point, of course, Renee would come back! Just after Kate and Maggie had their first kiss, Renee would be knocking on the door saying, "Hey, I'm back in town!" As a writer, I try to never make it easy for the characters – my feeling from the start was that Kate and Renee are madly in love, but they're *horrible* for each other. They bring out the worst in each other, they burn too hot. One of them is eventually going to have to grow up and say, "Okay, that's enough of that."

Q. *Batwoman: Elegy* is often recommended to non-comics readers – and women in particular – along the lines of, "You think you don't like comics, read *this*." But actually, quite a few of your titles appear on lists of books that women who are new to comics should read. Do you think this has affected your career? If so, how?

A. In all sincerity, I have a horrible, horrible sense of my career at any given moment. Apparently, I'm pretty well known in the comics industry, but that's kind of like saying, "Well, you're the biggest tadpole in this pond!" It's not a big pool. When our bestselling comic book barely breaks a hundred thousand copies, that's not a lot compared to a readership that should be, frankly, in the millions.

Look, you know how the Internet works. The people who don't like stuff are loud about not liking it, just as there are people out there who say, "Rucka's got an agenda." If that affects my numbers, then it affects my numbers. I don't know, and I frankly don't care, because at the end of the day it comes back to one thing: I want to tell the best stories I can tell about the characters I am writing.

Q. It sounds as if your interaction with the Internet, from your standing as a working professional, has left a bit of a bad taste in your mouth. Has it?

A. The Internet has made it impossible for me to read a review. For the most part, comics criticism is a fictional beast, it doesn't really exist. There are very few people writing comics criticism who apply a critical standard to it. Most people write comics criticism on the basis of, "I didn't like this and here's why...", and normally, the "here's why" comes out to "... because I wasn't the guy who wrote it." There's a common phrase in the industry – and I've heard it most often attributed to Mark Waid – that there are no fans, only people who want your job. There is, I think, a certain truth to that.

There's a difference between looking at the Internet for ego gratification and looking at it for fan and audience interaction. The problem is that those boundaries can get real, real thin. I want to be able to talk to people about the work, yes, and I want to make myself available to people who want to talk about the work. But I have no interest in making myself available to be a punching bag, and I don't think that's unreasonable.

Meeting people in person is entirely different. You know, I like going to conventions to meet fans. The only good thing about going to Comic-Con this year is that I'm going to see some fans – there will be some people who will want to talk to me about what they've read. Those are the reasons that make the trip worthwhile. Otherwise, I would not go to San Diego. I really wouldn't go.

Q. You've written quite a few creator-owned comics, but also DC and Marvel titles where you inevitably have to surrender the characters involved to the next creative team in line. In what ways do you go about making a particular character and situation yours for the duration of your custodianship? Conversely, when it's your turn to leave the book, how hard is it to let go of that character?

A. It's very hard. There are very few books that I've left of my own accord. The gaping wound in my soul that is my *Wonder Woman* run comes close to healing every now and then, only to re-open. I was removed from that book, and because of that, I wound up doing what in my opinion is a capital crime to do to a character: the equivalent of a drive-by. I wrote a story where Diana killed a guy [Maxwell Lord, to free Superman from his control], and there was a *lot* of story to follow that. But pretty much as soon as we had Diana kill Max, we were told, "Okay, you're done!" But – but – but – but

Talking about the things DC *didn't* do well, they in essence tried to hush this up. They loved that I sold books, but they didn't want to use the story. And I was like, "You can't *do* that!" I hate it when writers come onto something for two, three, or four issues just to chop off a character's arm and then leave again. If you do something that fundamental to a character, you need to own it and answer it. There was a long answer to what Diana had done, and I wish I'd been able to write it.

When I left *Detective Comics* the first time around, the editorial situation had deteriorated so badly that the editor at the time pretty much didn't have the balls to say, "I want you off the book." So, instead, he made me as miserable as he possibly could. He succeeded. He made me perfectly miserable. With *Checkmate*, at least, I left because of workload issues.

You asked me about what's involved in writing this stuff while you're there – and the answer is, you need to invest, and that's an emotional process as much as an intellectual one. You become the character's advocate. For that reason, departure is always going to be painful.

Q. Is it fair to say that if it doesn't hurt when you leave, you weren't doing it right in the first place?

A. I actually think that's an entirely fair way to put it. My daughter's been doing theater, and will tell me that she's very, *very* nervous before a performance. And I'll tell her how that's a good sign – the fact that you're nervous means that it matters to you. Be proud of that, and use it. It's not going to make you less nervous, but investing in what you're doing is a fine thing, and there's nothing wrong with that.

Q. Since you mentioned your daughter, are there any ways in which being a parent affects your writing and the kinds of stories you want to tell?

A. Not in the way I think you'd think. Before I became a parent, I could sit and watch episodes of *Oz* for hours on end.

I find that I can write some very dark, very scary things. *Walking Dead*, which is an Atticus Kodiak book, is pretty dark! It involves a lot of exorcism writing. Prior to having kids, I was aware of how a work would be perceived should children of a certain age read it, but I'm even *more* aware of it now. My 11-year-old son keeps asking, "When can I read your novels?", and I keep telling him, "Not yet! A couple more years, but not yet." Of our two kids, he is, in many ways, the more emotionally sensitive. Dashiell is very tough, very fierce – she externalizes, and doesn't hide what she's feeling at all. Elliot is much quieter, and internalizes things much more directly. He's very much a still-water-running-deep.

Q. Do you have any advice for female creators trying to get their start in the industry?

A. Oh, God. I'm really leery of answering this one, because I'm a guy.

Nobody enters comics the same way... that's No. 1. I got into comics because I was a novelist, which isn't a route that's feasible for everybody. It's not like I can recommend, "Go and get your first two novels published, and then get a deal for another two, and then hopefully know somebody who works at a comics company."

I would like to believe that the quality of the work that newcomers are doing will win out – but in all sincerity, that is not always the case. I will say to newcomers that the most important thing in any writing, to me at least, is emotional honesty. I have to believe in the emotional truth of the characters. If I do not, then you are wasting my time. I have to believe in them so I feel for them, I feel *with* them. And that isn't a gender issue, it's a human nature issue.

Also, while there are people in the mainstream – and here I'm talking editorial and publishing-wise – who are working to address the gender inequities, be aware that the comic book industry is still a sexist industry. And that may be because superhero comics – and I specify *superhero* comics – are a sexist medium. They are directed primarily, even to this day, at a fictional adolescent readership that is now in its forties! But they're still guys.

I had a discussion related to this with the artist on *Ghost Rider*, Matthew Clark – we've been friends for over a decade. If you haven't checked out the book, the new Ghost Rider is a young woman; I believe she's supposed to be 16. And Matthew told me that they'd gotten an email from a young woman who thanked them for drawing her as a 16 year old, for letting her look her age. Man, you could just see how proud Matthew was! But such a thing shouldn't be such an uphill-frickin'-battle! It should not be a stop-the-presses moment every time a teenage female character is drawn to look her age.

So, what's my advice to newcomers? I'm not sure I have any! My advice is, keep your chin down. Make sure your shell is pretty hard. Know the difference between constructive criticism and destructive criticism, meaning know the source. Stay off the Internet unless you have to. Don't read your reviews.

And tell the truth. That's advice I would give to anybody.

Comic Book Junkie

Jill Thompson graduated in 1987 from the American Academy of Art in Chicago and has been working non-stop as a cartoonist and illustrator ever since. She has illustrated books for nearly every comic book publisher in the United States, garnering acclaim for her work on *Wonder Woman*, *Swamp Thing*, *Black Orchid* and the award-winning *Sandman* with Neil Gaiman. In 1997, Jill's first children's book, *Scary Godmother*, was released to critical acclaim. More books and a series of comics followed, and *Scary Godmother* has since been turned into a series of television specials.

I remember the exact moment I became a comic book junkie. Oh sure, I'd already been interested in comics by now. I had moved from loving Charles M. Schulz's *Peanuts* to Dan DeCarlo's *Betty and Veronica*, *Archie* and *Jughead* comics, and spent hours upon hours drawing my own versions of these types of stories. I knew I wanted to be a cartoonist from the first time I had read anything with that lovable beagle Snoopy. When I told my mother that, "I am going to draw Snoopy when I get big!", my mother pointed out that, "The reason you get to see Snoopy in the newspaper is because somebody already draws him. You're going to have to make up your own character if you want to draw for the comics."

So I did.

Of course it was a total Snoopy ripoff, a low rent first-grade version of Snoopy, but I was wearing my influence on my sleeve as far as the main character was concerned. I called him B Dog. He was a simple cartoon. Easy to visualize. Close your eyes, I'll describe him to you. First of all, draw the capital letter B. Now on the back of that B at the top left corner, draw a big black teardrop for an ear. On the front of the top loop of the B, smack dab in the middle... draw a filled in circle for a nose. Inside the top loop of the B, draw a dot for an eye. Now at the bottom of the B under the loop, draw a flatter loop for a foot, and while you're at it, draw a tail on the back of the B and you are finished!

When the house down the block was having a moving sale and they had an orange crate filled with *Archie* comics from the 1950s and 1960s that I was able to buy for some small amount of money, my comics took on a Dan DeCarlo influence. I copied those beautiful drawings, I made up my own *Archie*-style characters based on the kids in my neighborhood and I wrote stories. My ballpoint pen creations were foisted on my parents to read once I was finished, and they always read them "cover to cover."

My little brother and I read that box of *Archies* over and over and over, digging to the bottom of the box to try and find an issue we hadn't read in a while. We had read them so many times that we could just look at the cover and we knew exactly what stories were on the inside. What were we to do? Well, there was that "scary comic" that my dad had picked up for me... you see, sometimes my dad would stop at the newsstand on the way home from work on Fridays and he would pick up a few new *Archie* comics for me. When I saw him come home with his newspaper tucked under his arm and a flat green bag sticking out of that newspaper, I knew there was a comic or two headed my way.

But sometimes there would be some other types of comics mixed in with the *Archies*. These were things I called "scary comics" because most of the time, someone on the cover was grimacing, wracked with pain, or generally in mortal danger. And there were some old Bernie Wrightson *House of Mystery* books in there too, which were meant to be creepy. Being a bit of a scaredy-cat, that was all it took for me to avoid them. But, with our lunchtime reading becoming almost committed to memory, I had to resort to drastic measures. I dug down to the very bottom of the comic box where the scary comics lived and pulled out a couple. How scary could it be? Not bad. Pretty colorful, actually.

Now, I'm not sure what the other comics were that I pulled up with it, but my addiction to comics was going to kick in full force once I opened up this issue called *Uncanny X-Men* #131. I got thrown right smack dab in the middle of "The Dark Phoenix Saga." And who was running right down that Chicago back alley towards my curly haired self? Why, that would be my comics heroin, oxycontin, coffee, cigarettes, booze, sugar... whatever the most addictive thing is that you can think of. In my case, it was Kitty Pryde. A 13-year-old Chicago area girl whose mutant powers were just manifesting. She kind of looked like me! She was the same age as me! I lived in the Chicago area! Boy oh boy, I identified with her immediately. I hit the ground running right along with that character. Lord knows, I always wanted magic powers, super powers, *some* kind of amazing powers (who doesn't?), and here was a comic filled with a bunch of women who had powers beyond belief.

There was Phoenix, who had the power to read minds, levitate, use her telekinesis to smash a car, and save the inexperienced, but also superpowered, Kitty. Storm controlled the weather and could fly. Even the evil White Queen, though a villain, was a powerful telepath as well.

I dove right into that world and never looked back.

After that first fix, I was using my babysitting money to mainline as many comics as I could get my hands on. I ate, slept, and dreamt comics. I would scour the drugstore racks to pull out any title that might be my beloved *X-Men*. I had no concept of back issues or when comics came out. I went every day just because maybe there would be a comic on the magazine shelf or on the spinner rack that hadn't been there before. I begged my father to bring me some more of these X-Men comics and he did. However, none of them were in order. They were random issues. The X-Men comic that had gotten me hooked had been a random issue left in the newsstand. So I was getting all sorts of parts of stories. But nothing complete.

Then one day, my father mentioned that he drove past a whole store in the adjacent town to ours that seemed to be a shop devoted solely to comics. He took me over one Saturday, and there my habit began in earnest. Whereas before I had spent my babysitting money on random comics shoved in a wire rack near the ice cream cold case at the drugstore, I now was introduced to the world of bagged and boarded back issues. I was hooked on the story and here was a veritable, albeit expensive, buffet for me to feast upon. I'd ride my bike over every Saturday when the shop opened to buy whatever back issue I could afford and a few new comics – because Rick, of Rick's One Stop Comics, was a very good "dealer" who was always saying things like, "If you like that Wolverine character, he makes a cross over appearance in this comic." Or, "Have you read any *Spider-Man*? I think you'd like Spidey, Jill." It wasn't long 'til I was picking up nearly every comic that had the Marvel logo on it. I'd try anything, but I'd continue with it only if I liked the art.

Rick introduced me to all the classics that I loved – John Byrne, John Romita, John Buscema (Sal, not so much, but I felt I had to be loyal to the Buscema name) – and I soon was able to understand how different inkers could make pencillers look different. I slowly expanded my comics world view to other companies with *The New Teen Titans* by Marv Wolfman and George Perez. I had found my hobby, my culture, my ambition.

I knew what I was going to do when I grew up. I was going to be a comic book artist.

Rick informed me about past continuity, what was coming out when, and introduced me to other comics I might like because of my taste in art and story. I dare to say I was his sole female customer. I don't think I ever saw another girl in that shop. Was it brightly lit? No. Was it organized? Pretty much. Compared to shops nowadays, it was actually rather diverse. Rick even had a corner devoted to British comics like *2000 AD*, independent publishers like Eclipse, underground stuff like R. Crumb (but he wouldn't let me look at those 'til I was old enough), and some well-worn, thick, Japanese mangas. No one knew what they were about, but they were there. Did it smell like old paperbacks and paper? Of course! It was amazing! There were rows and rows of stories waiting to be read. All waiting for me to earn enough money to buy.

My habit seemed to know no bounds. Soon, I was buying bags and boards to keep those X-Men books safe from the elements. Not safe from me, because I read them over and over and over! My love for them was actually destroying them at the same time.

Then one day, Rick dropped the bomb of all bombs on me. How could this comic thing get any better? How could this world expand even more?

"You gonna be going to that comic convention they got downtown?", said Rick so matter-of-factly.

"What's a comic convention?" I asked.

"Down there at the American Congress. It's all comics dealers with their comics and they got some of the artists and stuff, they come in sometimes." Again, Rick said these magic words as if everyone already knew the incredible information he had just shared.

"I'm selling tickets to it. Here!", he said, and handed me one. I don't even remember what the price was, but I think I rode my bike home the same way Charlie Bucket ran after getting the Golden Ticket in the Wonka bar.

My father graciously gave up a Sunday to escort me to downtown Chicago and wander around a hotel ballroom filled with boxes of comics, the odd movie poster, old pulp novels and the like. Once again, I was probably the only girl attending this show; any other females I saw were dealer's wives or girlfriends. But I didn't care. The place was full of guys who liked comics. That was good enough for me. People I could ask about stories and art! I bought a John Buscema *Conan* portfolio, and I think I got my dad to buy me a back issue of *X-Men* that Rick's shop didn't have.

My father was a sport, staying with me 'til late in the afternoon before he pulled the ripcord on my adventure. I picked up a flyer on the way out and to find that these little conventions seemed to happen every six weeks or so. Now my comics habit had a new habit. And I had just enough time to save up some more money.

Little did I know that Rick had one more surprise for me. "So, Jill..." He said one Saturday afternoon, "You know that John Byrne guy? The one who drew the *X-Men* you like so much? Well, He lives in Evanston, you know, so, he's gonna be at that next convention downtown..."

... but that's a story for another day!

From *Pogo* to *Girl Genius*:
A Life in the Funny Papers

Delia Sherman writes stories and novels for younger readers and adults. Her most recent short stories have appeared in the young adult anthology *Steampunk!* and in Ellen Datlow's *Naked City.* Her adult novels are *Through a Brazen Mirror, The Porcelain Dove,* and *The Fall of the Kings* (with Ellen Kushner). She is currently writing middle-grade novels. *Changeling* and *The Magic Mirror of the Mermaid Queen* are both set in the magical world of New York Between. Her newest novel, *The Freedom Maze,* is a time-travel historical about ante-bellum Louisiana. When she's not writing, she's teaching, editing, knitting, and cooking. She lives in New York City with partner Ellen Kushner.

My mother wouldn't let me bring comic books in the house when I was a kid. *Archie, Little Lulu, Casper the Friendly Ghost,* even *Donald Duck,* were forbidden to cross the threshold. *True Romance* and *Spider-Man* and *Superman* – don't even think about it.

I presumed that this was just another Mama thing, like her embargo on jeans and chewing gum. But, when I recently Googled "comics unhealthy 1950s," I turned up a bunch of articles about a book called *The Seduction of the Innocent,* written in 1954 by Dr. Frederick Wertham. In it, Dr. Wertham claimed to prove, through scientific study, that reading comic books – crime and horror comics especially, but even superhero titles like *Superman* and *Batman* – was likely to encourage children to become sadists, racists, homosexuals, and/or juvenile delinquents.

Almost immediately, a swarm of distinguished psychologists rushed into print with articles pointing out Wertham's sketchy methodology and the barking-mad illogic of his conclusions. But it was too late. Portions of *The Seduction of the Innocent* had already appeared in *The Ladies' Home Journal* and *Reader's Digest.* Comics became one of those dangers concerned parents warned their children against: You'll die of the bends if you swim after a meal. It's dangerous to take candy from strangers. Comics will turn you into a menace to society.

The hysteria was widespread enough to spawn a Senate Subcommittee on Juvenile Delinquency, chaired by Senator Estes Kefauver (senators just don't have names like that anymore). The Subcommittee did not, in fact, find that comics actually encouraged adolescent boys to pillage, murder, and rape, but as far as the press and the public was concerned, it might as well have. At the same time, other scientists, less rabid than Wertham, published studies that suggested that all comics, even the family-friendly ones, were bad for children's eyes, IQs, nervous systems, socialization, and reading comprehension.[1]

By the late '50s, the verdict was in. Comics might not be actively evil as such, but they were definitely the mental equivalent of living on soda-pop and sugary treats.

Which Mama didn't allow in the house, either.

Therefore, whenever Mama found me hiding behind the wire spin-racks at the drug store or in front of the comic shelves in the nickel and dime store, my nose deep in the latest issue of *Action Comics* with Supergirl or *Donald Duck*, she'd pluck the comic out of my hands and put it back on the shelf. "Comics make you stupid," she'd say. Or sometimes, "Only stupid people read comics."

I can't say I paid a lot of attention – other than being annoyed that I could never get to the end of a storyline. It certainly didn't stop me from sneaking peeks at comics whenever I got a chance.

It was the pictures, I think. When I was a kid, almost all children's books had little black-and-white chapter heads and spot-illos, plus maybe a color frontispiece and a couple of full-color plates, scattered through the text like raisins in rice pudding. The work of artists like E.H. Shepard (*The Wind in the Willows*), Edward Ardizzone (*The Glass Slipper*), Garth Williams (*Miss Bianca*), and Jessie Wilcox Smith (*A Little Princess*) trained me to see how an image could interact with and enrich the words of a story. I'd pore over the illustrations in Howard Pyle's version of *The Merry Adventures of Robin Hood* not so much to see what Robin Hood and Little John looked like, but to peer into their world of quarterstaves and longbows and deer running through the dappled glades of Sherwood Forest.

I was also a big fan of the funny papers.

The funny papers were the only part of the daily newspapers that held any interest for me – until I was in my teens, anyway, and realized that the news actually had something to do with me. My parents subscribed to *The Sunday Herald Tribune* as well as *The New York Times*

---

1. This led, in due course, to the Comics Magazine Association of America (CMAA) and the Comics Code Authority (CCA), which basically gutted the horror and crime genres and pumped new life into superheroes. So to speak.

(which didn't and doesn't and never will run comic strips). Every Sunday, Papa and I would squabble over who had first crack at the comics like (Mama always said) a pair of five year olds.

The funnies didn't count as bad-for-you comics because grown ups read them. Mama (who didn't really like novels unless they were Classics) was above such things, but Papa was a fan, in a low-key, grown-up way. Our Sunday squabbles would usually end up with our sharing the funnies, so that he could explain to me why *Krazy Kat* was funny and what was going on in *Apartment 3G*. Neither one of us could make head or tail of Sunday's *Dick Tracy* (we didn't get the daily *Tribune*, which contained most of the plot), but we liked his two-way wrist radio. It was Papa who brought *The Incomplete Pogo* into the house. Since it contained sharp political satire and was famously full of clever puns and malapropisms, not even Dr. Wertham (or Mama) could have called it stupid.

I read *Pogo* so many times, the spine broke and the cover fell off and half the pages fell out and the whole thing had to be held together with a rubber band. The political satire zipped right over my head, but I loved Pogo and Albert Gator and Howland Owl and Churchy LaFemme, their friendships and their tiny dramas – also the wonderfully wacky word-play, which put Papa's repertory of lame puns to shame. I used to know verses and verses of "Deck us all with Boston Charley, Walla-Walla, Wash and Kalamazoo!" (it would be impossible to know them all, since Walt Kelly changed them every year), but they've slipped through the cracks over time, along with the names of the girls in Apartment 3G and the principal of Miss Peach's school. What remains is a deep affection for swamps and the short, smart-guy hero/ tall, goofy sidekick pairing that made me a fan of *Rocky and Bullwinkle* from the first time I saw the opening credits, and the knowledge that comics could be smart and subversive as well as fun to read.

So there I was, in the middle of the Silver Age of the Super Hero, knowing everything there was to know about Beetle Bailey and Blondie, Prince Valiant and Charlie Brown, and next to nothing about Captain America or Green Lantern, Superman or Batman (except the ones on TV). I did manage to read a fair amount of *Donald Duck* and *Scrooge*, mostly because doctors with pediatric practices invariably stocked their waiting rooms with comics. The dentist had piles of Disney, and since he always ran incredibly late, I could get through two or three issues as I awaited my turn in the torture chamber. Mama let me, figuring, I suppose, that the comic cooties couldn't eat much of my brain in an hour or two – not to mention not having to listen to my whining.

Even before the dentist's office, however, I'd already learned to follow an extended narrative told by pictures from the Japanese screen that covered one whole wall of our good-sized living room.

It depicted the cycle of the seasons around a tea-house beside a river – not a very promising setting for gripping drama, you'd think. But you'd be wrong. The tea-house was populated by a whole continuing cast of characters – a princess[2] in flowing, layered *kimono*; her attendants (one of whom didn't seem to get along with the other ones); her prince and his attendants (a war-like group bristling with swords and staves); nobles (one of whom clearly didn't get along with the husband) and *their* attendants; plus horses, dogs, chickens, water buffalo, random peasants, and a black and white cat. The number of hours I spent, looking at these tiny, stylized characters, making up stories about what the peasants were doing in the background, what the noble had done to make the prince scowl at him, why the princess looked so melancholy as she viewed the autumn moon, what happened in the sections covered with swirling golden clouds, would surprise you. Or perhaps not. I did grow up to be a fiction writer, after all.

That screen and the Sunday funnies were pretty much the extent of my exposure to comics, though, until sometime in the upper reaches of middle school, when I began spending summer weekends at a friend's house on Martha's Vineyard. Although I really did like spending time with her, I blush to confess that the main attraction was her exhaustive collection of forbidden fruit, er, comic books. She kept them under her bed: stacks and stacks of real, honest-to-Pete, brain-eating comic books. There was *True Romance* and full runs-to-date of what I thought of as the Super Family (Girl, Boy, and Man – oh, and *Superman's Girl Friend, Lois Lane*, which I hadn't remembered even existed until I found myself typing the title). And, best of all to a girl who thought it grossly unfair that boys should get all the adventures, *Wonder Woman*.

Day after hot, bright summer's day, I'd lie on my stomach on the spare bed in my friend's room, potato chips and Coke easily to hand, taking in the image of a resourceful, independent, phenomenally strong, feisty heroine who didn't take any guff from anybody, male or female, yet was decent and kindhearted. Unlike most of the other heroines who

---

2. She probably wasn't really a princess. She might not even have been a noble's wife, but a very high-class courtesan. In either case, the man was probably her lover rather than her husband, and all those guests rivals for her favors, but I was a kid and more than usually naïve for my age.

crossed my literary path, she wasn't blonde. She didn't giggle, she didn't expend a lot of thought on boyfriends (or princes), and she got along with her sister Amazons just fine without backbiting and gossiping and playing favorites. She didn't have much of a sense of humor, but fighting crime will do that to you (look at Superman). All in all, Wonder Woman struck both me and my friend as a much more sensible and attractive and, yes, realistic person than Veronica or Blondie or any of the rather drippy heroines weeping and flirting through the pages of *True Romance*.[3]

My personal Golden Age of comic reading ended in 9th grade, when my friend went away to boarding school. None of my other friends having the slightest interest in such things, I led a more-or-less comic-free existence (except for the funnies, of course) which lasted through high school and college and a good part of graduate school. I read SF and fantasy avidly, hungrily, indiscriminately, whether anyone else shared my taste or not. But comics pretty much fell off my radar screen.

Looking back now, I really wonder why. It's easy (and true) to say that all my reading time was eaten up by graduate school and restoring the down-at-heel Victorian house I was living in. When I wasn't writing papers about Beaumont and Fletcher and John Jewel's *Apology for the Church of England*, I was helping my then-partner strip 50 years' worth of white paint off oak woodwork and turn a half-acre of brush and weed into a garden. And after the heavy lifting part of grad school and restoration was finished, I was teaching and learning to can vegetables – oh, and beginning to write fiction.

But that's just part of the truth. The rest of it is that Mama and Estes Kefauver had had a greater influence on me than I knew. When I looked in the windows of The Million Year Picnic comics store in Harvard Square, I saw an array of brightly colored covers featuring muscled, male superheroes punching out muscled, male supervillains, and assumed that there was nothing inside them (or the shop) that would appeal to me.

This meant I missed out on reading *Love and Rockets* when it first came out, as well as (among other books I've come to know and love)

---

3. The Internet informs me that *Wonder Woman*'s original illustrator, H. G. Peters, died in 1958, and that the 1960s re-boot model was a debased, girly, and marginalized figure. While I have to admit that I don't recall the any of the storylines, my memory of Wonder Woman is of a kick-ass awesome dame, so it's likely that a good part of the stash under my friend's bed was older than we were. On the other hand, I also remember Donna Troy, a.k.a. Wonder Girl, (born, comically speaking, in 1965). It was quite a collection.

Watchmen and the first volumes of *Sandman*. I might have missed everything, if the love of fantasy and SF that helped keep me sane through graduate school hadn't led me, in the late '70s, to buy my first membership to the venerable Boston SF convention Boskone. Since I didn't know anybody, and was pretty shy, mostly what I did was hang out in the Dealers' Room, looking for SF/ F The Harvard Coop (the university bookstore) didn't carry.

One of the things I found was *ElfQuest*.

ElfQuest was like no comic I'd ever seen or imagined. I loved Richard Pini's art, all bright and saturated and graceful and expressive,[4] and I loved Wendy Pini's story, all complex and character based, a heady blend of adventure, humor, tragedy, romance, and cultural commentary. As an extra added bonus, it was written by a woman, which made my feminist heart sing. I was, in fact, hooked. I bought (and still own) every issue as it came out – at The Million Year Picnic, as it happens – and read them multiple times, from cover to cover, including the letters section.

My second *Aha!* moment came in 1988 at Fourth Street Fantasy convention in Minneapolis, when Emma Bull told me about Kate Worley and Reed Walker's *Omaha the Cat Dancer*. Anthropomorphic animal erotica, she said, kind of noir-ish, with crime lords and strippers, and a plot with a feminist bent that arced and developed, populated by characters who changed and grew. Also written by a woman. I can't swear to it, but she may have said (because it is, after all, true) that *Omaha* isn't so much a comic book as, well, a serialized graphic novel.

I loved it. Of course I loved it. It contained, in its own particular way, all the things I look for in fiction: psychologically complex characters caught up in stories with sophisticated emotional arcs and complicated, human-sized stakes. I'm not that interested in stories about Saving the World (or Universe). I'm more of a small-picture kind of person. For instance, though I adore comics (and novels) set in the past,[5] it's not for the high-level political intrigue and epic sweep history. What rings my chimes are stories about the people that history happens to.

Turns out the French love them too.

French comic books are called *bandes dessinées* (BDs), and the variety of genres and styles they cover is bewildering. Mysteries, thrillers, high fantasy, erotica, SF, military, comic animals. Series like *Tin-Tin* and

---

4. And (I realize now) manga-like.

5. When they're well done. Alan Moore's *The League of Extraordinary Gentlemen*, for instance, makes me completely happy. As do all the *Sandman* story lines with historical dimensions.

Asterix, that are hard to classify. And historicals. Dozens and dozens of beautifully-drawn, exhaustively-researched, long, involved, exciting stories set in courts and kitchens and forests and town – mostly French, *bien sûr*, but in many other countries as well – in any period you choose to mention.

It was Ellen who turned me on to *bandes dessinées* while we were courting, by way of Francois Bourgeon's series *Les Passagers du Vent* (*Riders of the Wind*, roughly). "It's got a girl dressed as a boy, and ships and adventures and really good clothes," she said.[6] "And it's incredibly well-researched. You'll love it."

She was right. *Les Passagers du Vent* is set in the early eighteenth century, and follows the adventures of Isa, a young girl of considerable strength of character and an idiosyncratic sense of honor who (among other things) sails on a ship disguised as a man, rescues her true love from a British prison ship, does her best to disrupt the slave trade in Santa Domingo, and raises hell generally. I didn't understand all the words, many of which are not to be found in any French/English dictionary I own, but Bourgeon's detailed, glorious art more than filled in the blanks at least until I'd re-read it often enough to figure out what exactly was going on.[7]

BDs are an expensive habit. They're all hardcovers, they're large and heavy, and they cost the earth, even if you don't factor in the plane fare to France to buy them. I have to pick and choose carefully. Right now, I'm following two series.[8] One is a super-strange and surreal romp through the literature of at least three cultures called *De Capes et de Crocs* (a play on "cloak and dagger" that translates loosely as *Cloak and Claw*) by Alain Ayroles and Jean-Luc Masbou. The heroes are a wolf and a fox with plumed hats, sweeping cloaks, flashing swords, and a nice line in banter. Think Fafherd and the Grey Mouser, only fuzzier. The wolf, Don Lope de Villalobos, is afraid of rats. The fox, Armand Raynal de Maupertuis, is in love with a beautiful human girl who isn't as dim as she seems, even if she is blonde. At one point, they fly to the moon in a

---

6. Or something very like that. She may also have mentioned that some of it was pretty hot.

7. Probably. Bergeron writes really Byzantine plots. His SF series, *Le Cycle de Cyann*, has so far resisted all my efforts to follow it. Even though I love his art a lot, I gave up after the second volume.

8. Meaning, I buy one or two volumes when I go to France. Some BDs are translated, but the ones I like aren't the most likely to be exported. If they're going to be translated, I'll probably have to do it myself.

galleon propelled by a magic moonstone. Kind of steampunky, except seventeenth century. With swords and capes. It's considered a bit odd, even in France.

The same Alain Ayroles is also responsible for *Garulfo*, which is basically *Shrek* with a French accent. The hero is a transformed frog, and the requisite Beautiful Princess on the whole prefers hanging out with ogres[9] to romance. This is the French comic I may very well love enough to actually take the trouble of translating and finding an American publisher for. It's one of the funniest things I've ever read and Bruno Maïorana's art is wonderful – kind of children's book meets medieval illumination meets manga. Readers of *Fables* would love it.

But I'm getting ahead of myself.

Ellen's collection of comics included a whole lot more than BDs. She introduced me to Los Bros Hernandez and *Love & Rockets*, to Donna Barr's *The Desert Peach* and *Stinz* and Terry Moore's *Strangers in Paradise*. She put Neil Gaiman's *Black Orchid* into my hands and the first volume of *Sandman*. She even had a bound galley of Scott McCloud's *Understanding Comics*.

I've since gone out and bought the book itself, and realize that the galley was more of a script with occasional sketches than the masterpiece of word and image currently sitting on my desk. But it did help me see comics in a whole new light.

In his first chapter, McCloud points out that there's something fundamentally human in using pictures to tell stories. From the tomb paintings of the ancient Egyptians to the stained glass windows of half the great cathedrals of Europe, people have been using pictures arranged in a series to instruct, entertain and enlighten. Works as diverse as the Mexican Codex and the Bayeux Tapestry are elaborate and serious graphic texts. Physically, structurally, and perceptually, these narrative marriages of word and image are the ancestors of the comic book.

Obviously, I'm not suggesting that *Tales of the Crypt* is equivalent, on any level, to the Bayeux Tapestry, any more than *Slave Girls of Gor* (for instance) is equivalent to *Mansfield Park*. That would be as dumb as saying that *Mansfield Park* denigrates women or feeds adolescent male power fantasies because *Slave Girls of Gor*, which is also a novel, does those things.

What I am suggesting is that there are, and always have been, comics out there that don't insult the intelligence, that reflect emotional reality

---

9. Not green ones.

even if they offer escape from the laws of physics, that make you think as well as laugh or gasp or happily pass a lazy afternoon.

I can't write an ending to the story of Me and Comic Books because our relationship is still developing and growing. I still don't buy as many comics as I buy books, at least in part because I don't know as much about what's out there or whose work I might like. When I pick something up, it's mostly because a more knowledgeable friend has recommended it. That's how I fell in love with *Strangers in Paradise* and *Fables* and *Promethea* and *Lost Girls*. It's also how I found online comics, which are now as much a part of my morning routine as brushing my teeth and drinking my tea. With *Girl Genius, Digger, Hark, a Vagrant, Gunnerkrigg Court, Lovelace and Babbage,* and *For Better or For Worse,* I get a daily dose of graphic narrative, both short and long forms, to wake up my brain and get me ready to deal with the demands of the day.

Oh. I wear jeans, too.

I am Sisyphus, and I am Happy

Kelly Thompson graduated from the Savannah College of Art and Design with a degree in Sequential Art. She writes the *Comics Should be Good* column "She Has No Head!" and runs the bi-weekly podcast *3 Chicks Review Comics*. She also writes comic reviews for *Comic Book Resources*, and runs a popular blog, *1979 Semi-Finalist*. Kelly's short fiction and poetry have been published in *The Bukowski Review*, *The Main Street Rag*, *Aggressive Behaviour 2*, and *Pearl*. Kelly's novel about two teenage superheroes, *The Girl Who Would be King*, is currently on submission to publishers. Her first comics writing credit was for *Womanthology* from IDW. Kelly currently lives in NYC with her boyfriend and sadly, no pets. She really wants a kitten.

In 2009, one single image got me writing critically (and sometimes not so critically) about my beloved superhero comics. Until that image appeared, superhero comics and I had endured a love/hate relationship that flip-flopped like only a veteran politician can. That relationship, though frequently fraught, had up until 2009 at least for the most part been private.

But now I had a blog!

So in 2009 I blogged – with much more passion than reason – about a now-infamous promo image for the *Justice League* mini-series *Cry for Justice*, in which a young Supergirl in her traditional "cheerleader" costume is ogled by three much older male teammates (Green Lantern, Green Arrow and Shazam). Their eyelines were drawn so that they were looking directly at her chest. And, in fact, her chest was arguably the primary focus of the image. Unbelievably, this wasn't the biggest problem with the image. The problem was that either because of the way the image had been drawn or cropped, Supergirl had no head.

Let me say that again, SHE. HAD. NO. HEAD.

A powerful female character and the only female being represented in the image, had been made, officially, not Supergirl, not a superhero, and not even a woman, but rather an object. An object without a head. And, one can assume, an object without all those pesky thoughts, opinions, and personality that tend to go along with having a head.

It was a horrible message to send to readers, both male and female. To men, that it was not only okay, but approved by DC Comics, to view women this way; and to women, that they were obviously less-than. That they were objects, even when they were heroes. It was too much for me. I lost my shit on my own blog. But following the losing of my shit that spring and summer, repeatedly, and over a variety of comics issues, Brian Cronin approached me about writing a column for his *Comics Should be Good* blog on *Comic Book Resources*. I gratefully (and giddily) accepted, and since Brian was letting me write my own ticket, I decided my column would be about women and comics, and there was only one thing that column could possibly be called – "She Has No Head!"

Coming up on two years and some 116 columns and podcasts later, I can say I found great freedom and voice in finally talking about main-stream superhero comics from my decidedly feminist point of view. But I also found myself feeling like Sisyphus of Greek legend, constantly pushing a boulder up a hill, only to have it roll back down once I reached the top. It was endlessly frustrating. Even though there were many rewards just as Sisyphus surely had a moment of happiness get-ting that boulder to the top of that hill, not to mention his excitement as he approached the top (time and time again) – most of the time it has felt like more pain than gain.

So why doesn't one give up?

How do I give up on something that shaped me?

Picture this: I'm 15 years old (though dangerously close to 16), bored, naïve, and more than a little repressed (read: living in Utah – no offense, Utah!), while harboring vague dreams of a being a writer and even more vague dreams of being an artist. Possibly both with the equally vague idea that those careers would somehow allow me to wear pajamas all day and be a recluse, but a recluse with great purpose and at least a reasonable amount of respect. So there I am, 15 (in said pajamas) on a Saturday morning watching cartoons with my younger brother Scott on the couch. We're flipping, we're flipping, we're flipping (because as anyone over the age of five who watches cartoons knows, commercials during cartoons blow especially hard). And then all of a sudden, we're not flipping because my brother has stopped on something interesting. And I'm watching, wide-eyed, as an awesome chick without wings flies through a mall and punches a huge robot in the face. She has a white stripe in her hair and a Southern accent accompanied by massive amounts of sass. This was Rogue. In the same scene, a black woman with shocking all white hair and weather powers did some serious damage to that same robot. This, of course, was Storm. And this turned out to be the *X-Men* cartoon, and this was 1992 and those big robots were Sentinels. And for the first time in my young life, I was in love. It wasn't a classmate, or a sexy movie star I dreamed of, or a rock musician plastered on my wall, or even that kid I kissed one time at camp, but superheroes. More specifically, female superheroes!

And with this discovery, all my unrealized fantasies rose up suddenly that Saturday morning into realities – or, at least, the closest I'd ever come to fantasy and reality merging into one fantastic package. That morning, I began a lifelong love affair with superheroes. They captured something very specific in my heart. Something primal and powerful. Something I had never felt before and was desperate to hold onto.

I was officially, obsessed.

Years later, I can tell you the simple truth of that obsession and why it clutched me so powerfully – the world had *finally* showed me something that I could get excited about, and I responded in kind. I responded with a youthful enthusiasm (the kind I yearn for to this day), and I embraced this new love and swallowed it whole. I wouldn't trade all the cringe-worthy dramatic hijinks of those teenage years for anything, because it was the one and only time in my life that I recall being unabashedly devoted to something. And that devotion and enthusiasm for superheroes inspired both my writing and my art, unlike any other single thing.

It also totally freaked my parents out. Bonus!

At college, I floundered in my graphic design program at The University of Arizona. While other kids ate, breathed, and slept graphic design, I was taking secret comic book classes at night on the side at the local comic book store. My parents (though likely still freaked out) let me transfer to The Savannah College of Art and Design so I could enroll in their sequential art program. I still loved superheroes so much, I was going to study them in college. You know you love comics when you not only decide to go to college to study them, but also somehow manage to convince your parents that it's a completely reasonable choice. It was wholly *unreasonable*. But I don't regret a second of it. (Even though I still can't draw my way out of a paper bag. Well. Not a big one, anyway.)

Years later, while going through one of my "hate" phases of comics, when I had left comics behind to pursue other things, I began writing my first novel.

But that first novel was about two teenage girls with superpowers.

There was no escaping my obsession with superheroes, even when I tried to escape comics. Since superheroes and comics are inexorably linked, it was only a matter of time before I circled back around to comics again. But when I came back to comics, superhero and beyond, I found that the 15 year old that started out loving comics so blindly had grown into a pretty determined feminist. And you know what was filled with a surprising amount of sexism? My beloved superhero comics.

The feminist and the comics lover in me soon started coming to blows.

For some people, this is the point when they would gracefully exit stage left, leaving superhero comics behind forever. But not me, oh no, nothing graceful for me! There will be no grace! I decided that I loved superhero comics anyway and believed in all that they *could* be and thus I would *force* them to be those better things, come hell or high-water – kicking and punching, scratching and biting, pulling hair if necessary. In reality, this mostly meant a lot of reading, writing, and thinking critically about comics, and eventually getting in a lot of disappointing fights on the Internet. It's an exhausting battle to try to force change, and I frequently feel like I'm helping nobody, including myself. But every time I'm rolling that boulder back up that hill, I see a few more female comics readers; a few more positive female comics bloggers; a few more creators, books, articles and even tweets that suggest that change, she is a-comin'.

But I can't stop there. No comics lovers can. We need there to be something in mainstream comics for girls and women. And right now, I'm sorry to say, there ain't much.

In 2007, DC boldly tried a "comics for girls" line called Minx. It was fraught with problems, not the least of which was that they weren't committed enough to the idea and gave up within a year when it didn't meet with immediate success. There were other problems – the name "Minx" was not a great choice; and though they filled the books with wonderful creators, very few of those creators were women. Most importantly, however, they didn't manage to get the books into bookstores in large numbers, which meant that their intended audience didn't even know that they existed. It was a wonderful idea. Perhaps it was just ahead of its time. I like to think that that's true. And that it will be tried again with better success.

In the meantime, there are critical and important debates about women and comics going on right now; a powerful surge in the fangirl community; a steady removal of the stigma of being a woman who creates comics; as well as a groundswell of new female talent. In July 2011, an all-female comics anthology called *Womanthology* raised over $100,000 in funding on Kickstarter in a month, becoming the single most successful comics venture on Kickstarter ever. And the theme for that anthology? Heroic.

I frequently talk (some would say rant, but you know, tomayto, tomahto!) about how little change really actually has to happen for comics to become more accessible to girls and women. You don't have to do a major reconstruction. I firmly believe that all the same themes that men respond to resonate in women as well. I believe superheroes reveal universal truths that apply equally to women and men. But you do have to give things a minor facelift, a remodel if you will. You have to take down the implied "no girls allowed" signs that are formed by hyper-sexualized female characters at every turn and too few female voices as both characters and creators. You have to do a little bit of policing (some would say editing – and thus there is an entire job called, you guessed it, editor!) to make sure that images like a teenage Supergirl without a head being ogled by older male characters doesn't make it out the front door.

But this isn't rocket science.

It's being smart and thinking a little bit outside of your privilege, which we all have and are all guilty of being blind to from time to time. That privilege is one of the reasons that diversity in comics creators is so key to the success of this industry. It's much harder to make the mistakes of privilege when you have others with different backgrounds working with you. Sometimes mistakes are going to be made, it happens. But you should also have a slew of smart people at the ready to correct those problems when they do happen, rather than making things worse. Another symptom of not enough diversity and thus too many people blind to their own privilege.

At a time when mainstream comics are floundering heavily, it seems like insanity to ignore the money of 50% of the world's population just because change is a little bit scary. Change *is* scary, but if there's one universal truth about change, it's that it's constant. Change, especially for those used to the status quo, more than being scary is *hard*. And we as readers, creators, and lovers of comics have to force it from the outside more often than not by pushing that boulder up that hill every day. Though it can be exhausting to be Sisyphus, we must remember these words from "The Myth of Sisyphus" by Albert Camus: "The struggle itself towards the heights is enough to fill a man's heart. One must imagine Sisyphus happy."

Camus may not have meant it the way I'm choosing to use it, but from now on I'm going to try to think of myself as happy while I push that damn boulder, because maybe that needs to be enough.

At least for now.

Captain America's Next Top Model

Anika Milik has a lifelong interest in both fashion and superheroes. Think Mary Jane Watson: fashionista, fangirl, free spirit. And in love with Spider-Man. Anika runs *Red Carpet Superhero* (tightropemarvel.wordpress.com), a fashion geek and geek fashion blog, and is one of four contributors at the comic book culture blog *Fantastic Fangirls* (fantasticfangirls.org). She lives with her family in Connecticut and works at Wesleyan University.

What is the difference between Jim Gordon and Bruce Wayne? Both fight crime in Gotham City. Both hold themselves above the law. (Bruce is the masked vigilante Batman. Police/government official Gordon consults and conceals a team of masked vigilantes on a regular basis.) Both keep secrets from family, friends, and the public at large. Both have strong opinions and high ideals. Both are complicated. Both carry weapons as part of their job. Both wear specific clothes to do that job.

But Commissioner Gordon wears a uniform. Batman wears a costume.

Costumes are an excellent indicator of genre. Imagine yourself in the main character's clothes and answer the question, "If I go through my daily routine dressed like this, will anyone find it strange?" If – taking societal expectations on gender or age, etc., into account – the answer is "Yes," that's a genre film (or series, or novel, etc.).

Be True to Your School

Superhero comic books are considered genre fiction. It highlights the thesis that costumes – not just uniforms or fashion – are a vital element of a superhero persona. More vital, even, than the moniker. You can call yourself "Batman" all you want, but if you run around in a tracksuit, no one will make the connection. Take away the cowl and the cape, and it's not Batman. It's Bruce Wayne in a tripped-out tracksuit, most likely made by Armani. By the same token, Captain America can't wear what every other American soldier does, because he's *not* every other American soldier. He has to stand out. Comics are a visual medium, and costumes are key.

Costumes are, therefore, an excellent way to show devotion to a character. I have taken this to such a level, I freely admit to being a fangirl fashionista.

I have been cosplaying for 15 years, and I've been dressing up my whole life. I was that little girl who wore her Wonder Woman Underoos over her clothes, and I wore them *everywhere*. I have special outfits I only wear at Disney World. In high school, I had a favorite cardigan I called my "Eponine Sweater" after my favorite character in musical theater, and I consistently buy clothes in the style of Kaylee Frye (*Firefly*) or Jessica Jones (*New Avengers, Alias*).

Fangirl fashion is something I share with my daughters. Kiki, 15, and Aeris, 6, have both been to conventions in costume. Aeris had a brush with cosplay fame when she dressed as Hit-Girl from *Kick-Ass* for Free Comic Book Day, and posed with Darth Vader at our local comic store. The picture went round the web, reblogged and retweeted by Mark Millar and John Romita Jr. (the creators of the character), and Chloe Moretz (the young woman who portrayed her in the film – or as Aeris calls her, "the real Hit-Girl"). Aeris has not read the comic nor seen the film, but she understands Hit-Girl to be a little girl superhero. With her mask and cape and utility belt, Aeris *is* Hit-Girl, sprung to life from the pages of the book.

Stealth Cosplay!

But Aeris and I don't dress up only for conventions. She wore a tutu to her first day of first grade, and I've worn a Hogwarts school uniform to work more than once. We don't only cosplay, we also practice *undercover* cosplay.

"Undercover cosplay" is, essentially, when you cosplay and don't tell anyone. It's when you cosplay at work or school, out in the "real world." That T-shirt that you bought because so-and-so character on such-and-such a show wore it in your favorite episode? When you wear that to go to the grocery store instead of to a convention, that's undercover cosplay. It's also the easiest form of cosplay to accomplish. Entire websites are dedicated to finding knock-off versions of runway fashions, celebrity red carpet looks, and movie/TV appearances. There are also television shows and magazine articles. It's practically its own industry.

The older, slightly more sophisticated sister of undercover cosplay is what I call "Ready-to-Wear-Superhero." "Ready-to-Wear" is a fashion industry term for off-the-rack and mass-produced designer wear. Ready-to-Wear Superhero means using superhero costumes as inspiration for a fashionable outfit to be worn somewhere other than a convention. This is distinct from cosplay in that it's not meant to replicate the original look, but to refer to it. The process takes some creative thinking, but the result can be pretty spectacular.

Heroine Chic

Take this one step further, and you arrive at "Heroine Chic." (I am so inspired by the idea of this, I devoted a blog to it.) Superheroines, for better or worse, fight in clothes that are far more fashionable than practical, but I love – I *live for* – the moments when I see a celebrity or model on a red carpet or runway, and think "*Damn*, but she looks ready to fight crime in that." Because supergirls wear such ridiculous outfits anyway, I really, truly want a superteam made up of Hollywood It Girls in Gucci, Dolce & Gabbana and Chanel.

Captain America's Next Top Model... you know you want it.

Heroine Chic, like Ready-to-Wear Superhero and undercover cosplay, also exists on the rack and in the mall. It's out there, waiting for you and me and every other comic book fangirl or boy. We embrace Heroine Chic when we don boots that Ms. Marvel would wear, or a mini-skirt like Supergirl, or decide to streak our hair like Rogue. And when we embrace Heroine Chic, we embrace the idea that we are powerful.

Or put another, more direct and explicit way, that we *have power*. That's a message that all women and girls – and, for that matter, socially awkward geeks of all genders and backgrounds – deserve to, and possibly *need* to, embrace. No matter what we wear, we wear it to say something about who we are. Dress like a superhero, and you stand for what she does.

We have power. We, honestly, have *great* power. We should embrace it, take responsibility, get out there and save the world.

Therefore, I present...

Ten Tips to Creating Your Ready-to-Wear Superhero Who Looks Suitable For Saving the World.

1. Start with the silhouette. Comic books are, by definition, visual. And fashion design invariably starts with the silhouette – the way the clothes drape on the body. Take the big picture and break it down into elements. Is she wearing pants or a skirt? How long are his sleeves? Is it a jumpsuit? Is there a cape? How does it move, does it flow or is it stiff? How many layers are there? If this was one of those shadow art boxes that were popular in Victorian times instead of a comic panel, how would we differentiate Spider-Man from Superman from Wonder Woman from Wolverine?

2. Add the color palette. Of course, it's much easier to differentiate our heroes in a full-color panel than a shadow, even to a casual observer. The majority of superheroes wear bright, bold colors. They stand out, as intended. And a neat quirk in comics, especially older ones, is when colorists use the same color palette for a hero out of costume. To pick an example, in one of my favorite scenes from Peter David's original run on *X-Factor*, Alex Summers wears a bright blue suit and yellow bow tie – because those are the colors of his uniform as the superhero Havok.

Using color is one of the easiest ways to make any outfit *pop*, and to reference a character's look. And it's also one of the easiest ways to maintain the idea of a certain character while playing with the silhouette. Trade a skirt for short pants or jeggings for a jumpsuit – but keep the colors – and you achieve the same effect.

3. Branding. Toward the end of Neil Gaiman's *Death: The High Cost of Living* mini-series, Death (a.k.a. Dee Dee) replaces her stolen ankh pendant, the symbol of her power, with a similar one from a street vendor. The man who took her pendant assumed he was robbing Death of her abilities and therefore defeating her – but the ankh he stole didn't contain her power, it *represented* it.

In the same way, Superman's S shield doesn't grant him his power, it represents it. The Apple on the back of my laptop is decorative; without it, my computer would run exactly the same. And yet, the Apple logo does have a purpose – it says, "Hey, everyone, I'm a Mac." Superheroes have symbols for the same reason that corporations have logos and ponies have cutie marks – it's all easy, obvious and ubiquitous recognition.

But there is more to it than that. As Dee Dee says, "Symbols have power." They're not just advertising, they *mean* something. If a particular superhero stands for X, and X is something you admire and agree with, that superhero's symbol can stand for you, too.

The more popular heroes have branded merchandise available, which will simplify your adopting their symbol as your own. The less popular ones may take a little more creativity, but let's say that, like me, you are a huge Ms. Marvel fan – lightning-bolt key chains, belt buckles, or hats are not unheard of, or even scarce. Official merchandise is nice, but it's not necessary. Like Dee Dee's $10 knock off necklace, it's up to you to make it work.

4. Let's talk about capes. There are a few recurring elements in superhero costumes, and one of the best is a cape. I bought a "superhero kit" for a six year old's birthday once, and it consisted of a book of questions and catch phrases, and a bright red cape. That's all a kid needs to build his own heroic identity.

Lots of superheroes wear capes. Some supermodels, superstars, and royals wear capes. Very few average everyday ordinary people wear capes. That's not to say you can't! If you want to wear a full-on superhero cape to go live your not-precisely-superpowered life, go for it! But there are ready-to-wear alternatives.

First of all, there are capes that are less ostentatious than a standard superhero cape. There are capelets that fall only to the waist. There are shawls, and there are ponchos. But my favorite super-cape options are the ones that push past the obvious, such as a cardigan tied over your shoulders or a long scarf. The scarf idea is my absolute favorite, because scarves come in all colors and can be worn with absolutely everything. You can make any outfit at all a nod to superheroes with the addition of a long red scarf.

5. Life behind a mask. Masks are equally important to the superhero milieu. After all, a superhero identity is a secret. Even when a hero's identity is public, the mask exists to hide it because the hero isn't functioning as that person (e.g. Tony Stark), but as the superhero (Iron Man). Masks are integral to a superhero's costume, but they are frowned upon, and often unlawful, in real life. No matter how huge a fan you are, you can't wear a realistic superhero mask to work or school or the mall. So here are some options...

A hoodie is an obvious choice. There even are hoodies that are made to look like Batman, Spider-Man, and Captain America's costumes, cowl included. And customizing a hoodie is pretty simple; just use iron-on or sew-on patches available at fabric, craft, and even party stores. The same goes for knit hats.

Sunglasses are an accessory you can get away with most places, and there are plenty of frames that resemble various superhero masks – for instance, Spider-Man's bug eyes or Catwoman's slanted mask. A headband or other hair accessory can hint at a superhero's headgear; barrettes can emulate Thor's helmet, feathers can stand in for Hawkgirl's headdress. And though I might hold it back for special occasions, an actual mask worn up on the head – holding back hair maybe – is a pretty cute fashion statement.

6. Shoes are awesome. Whenever anyone asks me for fashion advice, the very first thing I say is: Spend money on shoes. Now, I don't mean only buy expensive shoes, or buy *so* many shoes, you need a separate room for them. I mean that you should pay attention to what you wear on your feet, and use your shoes to your advantage. I mean that any outfit can instantly become more interesting by wearing interesting shoes. (And the reverse is true as well, shoes can take away from an outfit just as easily. Wearing flip flops anywhere but the beach – why would you do *that?!*) Wear shoes that make the statement you want, and don't be afraid to mix it up. Wear combat boots with a sundress, and Converse sneakers with a suit. Just do it.

Superhero footwear, by and large, is silly. Many superheroes wear what amount to booties that may or may not be attached to their leggings. Then there are the brightly colored go-go boots and the stripper heels. As fun as these are, I don't really recommend wearing exact replicas of most superheroes' shoes. But you can use your shoes to show support for a favorite hero.

If you are a young boy or – like me – are lucky enough to fit into a young boy's shoe size, there are sneakers, boots, crocs and even the occasional buster brown shoe that feature heroes like Superman, Batman, Spider-Man and Thor (basically, anyone who headlines a movie). But if you can't fit into those, or like a more minor character, there is still a shoe for you out there. You just have to look.

For example, say you like a hero who wears red boots – which seems like half of them, easy – there are red boots. There are also red sneakers, red baby dolls, red china flats. I happen to personally love red shoes, and can tell you that they come in all shapes and sizes.

Black Canary is one of my favorite characters to see cosplayed. Her fashion look is biker-chick-superheroine, and that is both incredibly cool and incredibly hot. A lot of it is that she wears the kind of boots that look like they could hurt someone. When I wear boots like that, I instantly feel more dangerous and more powerful. I feel like *I* could hurt someone.

7. Don't ignore streetwear! I love superhero costumes, obviously. But I love a comic book superhero in street clothes almost as much. I firmly believe that what we choose to wear says a lot about who we are, how we see ourselves, and how we present ourselves to the world. Most superheroes designed their supersuits, but – as I said while discussing masks – the superhero and the hero inside are separate entities. And I am the kind of fan who calls my favorite superheroes by their "real" names.

A prime example of this: I don't love Ms. Marvel, but I love Carol Danvers. I want to *be* Carol Danvers... who happens to be Ms. Marvel. And so I pay just as much attention to what Carol wears when she's in her civilian identity. And what she wears – T-shirts emblazoned with NASA or Property of the Avengers, fitted baseball shirts and tight jeans, and the occasional red or black minidress – tells me that Carol, like me, wears clothes that (sometimes literally) say who she is: a tomboy who cares what she looks like, who wants to be perceived as tough, accomplished and attractive.

So why stop at Ready-to-Wear Spider-Man when Ready-to-Wear Peter Parker is just as fun? Because, let's be real, Peter Parker is the original hipster. He was a hipster before "hipster" was a thing (see what I did there?). Peter is an outsider – he's never been one of the cool kids, no matter how many people accept him or how popular Spider-Man becomes. He's so uncool... it's cool. He shops secondhand, he wears skinny jeans, he supports bands no one's ever heard of. He's accidentally fashionable, but he is, at the moment, entirely on trend.

Wanda Maximoff is a Bohemian. Nearly all the X-Men are preps. Tony Stark wears David August. There are so many possibilities.

8. Dress the why. Whatever superhero you want to dress in the style of, there is a reason why they have that style. Zatanna practices true magic, but she is also a traditional stage magician. Her costume reflects that showstopper side to her. Her top hat and tails have a reason.

In any good character or costume design, style is meant to say something to the audience. There are great characters with awful costumes, and awful characters with great costumes, but more often the characters we love have *costumes* we love because they are meaningful to that character. And maybe, just maybe, figuring out the "why" behind a favorite character's costume you *don't* like will change your opinion of it.

Also pay attention to why *you* chose this superhero. What is it about him or her that attracted you in the first place?

9. Be creative and have fun. This is the second thing I tell people when they ask me for fashion advice: You already know everything you need to know. You know what you like and what you want to show off. In fashion, more than in any other realm I have dabbled in, rules are made to be broken. Play!

10. Be yourself. Just like Batman isn't really Batman in a tracksuit, it's important to know your *own* character design. For example, about five years ago, I bought a knit hat in the shape of a monkey's face, complete with ears, at a country fair. I've worn it daily every fall/ winter for that last five years. And now that knit animal hats are absolutely everywhere, I've moved on to a cloche. I don't bring this up to boast that I am a trendsetter, but to give concrete examples of how I build my own character design and let it evolve. Once when I went to Starbucks, the barista wrote "Monkey Hat" on the cup instead of my real name. I took a picture of this that I will keep forever, because it was a "fashion defines me" moment.

I wear leg warmers and arm warmers regularly. I am always willing to reference Alice in Wonderland. I like heels because I am little. I love Spider-Man and frequent the Boys' clothing section to get T-shirts and shoes. I identify with My Little Pony Pinkie Pie, and try to work something pink into every outfit. Layers are my friend. My favorite styles reflect the Roaring Twenties and the subsequent Depression Era gloom. I love clothes.

What about you? What do you wear and how does it reflect who you are? Decide what you would say when I asked for your character design. Decide if you like it, and either enhance it or change it. Fashion is as easy – and as difficult – as that. It requires, most of all, bravery. But any comic book fan worth his or her salt knows that inside every one of us is a superhero. Stand with me and be that superhero. Don't be afraid to show it off with your own fashion – cosplay, undercover cosplay, Ready-to-Wear Superhero, heroine chic or something altogether different and personal.

Show it off. It's you. And you are super.

An Interview
with Louise Simonson

Louise Simonson has written and edited comic books for many years, including works in the superhero, science fiction, horror, and fantasy genres. Her Marvel work includes the award-winning *Power Pack* series; lengthy runs on *X-Factor* and *New Mutants*; *Wolverine: Meltdown*, co-written with her husband, Walter Simonson; and *Web of Spider-Man*. Her DC Comics work includes *Superman: Man of Steel*, which featured the "Death and Return of Superman" storyarc; *Steel*; and *World of Warcraft*, based on the multi-million-player Internet game, for DC's WildStorm imprint. She has also written 23 books for kids and adults, many featuring DC Comics characters. She is currently writing a Young Adult dark urban fantasy novel and a *Rocketeer* story for IDW.

Q. How did you come into the comics industry?

A. I was working in advertising-promotion for a magazine publisher, and I had a friend who worked at Warren Publishing. They published black and white comics magazines – it was genre stuff, horror, fantasy, and science fiction. My friend told me there was an opening in their production department, and the job paid more than my job. I had read the Warren comics back when Archie Goodwin was the editor and really liked them – they had great stories and art. So I applied for the job and got it. It was as simple as that.

A couple of months later, they created an assistant editor position, and slotted me into it. I was much better at editorial than at production! Then, when Bill DuBay – the senior, and only, editor – left, I talked James Warren, the company founder, into giving me that position. I edited there for four years, I think, until I moved over to Marvel in 1980.

Q. What were the challenges of being an editor at Warren Publishing, and in what ways were the challenges different when you moved to Marvel?

A. I loved working at Warren. It was a small company and, if they wanted, the people who worked there could fulfill lots of roles. I got made an assistant editor because I enthusiastically wrote ad copy for

James Warren's Captain Company and letters pages and did whatever else needed doing, in addition to my production work. I'm a visual learner, so, for me, watching and doing are my best ways to learn.

When DuBay left a few years later, James was looking for an editor and I had to talk him into giving me the position. His first comment was "Girls can't edit horror comics" – which was so wrong on so many levels. I don't think he honestly believed this, by the way. I think that he wanted me to fight for the position. He was pushing my buttons, to see which way I'd jump. So I said to him, "Look, give me the job for six months. I'll do it for my present salary, without an assistant, and I'll get the books on schedule. If I do it, you make me editor of the whole line."

James wasn't stupid. I mean, he was getting an editor for an assistant's salary and saving an assistant's salary on top of it. Of course he gave me a chance. I did what I said, and got the sales up as well. So he made me senior editor. Later, he made me a vice president. I was a big fish in a very small pond.

Another great thing about working at Warren – I don't know if you'd call it a challenge, exactly – was that during the summer months, James would mostly disappear to his beach house on Long Island, leaving us alone to carry on. I *loved* working without supervision, even though that was the time of year we put out annuals on top of our regular magazines, so we worked twice as hard.

Then, in the middle of summer, James would return for a few days, and yell about how everything we'd done was wrong, and explain – at the top of his lungs – how it would have been so much better had he been standing over us. I call this the Dominant Gorilla Syndrome. In the jungle, the greyback will wander off and do his thing for a while. When he returns to his troop, he knocks the lesser gorillas around, just to prove he's still dominant. That was James in summer, then he'd go away again for a few months.

In the fall, he'd return and create a problem – such as insisting that there wasn't enough contrast between the logo and the cover, for instance. He'd yell about it for a while, then he'd solve it. He'd say, "See how much better yellow works than red?", and I'd say, "Wow! You're right!", and then he'd say, "Why didn't you think of that?" And we'd both go back, happily, to our daily routines. It was kind of funny, once I recognized the pattern.

Two things grew out of this. One was that I told James I didn't like being yelled at, and he wasn't to do it. He was allowed to yell all he wanted *about* stuff, but he wasn't allowed to yell *at me*. And he didn't.

Second, once I recognized the gorilla pattern, I learned to say: "Yes, oh great greyback!", but not in those words. It was like a ceremony of acknowledgement that he was the boss that we had to go through each fall.

And he did have really good instincts, including a terrific eye for spotting talent. I learned a lot from him. And he was the boss. He *was* Warren Publishing. He was *king*.

Beyond that, I could do pretty much anything I wanted. Theme issues, contests, and different experiments on the readers to see what they'd do and what they wanted. There was a predominance of Spanish artists when I took over – wonderful, brilliant artists from the Selecciones Illustradas agency in Spain. But, I fought to be allowed to include more of the young American and South American artists, as well. And I had some great writers – Bruce Jones, Jim Stenstrum, and others. I loved working at Warren.

But then I accepted Jim Shooter's offer to work at Marvel, beginning in 1980. Shooter had a reputation for being a tough editor-in-chief to work under, but, after the time I had spent dealing with James and mostly enjoying it, working under Jim was fine.

For one thing, Jim and I had similar ideas about what each issue needed to have: clarity; good characters; conflict and resolution on more than one level; and beginnings, middles, and ends – all within the context of the larger continuing Marvel sagas. Jim may sometimes have carried these ideas a bit to extremes, but his heart was in the right place, so mostly we got along. And for the most part, if he was mad at me about something, I had earned his wrath.

I was given the licensed properties – *Conan*; *The Savage Sword of Conan*, which was similar to the Warren books; *King Conan*; *Battlestar Galactica*; *Micronauts*; and eventually *Star Wars* and *Indiana Jones*; as well as Chris Claremont's books, *Uncanny X-Men* and *Man-Thing*. Chris had a reputation for being difficult, but I thought he was great and loved working with him every chance I got. He's so smart about story and has so many ideas. He had a way of making his stories feel important.

There were a few others – movie titles, like *Xanadu*. We added *Ka-Zar*. Later, *Uncanny X-Men* became its own franchise, with the spinoff title *New Mutants* and several mini-series and graphic novels.

My first challenge at Marvel was dealing with "The Dark Phoenix Saga" storyline. I was put on that one half way though, after there was a dispute between its editor, Jim Salicrup, and Shooter about one of Phoenix's acts of destruction – she destroyed a planet with people on it, killing them all – and whether Shooter had okayed it or not, and what the results of that destruction would be on the character's future. With Chris's reluctant okay, it was decided that Phoenix would die. Oddly enough, that probably helped cement the popularity of X-Men as a fan-fave book. After that, X-Men fans knew they couldn't look away for a minute, or they would miss something really vital.

In addition to everything else that was going on at the time, Chris and John Byrne were engaged in a creator conflict. John really wanted a book he could totally control, and I wouldn't let that be *Uncanny X-Men* – I just liked Chris's writing and ideas too much. So John quit and went off to write and draw the Fantastic Four! It was the best move for him. I was worried I'd killed the X-Men franchise with John's departure, but it survived and prospered.

While I was an editor at Marvel, there were a lot of changes with major impacts on the medium – to name just a few, comics as graphic novels began to come into vogue, comics began to be sold through the direct market, and creators began to get royalties. It was an interesting time to be in comics, and I was very lucky to have been part of it.

Q. What editorial works are you most proud of, and why?

A. At Warren, it would be bringing more American artists into the company, although Bill DuBay had started that trend; hiring Bruce Jones as a Warren regular, 'cause his work was just so good; and some of the fun experiments I ran.

At Marvel, there's quite a few worth mentioning. There was "The Dark Phoenix Saga" and "Days of Future Past" (here I came to realize that death sold, big time!), hiring Paul Smith to be the ongoing *Uncanny X-Men* artist, because his work was wonderful; hiring John Romita Jr. after him – both Paul and John worked well with Chris – and Frank Miller and Chris's *Wolverine* mini-series. Heck, our whole *X-Men* run.

I'm also really pleased to have created the Ka-Zar book with Bruce Jones and Brent Anderson; of the work we did on the *God Loves, Man Kills* graphic novel (again with Brent Anderson and Chris); of having created *New Mutants* (with Chris again!); of our *Star Wars* run with David Michelinie, Walter [Simonson], and Tom Palmer; and the X-Men-Teen Titans crossover with DC, which had Chris and Walter again, and Terry Austin. It was also satisfying to help raise the sales on everything – because publishers are in the business of selling books! – and the way that we doubled the sales on the black and white *Conan* magazine.

I'm sure I've forgotten lots of stuff.

Q. How did you transition from editor to writer?

A. Shooter had wanted us editors to freelance in addition to our editorial duties, I think so we'd know what it was like to be freelancers. It was a good idea, but I was reluctant since I had a job, and thought anything I did would take food from some freelancer's mouth. I thought it wouldn't be fair. Then Shooter hired a batch of new editors, so our workloads were cut in half. Since I could do my work easily, I began to have time on my hands. So I revisited the "freelancer" idea. I figured if I created something, it wouldn't be taking anything away from anyone.

I had the idea for *Power Pack* and wrote it up. Then I had a stroke of luck when June Brigman came into my office looking for work – all of the books I was editing had artists assigned to them, but it turned out that June could draw kids. She did illos of the Power Pack kids on spec – they were wonderful! – and I submitted the proposal to Shooter with June attached as artist. Shooter loved the proposal, and told me that June and I had a monthly series.

After that, I found I really liked the challenge of writing, and after a while other people offered me more writing work. So I quit editorial and started writing full time.

Q. You worked for Marvel during a time when some big names and big personalities were also at the company. What can you tell us about some of those people? Are there any stories or anecdotes that stand out in your memory?

A. Some aren't printable, and it would take too long here to tell them all. But here's one that I wasn't involved in, I was just an amused bystander...

Shooter, in his demand for clarity, wanted Frank Miller to stop putting little blowing pieces of paper in the cityscapes of his *Daredevil* stories, since people "wouldn't know what they were." This pissed Frank off. Walter and I were out to dinner with Frank and he was telling us about it – pretty indignantly – when he got a great idea! Frank wrote a story where Daredevil fought someone – I think it was Bullseye – in the middle of a tickertape parade. This was a perfect dilemma for Daredevil, because the tickertape screwed up his radar sense. And all through the story, all very necessary, is page after page of blowing paper. The opening page, even, has the credits on blowing pieces of paper. And Shooter's paper is upside down. It was a great character story. Great story period. I don't think Frank heard that complaint from Shooter again.

And the moral is... I dunno. There are so many. Pick one.

Q. You worked in a predominantly male industry for quite some time. What, if any, were the challenges for you as a woman?

A. Actually, over the years, I've pretty much been treated like one of the guys. I was – and I know this will sound weird – sort of innocently unaware that the industry was so male-dominated while I was at Warren, and when I was first at Marvel, until people started pointing it out to me. I hadn't thought my being included was anything special or unusual. I just loved doing the job.

I only ran into the "girls can't do (whatever)" thing a few times, and that was never an overt statement except for that time with James Warren – it was more a feeling I'd get from one person or another. Generally, it wasn't a big deal, since I had plenty of options. As an editor, it may even have worked in my favor. For instance, Chris seems to work really well with female editors. He loved working with Ann Nocenti.

As a writer, I did avoid doing "female character" books too often for fear of being typecast as a "girl writer," although I did do a *Spellbinder* and a *Red Sonja* mini-series, and a couple of issues of *She-Hulk*. Too bad, in a way, but it made sense at the time.

I really enjoyed writing female characters as part of a group – in *Power Pack*, *X-Factor*, *New Mutants*, and *Superman*. But then, I love writing group books in general.

Q. You have worked for both Marvel and DC, taking on some of their most iconic characters. Do you find that you approach writing in different universes very differently?

A. Not really. I'm at heart an old school "Marvel style" writer, which means I like working plot-art-script-inks. But you do have to understand the world your characters live in, and that the tone of each world will be a little different, as will be your characters' place in it and the agenda they bring to it.

I like active stories, where the conflict is physically defined, but hate it when slugfests are about nothing but one big guy hitting another one. For me, the question is always "Why"? What drives this character? What drives the action? Once I've answered that, I pretty much have my story, no matter what universe a character is in.

Q. When you sat down to create *Power Pack*, what did you hope for those characters and that title?

A. I hoped I'd be allowed to write the kind of story I'd loved as a kid, in comic book form, but my hopes weren't that high. When I first proposed the idea, verbally, Shooter wasn't all that enthusiastic. He said something like, "Write it up... maybe a mini-series," and I could practically see him rolling his eyes. But, once I turned in the full proposal – with the plots for a four-issue arc – he loved it. It was a shock to me and June. Neither of us had ever done a whole comic before.

I never expected *Power Pack* to win awards or be as popular as it became. I never thought it would be a cult hit. I never thought it would have the best – the kindest, warmest and friendliest – fans in the world. I never thought it would still be going, in one form or another, decades later.

I was very lucky with *Power Pack*.

Q. Your X-Factor comics are among the first that are now sometimes read as having gay-coded characters, specifically Cameron Hodge. Can you tell us a bit about the process of introducing his character, and what you intended for him? Did the gay angle become more troublesome once Hodge became a villain?

A. I thought I was pretty subtle about "gay" Hodge. Heck, I wasn't even totally sure Hodge was gay, myself.

I didn't introduce him. He was there when I took over the book, with *X-Factor* #6. But his position with the team and his behavior was so against the team's best interests that I asked myself "Why"? As I've said before, "why" – i.e. motivation – drives the story for me. It was in answering this question that the idea emerged, that his love/hate relationship with Angel and X-Factor as a whole might have its roots in jealously.

But what *kind* of jealousy? Might it have been only over X-Factor's powers? But it was more fun if it was personal. So then, what kind of love? What kind of hate? And thus a character emerged. Hodge became the driven, single-minded, mad sort of character who, if he couldn't have something, decided that no one else could have it either.

Poor Hodge. So conflicted. So crazed. He was a very fun character to write.

Q. You sometimes created comics with your husband Walter. Did you have any sense that pairing up with him changed how you were viewed as a writer?

A. I didn't work with Walter all that frequently, and I made that choice deliberately. I figured, that way, if one of us got fired off a book – or a book we were on crashed and burned – the other one would still have a job. Though Walter did write his first comic story for me when I was an editor – a *Battlestar Galactica*, which spring-boarded his career as a writer. And he drew *Star Wars* and *The Uncanny X-Men and The New Teen Titans* one-shot, which I edited. But face it, if you write as well as Walter does, you mostly don't need another writer around.

We did do *X-Factor* together – me as writer, Walter as penciller – and we teamed-up to write the gorgeous *Meltdown* mini-series together, which was painted by Jon Muth and Kent Williams. And years later, we team-wrote *World of Warcraft*, partly because there was too much continuity in *Warcraft* for one writer to handle. But mostly, we've worked separately.

I don't think teaming up with him made any difference, one way or another, in how I was viewed, except that we did good work together. Your readers would have more of a sense of that than I would.

Q. What is the most positive change in the comics industry that you've seen over the course of your career? The least positive?

A. The most positive would be that creators now get royalties, that comics are presented well in other media, and that there's been such a rise of independent publishers who focus on other material than just superheroes. I do love superheroes, but it's a big world out there. Also, the expansion of e-publishing, with individual creators beginning to figure out how to make it work for them.

The least positive would be that at Marvel and DC, story creation is too often handed down from the top, with single creators – sometimes very talented single creators, but still... – controlling storylines across a whole lines of books, including massive crossovers. I think it stifles creativity and plays to a smaller and smaller niche audience.

Q. What advice do you have to budding female writers and artists in an industry that, on the creative side, is still overwhelmingly composed of men?

A. Do what you love. Make every single story you write or draw be the best that it can be. Be deadline conscious. Don't settle for second best, and don't give up. If one door closes, look for another that's open.

Also, be friendly and open to constructive criticism. If someone takes the time to look at and evaluate your work, be grateful and say thank you. If you hear the same criticism two or three times, it's probably something you need to work on. So do it!

Be willing to get your work published in smaller venues, if that's what it takes. If it's that good, people will notice. Just remember that you're competing with the best guys in the field, so you have to be as good as they are... or better. If you're that good, you'll get your break. Then all you have to do is prove you can play in the big leagues.

Me vs. Me

Sarah Kuhn is the author of the geek romantic comedy novella *One Con Glory*, currently in development as a feature film. She has written for *Back Stage*, *IGN.com*, *Geek Monthly*, *The Hollywood Reporter*, *Creative Screenwriting*, *Consumers Digest*, and *StarTrek.com*. She is one fourth of the Alert Nerd collective (Alertnerd.com) and can be found blabbing about gender and genre on popular panels like GeekGirlCon's "Character Studies: Geek Girls in Popular Culture." In 2011, Sarah was selected as a finalist for the CAPE (Coalition of Asian Pacifics in Entertainment) New Writers Award. She lives in Santa Monica with her gamer husband, an extensive *Buffy* action figure collection, and way too many comic books.

"Who would win in a fight?"

How many times have we comic book junkies heard this simple, six-word utterance? How many times have we used it, thought it, or typed it into our handy Internet time-suck of choice? If my mutant power was to amass all occurrences of this phrase as it was articulated outside the ArcLight Cinema's premiere midnight showing of *Thor* alone... Well, first of all, that'd be a really shitty mutant power, but second, I would surely end up with a number somewhere in the quadruple digits. "Who would win in a fight?" is both ultimate nerd ice-breaker and ultimate nerd debate tool – a means of bonding swathed in the fiery coating of fan passion.

I kind of hate "Who would win in a fight?"

I didn't always. I used to jump into such debates with unabashed gusto, brandishing my dog-eared issue of *X-Men* #30 (1994) as if the very existence of that one panel wherein Rachel Summers wore a horrifically ugly dress took my argument to a place of undeniable rightness, a place where no amount of point-refuting "actually..."s could take me down.

The realization that I no longer enjoy "Who would win in a fight?" hit me with the blunt force of Mjolnir during a recent Internet-based tournament wherein female characters from the DC Universe were pitted against each other, bracket-style, and fans voted for their favorites. To be clear, this tournament was not in the context of "Who would win in a fight?" It was just, "Who do you like better?" or "Who is more kickass?" Also, I would like to state up front that I do not begrudge anyone for setting up or voting in such contests. This one, in particular, seemed quite fun and lady-empowering. My realization was of a personal nature, not meant to rain on anyone's "vs."-style parade.

I voted in a few of the early brackets in a fairly cavalier fashion – I'd glance at the poll, have some sort of *That one!* gut reaction, and click the appropriate bubble. And then came the bracket that broke me. Then came Lois Lane vs. Oracle. The tough girl reporter who inspired my first career choice vs. the super-smart star of one of my absolute favorite books.

As my cursor hovered back and forth, I realized this was an impossible choice. I just couldn't do it. Both bubbles remained unclicked, and I declared on Twitter that I was abstaining from this particular poll because there was no way I could choose.

"But you must declare yourself!", exclaimed Twitter. "You must make your allegiances known! Otherwise, how will we know what You're All About?" In the midst of this, there was also the expected campaigning for each character: Lois is the best girlfriend ever! Oracle has an incredible dramatic arc! Lois is better represented across different mediums, like film and television! Oracle's hair is basically amazing!

As this continued, building to some sort of fan battle fever pitch, I started to feel a little left out. Was I a bad fan for not being able to pick a side and clearly articulate *why* I picked said side? Was I not as passionate? Not as pleasingly obsessive? As these thoughts cycled through my brain, a few folks engaged in a new strain of Twit-campaigning: Basically, "You should vote for *this* character, because the other character is *lame*." Lois is *just* a girlfriend: not a superhero! Oracle's hair is basically stupid!

The tournament was, as I understood it, designed to champion female characters, and most people seemed to be doing a good job of that. But I was bothered by the few folks who resorted to the old "let's praise one lady by denigrating another" thing. I wanted to be able to find both of these characters awesome – for very different reasons – without being forced to pick a side.

As I mulled things over, brow furrowed in overly serious thoughtfulness, I started to realize that maybe I was obsessing over this particular "vs." issue because I'd been picking sides all my life. Even in fandom. *Especially* in fandom. And it was finally time to stop.

Me vs. Me

#

I vividly remember the one and only time I uttered a bad word in front of my mother. This woman – a second generation Japanese-American with a penchant for seemingly mild pastimes like sewing and Sue Grafton novels – could fillet you with a mere look, the smallest narrowing of her gaze accented by a disapproving eyebrow raise. My brother and I *never* wanted to be on the other end of The Look, so we usually managed to keep our language as vanilla as possible.

But there was one time I let a blue word slip and not only did I get away with it, my mother actually agreed with the sentiment I was expressing.

Allow me to back up a little.

I grew up in a tiny Oregon town. It had one main "street" and one all-purpose "Asian" restaurant, where you could get a burger with a side of fried rice. The environment was overwhelmingly white and more than a little strange for a half-Japanese/quarter-German/quarter-English mutt with a deep love of comic books and a Major Kira Fan Club membership card.

Comics were an escape, a portal to another world. I liked to imagine that someday my mutant power would manifest and I'd be outta there (but not before I demonstrated said mutant power for my more popular classmates, causing them to finally realize how cool I was). My obsession wasn't limited to the Marvel Universe, however. I also thrilled in the teen dream adventures of Archie Comics's Betty and Veronica: two best buddies engaged in a constant, epic battle over a boy, capital-F "Frienemies" before that was even a thing.

The books seemed largely sympathetic to Betty, a ponytailed middle-class sweetheart adept at wholesome activities like volleyball and diary-writing. Archie, however, tended to prefer scheming rich girl Veronica, who was so concerned with looking hot that she once donned a figure-hugging bodysuit with a built-in heating device rather than surrender to the bulky, unflattering cocoon of a winter coat. (In truth, I thought that was pretty dang genius, but I don't believe you were *supposed* to think that.)

I wasn't sure why I had to choose an allegiance. My favorite stories were the ones where Betty and Veronica just went shopping or whatever and Archie didn't even enter the picture. In fact, my favorite of all time was probably the one where Betty got depressed over the general shittiness of her "artistic" (but actually pretty shitty) macaroni sculptures and Veronica went around strong-arming/ threatening/ blackmailing everyone else in the gang into buying one.

And yet, the books made it seem imperative that I choose – Archie always faced this dilemma, after all – so I expended a decent amount of tweenage brain cells considering both options. In my head, I wanted to be for Betty (so nice! So ponytailed!), but my heart kept falling for Veronica. Much of this was likely aesthetic: A lot of the tween-focused media I was consuming offered up pretty blonde heroines and jealous brunette witches/ villains/ megalomaniacal dictators. What is a severely brunette Asian girl supposed to do with that? The fact that stories were sometimes written from Veronica's point of view, and the fact that she was occasionally portrayed as borderline sympathetic, was *huge*. This, I now see, was very likely the genesis of my tendency to root for the Misunderstood Bitch (see also: Blair Waldorf, Emma Frost, Kitiara Uth Matar), even when what she's doing isn't exactly a rootable action.

As I was considering Betty vs. Veronica, I was also moping my way through my first big racial identity crisis, spurred largely by the heady cocktail of pre-teen angst and my classmates' unending litany of "But what *are* you?" queries. My initial answer ("half-Japanese, half-white, all mutt") never seemed to satisfy, so I just started responding with a defiant "Um, *American*" and then giving whoever was asking a gimlet-eyed stare, daring them to take their line of questioning any further. I also made every effort to play down my mixed-ness, to seem completely non-exotic, completely *American*: I might've looked different, but I could wear Guess jeans, read *Bop* magazine, and hoover McDonald's French fries with the best of them. I felt like, just as the comics I was reading asked me to make a clear choice – Betty or Veronica – my little hometown wanted me to define myself in easily understandable, easily digestible, easily explainable terms. And if I did that, maybe people would stop asking me stupid questions.

And then, naturally, there was the day my perspective on all this underwent a multiverse-shattering shift.

My mother and I had stopped by our favorite little hole-in-the-wall donut shop, conveniently located next door to the shopping bonanza that was the local Goodwill. We ordered our usuals – plain cake for her, pink frosted for me – then waited for the kindly elderly donut shop lady with the comforting helmet perm to bag them up for us. While we were waiting, a hulking, bearded beast of a man lurched over and spat out sentences laced with a kind of gut-level venom I'd never experienced before.

"The Japanese take all our lumber," he hissed, towering over us. "*All* of it. Can't trust them. *Japanese.*"

I remember being scared in this moment. I remember feeling cornered, hated. I remember a general sense of confusion because, even though I felt his anger, his sentences had a slurry gibberish quality to them that made no sense. I also remember that I looked to the kindly donut lady, expecting her to say or do something: She was our friend, our regular dispenser of sugary carbs. And I remember that all she did was laugh, as if this terrifying giant in front of us was a floppy-eared puppy who'd just pissed – *adorably* – on the rug.

My mother turned to the kindly donut lady and simply said, in her clipped way, "I won't be coming here again."

When we got outside, I unclenched my balled-up fists, the fingertips bright with chipped, ill-advised neon nail polish, and blurted out: "What an *asshole.*"

My mother met my gaze, her eyes wide and serious – no narrowing, no disapproving eyebrow-raise – and simply said, "Yes."

Then she took my hand in hers (even though I had long claimed to be too old for that) and we went to Goodwill.

That was the day where I clearly saw, for the very first time, that it doesn't matter what side of the "vs." coin you choose when it comes to defining and presenting yourself: I'd never be *American* enough for hulky bearded man, no matter how many *Bop* magazines I owned. People will see you however they want, so you might as well be what *you* want.

I also decided to stick to the stories where Betty and Veronica just went shopping or whatever. For all the times he had to face the "vs." dilemma, Archie never *actually* chose. Not really. So why should I?

# # #

After high school, I used my mutant power to escape to college in California. This was where I met Sonjia, a delightfully snarky-mouthed cinephile with little patience for low-level dumbassery. Sonjia was key in introducing me to black-and-white "real life" indie comics where people felt all their feelings and spent multiple panels having moments of extreme honesty.

She showed me Daniel Clowes's *Ghost World* one hazy day when I was sprawled on her rickety dorm room bed with my arms flung over my face in a classic "Woe is me over some dumb boy drama" pose.

I immediately loved the way the book honed in on the simultaneous importance and non-importance of tiny moments between two aimless girls, the way the fragility of friendship was captured in lines like, "I just totally hate myself." My favorite panel in the book featured Enid and Rebecca, our compelling teenage misanthropes, slumping into each other on a lonely-looking bench, looking utterly defeated. It's right before their friendship's about to implode in on itself and it's the quietest, truest punch to the gut you'll ever feel.

Upon graduation from college, my obsession with the more minutiae-laced corners of the Marvel Universe helped me land my first big job: writing and editing for a major geek-centric site about television, movies, and, yes, comic books. I was one of two female editors site-wide – and the sole female editor on my section.

I still remember one of the marketing people chirping at me, "How cool are you? A *girl* who likes all this stuff. That's so... *different.*" I suppose that sentiment seems downright quaint now, in an era where we have, oh, I don't know – an entire anthology dedicated to women writing about comics? But this was a decade ago: the gender breakdown at San Diego Comic-Con still erred heavily on the testosterone side, and I do remember being on the receiving end of various levels of "hey, a unicorn"-esque fascination from my male counterparts.

Because of this, I felt the need to *define* myself, loudly and clearly, as a certain type of geek. And when you categorize and label in geekdom, you usually do it by declaring which pop cultural products you most enjoy. When asked, I streamlined: I was a *geek*, man. *Different*, like the marketing lady said! I liked *Deep Space Nine* and didn't know how to put on lipstick! Indie comics didn't come up, cause those were, like, girly or something. If I wanted to be accepted as one of the uber-nerd tribe, I couldn't muddy the waters by sharing *all* of my likes. Superheroes all the way! What's *Ghost World*?

This, of course, had to shift. And this time, the shift came when my mom was diagnosed with cancer. When it happened, it was too late, a mere matter of counting down the horrible days. I found myself unable to vocalize this to people, because saying it out loud made it real. The words wouldn't form, wouldn't make themselves known. But maintaining a daily veneer of "everything's fine"-ness sapped my strength like nothing else – I still remember bursting into tears in aisle fourteen of the grocery store cause I couldn't decide which mustard was the absolute right mustard to buy, the one that was going to make me feel *normal*.

I started telling people. And the first person I told was Sonjia.

I remember her eyes getting big and glassy, like buffet dinner plates that have been washed into shiny oblivion. I remember that she didn't say "It'll be okay" or "I'm sorry" or any of those prepackaged statements that sound nice but ultimately don't mean anything. And I remember that she squeezed my hand and asked me a few questions and then took me back to where I was comfortable, talking about other things. We shared stories about hanging out with exciting post-collegiate groups of people, at new jobs and internships.

"It's nice to make new friends, isn't it?", she said.

I said, "Yes," and secretly thought, "But none of them are you."

Later that night, I thought about moments of extreme honesty. Moments like Enid and Rebecca on that sad bench. Moments like me finally breaking down and letting the words come out and telling Sonjia about my mom. Moments like her perfect response to my confession.

If moments like this are what we're always chasing, then why did I keep trying to stuff myself into a confining little "vs." box? Playing up one side of myself over the other was far more work than just being honest. So I stopped. At my job, I still wrote about superheroes, but I also wrote about *Strangers in Paradise* and Lynda Barry, and the entire circa 2000 output of Oni Press.

Shockingly, no one doubted my nerd cred: that was a perception I'd built up in my own mind, a barrier I crafted out of my intense fear of not being taken seriously. I was glad to be done with it.

I even got a couple of my dude co-workers into *Ghost World*.

# # #

I did not have a conclusion to this piece until two days ago. In theory, I know why I've been able to fully move on from "Who would win in a fight?" Even though the Internet is often still home to these battles, it's also connected and opened up fandom in such a way that the pressure to box yourself on one side or another doesn't seem as prevalent. Now I know other mixed race kooks who once dreamed of having mutant powers. Now I know plenty of ladies who follow Terry Moore and *Batwoman* with equal gusto. And now I know that championing one thing by denigrating the other is almost always harmful – and a bad argument to boot.

I became aware of my distaste for the idea of "vs." when faced with Lois Lane vs. Oracle. But the thought of actually rejecting this idea didn't fully solidify for me until earlier this week, when I was sitting on a stage being filmed for an episode of *ComiCenter*, a web show dedicated to discussing issues in the comics industry and fandom. I had been summoned there, along with three other nerdy ladies, to talk about some recent controversies in geek girldom.

One of the hosts said something about how a certain prominent geek girl TV host should be "the standard" for geek girldom and then contrasted her with another female host who he apparently found lesser in some way. The four of us nearly jumped out of our chairs, pointing out that pitting women against each other in some kind of "vs." match isn't cool – and besides, we're all very different and proud of it.

There is no standard. There shouldn't be.

One of us is a self-described Sith who cosplays as Lady Vader. One of us has an extensive collection of swords in her home (and at least two lightsabers in her car trunk). One of us threw an elaborate *Firefly*-themed birthday party and transformed her living room into Captain Mal's *Serenity*. And one of us really wishes there was an *X-Men* storyline wherein Jean Grey and Emma Frost became best friends and went shopping together (a la Betty and Veronica).

Sitting on stage alongside one another, we were all willing to share these things, to be nothing less than ourselves. There was no downplaying different pieces of our fandoms or personalities because they might not fit with what people perceive as "geek girl." There was no dissing each other because we might disagree on which *Star Wars* comics are the best. There was no "vs.," no "Who would win in a fight?"

Instead, we all presented ourselves on our own terms. And we all won.

A Road that has No Ending: Revenge in *Sandman*

Sarah Monette lives in an 105-year-old house with a great many books, two cats, one grand piano, and one husband. She has published more than 40 short stories, and has two short story collections out: *The Bone Key* (Prime Books 2007, with a shiny second edition in 2011) and *Somewhere Beneath Those Waves* (Prime Books, 2011). She has written two novels (*A Companion to Wolves*, Tor Books, 2007; *The Tempering of Men*, Tor Books, 2011) and three short stories with Elizabeth Bear, and hopes to write more. Her first four novels (*Melusine, The Virtu, The Mirador, Corambis*) were published by Ace. Her next novel, *The Goblin Emperor*, will come out from Tor under the name Katherine Addison. Visit her online at sarahmonette.com.

There are many reasons I love Neil Gaiman's *Sandman*: the depth and richness of the world(s) Gaiman and his artists create; the characters, both human and otherwise, who are by turns wise, funny, sad, and sometimes breathtakingly stupid; the delicate intricacy of the plots, both within issues, storyarcs, and within *Sandman* as a whole; the way in which ideas, themes, problems may be put down for a while, but are never entirely forgotten. I love the vast scope of the material he uses, from classical mythology to John Aubrey to the Chordettes. And I love Gaiman's intense metafictional awareness of the story he's telling and the genres he's using to tell it, the way that his stories always comment *on storytelling*. I love that *Sandman* is morbid and that it is gruesome and that neither of these qualities interfere when it decides to be heart-rending.

There are also many reasons I love revenge tragedy. Revenge tragedy is a genre of play that flourished in English theaters between, roughly, 1592 and 1642. It's not actually the kind of thing you think of when you use the words "tragedy" and "play" in the same sentence; you'll get much closer to the distinctive flavor of revenge tragedy if you think of it as horror movies for the stage. Like horror movies, revenge tragedy is in love with the grim, the ghastly, the grotesque; people drop like flies in revenge tragedy, and the bloodier and more exotic their deaths, the better. Characters die from kissing poisoned corpses in revenge tragedy.

These would be some of the reasons I love it.

Which, I suppose, would lead you to wonder about me and whether I am safe to sit next to.

I'm a horror writer, among other things, and one of the things horror writers have in common is our taste for the morbid. ("I have the heart of a small boy," Robert Bloch once said. "I keep it in a jar on my desk.") As far as I can tell, this propensity is in-built; certainly, in my case, it was deep-rooted and blooming great carnivorous flowers well before I reached puberty. The first story I ever tried to write was a horror story.

I can't explain the well-spring of my love for horror, but I can suggest some reasons why – while its popularity has ebbed and flowed over the course of human civilization – it never entirely goes away. At its root, horror is about the fear of death, which is something we all have to contend with. But more than that, horror gives us access to a part of our psyche we normally keep bricked up (like Fortunato from Poe's "The Cask of Amontillado"). We *have* to keep it bricked up, or that human civilization thing I mentioned would never have gotten off the ground, but at the same time, it's not a good idea not to go down there into the cellars and talk to it occasionally. Sigmund Freud said some very stupid and toxic things, but one thing he got right was the idea of the return of the repressed. The harder you try to bury something, the more it tries to claw its way out of the ground.

There's a lovely meta encapsulation of horror as a genre in the sixth issue of *Sandman*, "24 Hours." When John Dee forces one of his victims to tell the truth about herself ("Hour 12: It Is Time For Them To Get To Know Each Other Better"), the story that this nice, middle-class woman – a woman you'd think had no darkness in her soul at all – tells is a horror story. All the gory trappings of horror, the monsters and the madmen and the heart-pounding fear, are a way of forcing us to face up to the part of ourselves we keep bricked in the cellar. Revenge tragedy knows this, and *Sandman* knows it, too.

I was introduced to *Sandman* before I encountered revenge tragedy, thanks to my first boyfriend's evangelical fervor. He adored comics and in his whole-hearted, geeky desire to share his passion, he would tell me for hours about whatever comic he'd been reading most recently. He told me more about *Justice League* 1990-1992 than I and the entire Library of Congress ever needed to know. But he also told me about *Sandman* and – greater love hath no man – let me read the issues that he had. *Justice League* didn't click with me, but *Sandman* did. Although I never collected comics, I bought the *Sandman* collections as they came out, and two of my dearest possessions are *A Game of You* and *The Kindly Ones*, which Neil Gaiman signed for me.

So I loved *Sandman*, but it was revenge tragedy that, for a time, took over my life. The more revenge tragedies I read, the more I loved them: their moral ambiguity, their morbid ingenuity, their shameless wallowing in gore. In the intensely respectable field of early modern English literature, revenge tragedy capers like a demon toddler, smearing blood on the walls and shrieking with half-hysterical laughter. I realized I could write about horror, which is possibly my truest, deepest love in all literature, and yet write a dissertation that was impeccably academic. I wrote my doctoral dissertation on ghosts in revenge tragedy, discussing plays like *The Spanish Tragedy*, *The Changeling*, *The Revengers Tragedy*, *The Atheist's Tragedy*. And, of course, *Hamlet*, which might have been devised as a blueprint for how revenge tragedy should run: complicated plots, madness, multiplying revengers, and – the thing that everyone knows about Elizabethan drama – the stage covered with corpses at the end. It's gruesome, but it's also an integral part of what makes the genre tick.

Revenge tragedy's point is that murder is a contamination; the more people you kill, the more people have to die. The saddest characters in revenge tragedy are those who just happen to be in the wrong place at the wrong time, like Ophelia. Loki says to Carla at the end of Part Five of *The Kindly Ones*, "And do you know your tragedy, Carla? It's that, for all your goodwill, for all your willingness to help, you never knew what any of this was about, what was going on. You don't know how it ends. And you'll never get to find out." Carla's horrible death marks the genre she has become trapped in; like Ophelia, Carla dies for someone else's revenge.

It doesn't take much to see that *The Kindly Ones* is a revenge tragedy. Lyta Hall gets her revenge on Morpheus, and in the process destroys the Dreaming and everything she cares about. She is a revenger. She is also, like Laertes in *Hamlet*, a patsy, a puppet for forces which she cannot understand – and which she makes no effort to understand. The tiny pocket universe in which Lyta and Hector live in *The Doll's House* is a perfect symbol of Lyta's own mind: closed, airless, and impervious to reality.

(I am not a fan of Lyta Hall.)

But at the same time, Lyta could not achieve her apocalyptic revenge if Morpheus had not *also* played into the hands of the Eumenides, the "kindly ones," those terrible personified forces out of ancient Greek mythology and tragedy... and the truth, of course, is that tragedy and mythology, in ancient Greece, were very nearly the same thing – as are tragedy and horror. And Gaiman does a brilliant thing, because Morpheus's *hamartia* (to use a word from Aristotle's theory of tragedy, a word which can be translated as mistake, or flaw, or sin) is the same as Lyta's.

Morpheus cannot forgive.

Morpheus, too, is a revenger.

We see this immediately, in the first issue of *Sandman*. The first thing Morpheus does when he escapes imprisonment is to take his revenge on his captor, Alex Burgess. We see it again and again throughout *Sandman*'s run. He revenges and he does not forgive. Richard Madoc, Nada, Orpheus, Lyta herself. Morpheus is capable of compassion, although he's not very good at it, but he does not, *cannot* forgive. In the end, he cannot forgive himself.

When Abel says, in *The Wake*, that what they're mourning is a point of view, I think it is this, specifically, that he means. The point of view that was too rigid to bend, that could only revenge, not forgive. The point of view that was Morpheus and not Daniel.

And it's interesting that it's Abel who says it, not only because it's a secret, but because Cain and Abel are themselves a revenge tragedy that never makes it past Act I. Over and over, throughout *Sandman*, Cain kills Abel, and Abel comes back to life. Over and over, Abel fails to take, or even contemplate, revenge. One may think – as Cain says loudly and often – that Abel is weak and stupid, but we see the obverse side of Abel's forgiveness when Cain, prickly and pompous and bullying, comes to Daniel to get Abel back. And when bullying won't work – Daniel is gentle in a way Morpheus never was, but he's not weak – Cain actually begs, and we learn that, as necessary as Cain is to Abel, Abel is no less necessary to Cain. Where revenge begets nothing but more revenge, Abel's forgiveness is recognized and returned as a kind of love.

And I think it is not an accident that the way Morpheus deliberately opens the door for his own death is through an act of forgiveness: granting death to Orpheus. Because Daniel, from the beginning of his reign as Dream, forgives. He forgives Alex Burgess. He forgives Richard Madoc. He forgives Lyta Hall. And with each forgiveness Daniel offers, we are shown another place where Morpheus, because he could not change or bend, created a dead end for himself. In the end, we understand that Morpheus had to die, not because the Kindly Ones were pursuing him, but because he had backed himself into a corner where he had no other options. He says to William Shakespeare in the final *Sandman* issue ("The Tempest"), "I do not change," which neatly sidesteps the question of *can't* vs. *won't*. And in the end, for Morpheus, it turns out to be the same thing.

He could not forgive.

Daniel can.

Revenge tragedies do not end on notes of hope, for no one can walk away from being a revenger. The plays end with most, if not all, of the characters dead. The survivors are most often grief-sick, blood-sick, like Horatio in *Hamlet*, alive only because Hamlet insisted that someone remain to tell the story. They end, in other words, where *The Kindly Ones* ends, and possibly the thing I love most about *Sandman* is that it *does not end* with *The Kindly Ones*. It talks about what happens after the story is over, both the grief and the rebuilding. It gives us a space to understand Morpheus as well as to mourn him.

The Wake also deconstructs the story of *Sandman*, as Gaiman has been doing all along. Morpheus has been the central character, but the story does not end with his death; the other characters – his friends, his lovers, his enemies, his victims – all have to figure out what they're going to do, now that he's gone. Morpheus chose – and was chosen by – tragedy, but it is not the only genre at work, and Gaiman suggests it isn't even the most powerful one. Cain can kill Abel, but he cannot make Abel hate him.

"You sought vengeance," Daniel says to Lyta. "But that is a road that has no ending." And he gives her the opposite of the Mark of Cain (which we saw perfectly plainly on Cain's forehead in *Season of Mists*) – for while, as with the Mark of Cain, Daniel's mark means that no one will harm her, he also tells her, "Put your life together once again. Go in peace."

The older I get, the more interested I become in stories that try to talk about what happens after the story is over, stories that understand that all endings are artificial, even tragic ones. And thus the final thing I love about Neil Gaiman's *Sandman* is that after all the tragedy and catastrophe, loss and disaster and failure... after all this, it ends with a beginning.

Mutants

Marjorie M. Liu is an attorney, and a *New York Times*-bestselling author of paranormal romances and urban fantasy. In the world of comic books, she is also the writer of *Astonishing X-Men, NYX: No Way Home, Black Widow, X-23*, and *Dark Wolverine*. She lives in the American Midwest and Beijing, China. For more information, please visit her website at marjoriemliu.com or follow her on Twitter: @marjoriemliu

I remember, I remember so well – the title, that first page, a splash for the contents of the story to follow, and those words, words that hit my teenage heart a little too close:

My father bleeds history.

My father bleeds. I bleed. We bleed. All of us, together, in that book – the first graphic novel I ever read, and maybe the most powerful novel, prose or illustrated, that I have *ever* read.

Maus: A Survivor's Tale.

My first step. No capes. No powers. Just truth. About the Holocaust and its survivors, and the children of those survivors.

Some stories, some *histories*, are too awful – too incomprehensibly terrible – to explain through words alone.

This is why I love comics.

#

Here, take a moment for a different history.

In the 1930s and '40s, comic book characters such as Superman, Wonder Woman, and Batman provided escapist, crime-fighting fantasies. Men leapt over tall buildings, caped vigilantes prowled the streets, golden lassos compelled the truth.

Stories, however, changed after America's involvement in the second World War. Hundreds of thousands of comic books were being shipped to service personnel, and current affairs trickled into the lives of superpowered heroes. No retreat from reality, on the part of the comic book industry. No way to ignore what the world had become.

Even America's triumph at winning the war was short-lived. We had a nuclear weapon – but then, the Russians acquired one, too. Communists became our new foes, and the Korean War cemented our sense of vulnerability. Comic books offered few escapist fantasies where it concerned the portrayal of American soldiers. On those pages, men dropped like flies, and fears of death were described in graphic detail.

Comic books geared towards the mainstream reflected a society that now dreaded the true, physical destruction of the world – the American world, that is – by nuclear weapons, war, or a foreign power out to conquer.

Heroes were created who could battle the people responsible for these terrible threats – villains who sought to bring about an end, an *apocalypse*. They told stories from the points of view of a society unwilling to face the end-times. Stories about men and women with the strength to prevent such apocalypses – or survive them with honor.

Even when life is at its bleakest – there is hope.

A hero comes, and we are saved.

#

Also, there's a girl.

There's always a girl. Only this one is raised in a lab, manufactured by scientists for a single purpose:

To kill.

Imagine that. Imagine the loneliness of that life, and the coldness. No love. No kindness. No compassion allowed. The girl is stripped of her humanity in order to become a thing that will follow orders. She is conditioned to tolerate pain, and abuse, in all its most terrible forms.

Yet, there is a part of her that remains unbroken – that still thinks, and feels. Even if she does not understand those feelings.

The girl wants to understand, and she wants to be free – if she can figure out what freedom means.

She is X-23.

She is an assassin, but there are spies in her world, too – and thieves, and men with claws in their hands, and women who can read minds and walk through walls. Good people. Bad people. Crazy, otherworldly, people. Hundreds, thousands, each one with a life inside a comic book, suffering prejudice and broken hearts, forbidden love, uncontrolled power, terrible danger.

Someone's world is always ending. Someone's world is always being saved, against incredible odds. And always, the bonds of friendship become as strong as the bonds of blood, built on sacrifice and hard choices.

This is what I remember when I write. Heroes are those we can admire without apology, and the privilege of participating in their journey, both as reader and creator, is that we are also granted moments when we live as heroes with them.

# # #

Simple, really.

We love stories about heroes.

We talk about how the modern world is an unfriendly place. The world has always been unfriendly. We fear devastation, and yet we embrace stories that show us an endless parade of apocalyptic futures. We fear the end-times, but we create them in our fantasies. We face evil. We search darkness.

And we discover the power that comes from mastering the darkness.

We live with the heroes of those stories, and watch them overcome malevolence and destruction. We become empowered, inspired, through their strength and determination.

If pop culture is an institutional religion reaffirming the values of the masses, then the continued existence of comic books and superheroes, and the resurgence of them on film and television, reflects well on our society – which is so often painted in shades of gloom and doom. Indeed, our obsession with the end of the world in popular media is as much an obsession with heroes.

A reflection on our own hunger to matter, and make a difference.

Life is precious, and precarious. We cling to this rock and each other, and dream for the best. We search for *revelations* – often in what frightens us the most, whether that is the apocalypse or some quieter devastation: isolation, heartbreak, loss.

This is why I love *stories*.

From a young age, I remember reports about bombs and wars, outbreaks of disease, murder-sprees – leaving me concerned that some force beyond my control would steal away all I cared about most. I took solace in heroes – who overcame, who took control, who did what was necessary – without losing the humanity that made them great.

It will never be the end of the world. Not in the true, physical sense. Not unless some cosmic accident blows our planet to smithereens. Not until our sun goes supernova, five billion years from now. If humans are wiped out tomorrow, the planet will spin onward, and life will keep busy, and another intelligent species will take our place and dream their own heroes.

But the end of our existence isn't the point, not in any fantasy. It is what we do when it falls apart that matters to us.

What do we do? What do heroes do?

Heroes are varied, some flesh and blood, others who have never existed beyond the page or screen, or some storyteller's tongue. Some are human, some are mutants and vampires, or aliens. Some heroes are children with quick wits. Throw in a dog or two.

What they all show us is hope. What they show us is that we, as a people who love them, are *hopeful*.

We can do anything, with hope.

Hope is our superpower.

This is why I love comics.

You're on the Global Frequency

Elizabeth Bear was born on the same day as Frodo and Bilbo Baggins, but in a different year. She is the Hugo and Sturgeon Award-winning author of – most recently – *The Tempering of Men* (with Sarah Monette), *Grail*, and *The Sea Thy Mistress*. She lives in Massachusetts with a giant ridiculous dog, and spends rather a lot of her life on planes.

I grew up in Snowtown.

Not *exactly* the Snowtown of the inside of Warren Ellis's head – the Snowtown that features as the antagonist in his-and-Ben-Templesmith's brilliant, intermittent, intentionally low-budget little nine-panel-to-the-page comic *FELL* – but a real-world version: a little less violent, a little less weird, a little less urban. But just as poor, and just as hopeless, and just as full of people who were going nowhere and didn't exactly understand how they'd missed the bus to life.

The secret is kind of simple: There are places where that bus doesn't run, anymore. Or any buses at all – even the less figurative one. Where there are no city services; no social services; where in some places the infrastructure has failed to the level of Elizabethan London, and nobody is coming to fix it.

My neighborhood in Rockville, Connecticut, was one of those places, back when I lived there. Okay, there was city water... but there were collapsed retaining walls and burnt-out houses, as well. A failed municipality, a derelict milltown, it had actually been absorbed by the neighboring town of Vernon. So it was a town that wasn't even a town, and while it had its better neighborhoods, the street where I lived was, not to put too fine a point on it, a half-step up from a rookery – decaying three-story mill-worker's housing broken up into apartments, inhabited by the usual assortment of poor families, dysfunctional families, local color, the mentally ill, the substance-addicted, unemployed men cleaning their guns on the stoop on hot days, and people outside of the confines of regular society for whatever reason. (We were the queer family who yelled a lot. You go where they'll rent to you.)

There are things about a town with a totally collapsed economy that are a bit different from your standard suburbia, but the thing was, those of us who lived there were aware that it was a slum... but we were also aware that it was where we lived. Our neighborhood.

That's one of the things that I find compelling about *FELL*. Ellis captures that sense of neighborhood, even in a book that is largely about the horrors of a town that wider society has abandoned. He brings in that sense that it is a community – a community full of people who may be powerless, but that does not mean they do not *care*.

True, my town was devoid of creepy recurring nuns in Nixon masks – and I don't think Rockville actually had a malevolent intelligence behind its decay, as Snowtown seems to – but I think that very real tension of people going about their lives and dreaming their dreams in the belly of the beast is symptomatic of the thing I find most compelling about Ellis's work.

Which is its peculiar, bleak, indomitable humanism.

To stay on *FELL* – and its titular character, Detective Richard Fell (yes, I rather imagine it's intentional that his name is also a sentence) – for a moment, this is evident in the unusual nature of Fell's heroism. He's tired, and broken, and an egoist, and he's facing impossible odds in a struggle he seems bound to lose. He's been sent down from the nameless city to which Snowtown serves as slum and dump and charnel ground for an unnamed sin, which he characterizes as having done a good thing.

He despairs and he's brutal and he does not play by the rules, because where he lives there aren't any rules. When Fell arrives in Snowtown, someone immediately calls him "devil cop." The first person who is kind to him also (literally) brands him – on the neck, with a mystic symbol intended to keep him safe. And this is par for the course in Richard Fell's life.

In Snowtown, he – and so, we – finds a girl whose physically abusive alcoholic father is the best thing in her life. We meet a police lieutenant who "doesn't care" how Fell does his job and who "takes a lot of pills." We encounter a woman distraught because her husband left her for the family dog, and a child whose father keeps her in an attic and injects feces under her skin.

(*FELL* has a lot of recurring images of fathers and children and the legacies of the former to the latter – almost all of them painfully toxic. Although there is Fell's not-quite-girlfriend Mayko's father, who left her a bar.)

This is all part of the normal run of events in this cold city on the borderlands of unreality and Hell.

Fell actually can't do much about most of this evil: The majority of it is so far beyond his power to affect that the only sane response – the response of just about every other person, besides Fell – is to shrug, feel bad, and move on.

What makes Fell a hero – a "good man" as Mayko puts it – is that he looks at all this world of misery... and he does not look down. He finds ways to fight back, to throw a crumb of comfort and justice to anyone he can. He responds to Snowtown by becoming as arbitrary and unfair as Snowtown itself – but under the circumstances, there is a heroism in that.

Fell keeps struggling to understand the people around him, to help them, to preserve as many of them as possible in the face of more awfulness and indifferent malevolence than any human will can withstand. It is simply – and indelibly – a refusal to surrender to evil, no matter what the personal cost of fighting on.

No matter how tired he gets. Because somebody has to do it. And he happens to be the guy who is standing there.

My favorite issue revolves around Fell's day off: Having ruined his only two decent suits (through the simple expedient of having been knifed twice in his first two weeks on the job), he stops by a thrift shop. This being Snowtown, realm of coincidence and very slight unreality (and nuns in Nixon masks), the thrift shop is also a little bit of a magic shop. It's staffed and owned by an elderly woman who is selling, among other things, the possessions left to her by her father (fathers again, and legacies). Which include his suits.

We also learn that Fell has nothing from his own father, because his older brother absconded with it all – not because he wanted it, but because Fell did.

Being taken with Fell (who is both a perceptive and a personable man, in his own quizzical, reactively violent sort of way), she offers him one of her father's suits to try on, insisting that it won't matter if it's a bit too large. "My momma always said, how a man wears a suit is about the man, not the fit." Which might serve as a sort of allegorized thematic statement for the entire (so far incomplete) work, come to think of it – but more on that later.

Because when Fell enters the changing room, he discovers it is already occupied – by an older gentleman in a plaid shirt with a homemade bomb strapped around his waist.

"I'm a suicide bomber," he says to Fell.

And Fell, with Midwestern deadpan aplomb, replies, "I can see that."

The ensuing, more or less eerily calm and reasoned conversation between Fell and the bomber (Jeff) and the elderly woman (Ellen) ranks as one of my favorite moments in all of comicdom. It transpires that Jeff wants to destroy Ellen's shop (and Ellen) because – as a sort of charitable sideline to the thrift store business – Ellen gives away guns to the elderly and afraid, and one of those guns was used to shoot Jeff's brother while he was robbing someone's home. Fell reminds Jeff that he still had everything his brother left him – "the music, the games, the things he touched" – and distracts him sufficiently to pull off a last-minute save that is as elegant in its simplicity – and stupid bravery – as it is in its brutality.

Fell may be a "good" man – but he's not a nice one. And not everything he does is morally unambiguous. In fact, some of his most heroic acts are also his most indefensible – for example, when he brutalizes a killer, frames him for another crime, and then informs *the city of Snowtown itself* that for every one of Fell's it takes without justice being served, Fell will take back one of its.

It's an impossible promise, of course. I'm reminded of a scene in the television show *Criminal Minds* in which Mandy Patinkin's character informs a vigilante, "You can't kill fast enough to keep up."

It's an impossible promise. But it's a heroic one. Of a sort.

And yet, Fell is presented without the gloss of auctorial approval so often offered to protagonists who do morally muddy things. Even though Fell is a first-person point-of-view narrator (every scene we see, we see narrated from his perspective – sometimes literally, including one issue in which every single panel is a shot taken by him through the digital camera that is his constant companion), the *narrative* never stops being aware that some of what he does is not just questionable but reprehensible. That Fell's actions can be understood as reprehensible and *simultaneously* as heroic is a peculiar gift or skill of Ellis's.

It's not just about the morally ambiguous hero: Those are common enough, after all. There's something more going on here than the anti-hero, the gray-scale, the tarnished knight of the Dashiell Hammett and Raymond Chandler-influenced noir tradition.

Because Ellis also often gives us an inside view into horrible people doing horrible things. He's perfectly capable of showing that without committing the error of either softening the edges of the evil *or* removing culpability, agency and motivation from the characters who perform it. His work is aware of the evil by which human beings so often exist, and more – he doesn't glamorize it. He shows it as banal, and tawdry, and as narcissistic as it really is.

That he balances this with a similarly banal and nuanced and everyday heroism – and that he doesn't glamorize or valorize the flaws of his protagonists – is, for me as a reader, the real core and draw of his work.

On the topic of the banality of heroism (and isn't *that* an interesting concept? We hear so much about the banality of evil, or of pain, but it takes real art to demonstrate that heroism, too, is a quality of the ordinary human being – and that the two extremes can exist simultaneously inside the same skin, and, in fact, arise from the same root), let us consider another Ellis project, *Global Frequency*.

While *Global Frequency* has an apparent pair of central protagonists – the pseudonymous Miranda Zero and her human nerve and command center, Aleph – the narratives themselves revolve around a familiar trope: In each episode, a different team of carefully selected private citizen volunteers respond to some sort of superhuman-level crisis situation, usually caused by the machinations of some world government or another.

These agents are said to be "on the Global Frequency." And Global Frequency itself is described as a "rescue organization." It is multicultural, transnational, and completely apolitical. All it cares about... is saving the world. In some ways, it's a modern outgrowth of a great fictional concept of the 1960s – the United Network Command For Law and Enforcement, fondly known to millions of television viewers the world over as the U.N.C.L.E.

But where U.N.C.L.E. was a quasi-governmental organization, Global Frequency is presented as ambiguous in its origins and sources. Obviously, there is money and technology behind it... and a great deal of both. Where that expertise and capital comes from is never established – but it's pretty clearly not from the governments that, time and again, Global Frequency rescues from the consequences of their own hubris and folly.

These governments resent the Global Frequency... but they also need it, because when one of their ill-conceived experiments in transhuman power-mongering goes awry, somebody has to clean up the mess. It's fairly clear that Global Frequency is a citizen agency – a nonprofit, of sorts. In a world without superheroes, it's everyday human beings to whom that task falls.

As I said, it's a familiar trope, but as Ellis works it, it's also a rewarding one.

One of the things I love best about *Global Frequency* is how strongly it presents this human heroism as something latent in everyone. Global Frequency operatives appear in every ethnicity, sexual orientation, and level of neurotypicality. The world is as likely to be saved by an MIT computer scientist who doesn't bother to pull off his zipper-mouthed bondage mask to engage in a little light hacking as by the true love of a lesbian operative for her civilian partner. Our heroes – the agents of the Global Frequency – include punks and police officers and contract killers and psychopathic Soviet assassins. They are scientists and spies, cat burglars and computer technicians.

And every one of them is ready to die in order to rescue the world from the people who are supposed to be protecting it. It's a wonderfully subversive series, and it undermines and strips away the idea that only governments and corporations are powerful enough to have a positive impact on the fate of humanity.

Through this metaphor of world-saving, in other words, Ellis illustrates that personal responsibility – personal choice – does have an impact on reality for the better. It's a powerful refutation of nihilism, couched – even as it is – in existentialist terms that deny the existence of an objective morality.

The subjective morality of the protagonists, this book says, is sufficient unto the decisions they must make. Even when those decisions are life-shattering, life-evolving. World-changing.

World-ending, potentially.

If subjective morality is all we have, if the tools at hand are what is offered – well, an ideal universe isn't about to pop out of the shipping box any day soon. We work with what we have.

Sometimes, in fact, it's the weapons themselves that save the day through their own self-sacrifice, because Ellis never forgets that his superhuman monsters were human once, themselves – and something *made* them monsters.

And he never forgets that it's *important* that every human being see her or himself as a potential hero. Not the blonde, butt-chinned Hollywood hero – but a scarred ex-soldier, or a child, or a widowed detective, or a weedy mohawked genius punk with big tits. There are scenes in which one of Miranda Zero's operatives charges into a crisis scene and deputizes everybody in sight. "You're all on the Global Frequency now."

All of you. Citizen operatives. Saving the world.

I think the thematic freight there is plainest in a single wonderful

panel near the end of the issue entitled "The Run," in which our protagonist for this particular episode – a parkour traceuse named Sita Patel
– is climbing the outside of the London Eye to reach a terrorist armed
with a biological weapon. A little subcontinental Indian girl, clutching
her father's hand, sees her – and cries out – "Daddy, look. Spider-Man's
a girl. And she's just like us."

She's just like us. In Snowtown, in London, in New York, in Tokyo
– anywhere we go. Spider-Man's the everyman hero, the banal hero,
the guy with a dayjob saving the world because it's the right thing to do.
And so is Sita Patel.

And she's on the Global Frequency.

And if we're honest with ourselves, so am I. And so are you.

Crush on a Superhero

Colleen Doran is an illustrator, film conceptual artist, cartoonist, and writer whose published works number in the hundreds. Her clients include The Walt Disney Company, Lucasfilm, Marvel Entertainment, DC Comics, Dark Horse Comics, and many others.

I had a crush on Aquaman when I was a little girl.

I saw him in the 7-11 store, on the cover of a comic book, the King Arthur of the Seven Seas in goldfish colored hues. He was handsome and noble and ruled three-fourths of the Earth. What more could a girl want?

Aquaman cost twenty-five cents, which was the price of five recycled bottles. I spent hours scouring the gutters and trash bins fishing for cash so I could reel in the Aquacutie catch.

Lucky me found a pile of discarded comics under the school bleachers, and added them to my stash. Wrinkled and coverless, to me they were treasure... but Peter Parker as Spider-Man was not nearly as smoochtacular as Arthur Curry/ Aquaman.

Then we moved away from the city, and my parents tossed my comic book hoard in the trash.

Oh, woe.

I didn't see a comic book again for years. Our little town of 1,500 people didn't even have a magazine stand at the local store.

I settled for Saturday morning cartoons. The *Super Friends* show restored Aquaman's prime place in my Temple of Crushdom, and even though the writers did not seem to have a clue what to do with a super powered being who ruled most of the planet, he was still blonde and wore a shiny gold top, so I was content.

I eventually forgot comic books existed. The 7-11 stores stopped carrying them, and mom and pop stores went out of business everywhere. No newsstand carried comics anymore.

When I was 12 years old, I got a bad case of pneumonia. A friend of my dad dropped by with a huge box of comics for my entertainment. One shot of my old habit, and I was hooked again. Stories made with pictures, exciting images, cosmic turmoil, and romance!

However, this pile of mostly Marvel books had a darker, more intense sensibility than my old DC Comics. And the guys weren't as cute.

Captain America had some sort of identity crises and became Nomad. Peter Parker was such a loser that no matter how many people he saved while wearing long johns, he couldn't seem to get a decent apartment. Tony Stark as Iron Man was kind of a jerk. Comic books weren't the colorful escapism I remembered as a very little girl, and none of these had really yummy guys in them. The men snarled a lot. I disliked the stack of *Conan* comics so much that I tossed them in the trash. Later, I found out they were incredibly valuable early issues drawn by Barry Windsor-Smith.

I wanted escapism, and bright colors, and fun, and cute boys to giggle over. I'd started reading comics just in time for them to become dark and gritty.

I'd had enough dark and gritty in real life already.

When I was a little girl, we lived in a small Southern city where black people could not marry white people without getting arrested.

I saw my first riot when I was six, on the steps of my elementary school. My father was a policeman. I ran to him in the middle of the fray shouting, "Daddy! Daddy!" Someone was swinging a chain about, and blood spattered everywhere. Dad shouted, "Go home, Colleen! Go home!" I ducked and dodged my way out of the mess, and quietly walked home. I think I was in shock. Then I went to the bathroom and rinsed the blood out of my little navy sailor dress.

Even though my parents had once been homeless and were still very poor, my father risked his job by refusing to arrest a serviceman and his Asian wife for the crime of miscegenation. People used to shoot at our house, and die in our front yard.

So, I'd had enough of grim and gritty and snarling already.

In Marvel Comics, everybody snarled.

Aquaman was cute and he talked to fish. And he lived in a world where the good guys always won.

I wanted more Aquaman. But Aquaman didn't have his own comic anymore. He was reduced to an also-ran in *Adventure Comics*, and a side-bar in *Justice League*, books to which I had no access except as a tantalizing glimpse in the ads of the few DC Comics I'd been given. The only way to get these treasures was to subscribe.

I developed an intense, temporary interest in babysitting. I'm sure this is why I have no children today. But I earned enough money to buy my first comic book subscription.

The *Super Friends* comic was dreadful, and I wrote the publisher to complain about the art. Even though I was only 12, I had ten people's worth of opinions. DC Comics printed my letter and edited it to be far kinder than I remembered when I wrote it.

My dad popped a gasket when he saw I'd had a letter printed with my name and address in a public forum, certain 342 people he'd arrested were coming for the house. That didn't happen. However, some pervert wrote me asking me for a pair of my panties, and a random convict asked me to be his pen pal.

I did not discuss these disturbing developments with my mom and dad because I really hated it when they were right. And I was afraid they'd make me stop reading comic books. I didn't write any more letters to comics for a long time, but I got an early lesson in just how much unwelcome baggage goes along with being a girl comics fan.

While *Super Friends* the comic was bright and sparkly and cheerful, it also sucked. When you're turning off 12-year-old girls who have hopeless crushes on comic characters, you're doing it wrong. *Super Friends* got a mercy killing after a short run.

So, it was off to *Adventure Comics* and *Justice League* for me.

I read each issue over and over. I read them until their covers disintegrated. I drew pictures from them. I learned how to draw wonky knees, just like Jim Aparo, and plasticene hair, just like Dick Dillin.

I also learned that Aquaman was married, and went into a period of mourning. I'm pretty sure Aquaman was married even when I was a little girl, but I blotted the horror of being separated from my one true love from my mind. And I kept hoping his wife Mera would get hit by a bus. Or a sperm whale.

Comics ate up more and more of my time, and my parents fretted. I spent hours alone drawing and making up stories. Household infractions were punished by the removal of comic book privileges. My subscriptions were snatched from the mail and stored in my parents' closet, where I was not permitted to read them for six solid months. I snuck in and read them anyway. Much tastier when the fruit was forbidden.

While avoiding real life by sneaking into my parents' closet to read comics, real life crept into Aquaman's tale. The real life comics problems I had once rejected, now riveted. Aquaman's baby was slain by the villainous Black Manta, and I sobbed and sobbed. I sobbed so much that my folks came home to my swollen face and red eyes and thought I'd been beaten up in school.

Aquaman and his wife separated, and I felt genuinely sorry.

Over at *Justice League*, writer Steve Englehart pumped new life into the old franchise, bringing soap opera-ish elements and complicated multi-part storylines to the series. I loved all the little character touches: Aquaman ice skating, while the Atom perched on his shoulder. Such a nice break from saving the world.

But what really got my interest was a crossover epic featuring the Legion of Super-Heroes. It was my first introduction to this teen super group from the future, and I was dazzled by the myriad of funky costumes and wild powers. I was skeptical that any of these people were supposed to be teenagers, since they were all drawn to look aged 32, but that didn't matter. I wanted more. And how to get more, living in the land of no-comics-except-by-subscription?

I ached for comics. I pined. I fretted.

Out with my parents scouring the flea markets for antiques, I spotted comics for sale at only 25 cents each. I bought everything I could afford. Tattered and torn, it didn't matter.

By now, my parents glommed on to the fact that my interest in comics wasn't a problem, and had some nifty side benefits: My drawings won awards. While in a bookstore, I found a flier for a science fiction convention where I displayed my art in a show for the first time. I sold every piece I had for sale and landed my first job for an advertising agency.

Now with cash, and old enough to drive a car, I went on a wild comic book buying tear. The only comic shop in the nearest city was a dive where my father had once confiscated child porn. I was forbidden to go there, so I went. The comics were displayed right next to the pneumatic women porn, and once some old guy next to me enjoyed himself a little too much. At first I thought he was having an asthma attack.

Undaunted by pervy customers and pervy old men who wrote asking for my used undies, I forged ahead. Nothing would keep me from my comics, and nothing would stop me from becoming a real cartoonist.

Now devoted to the Legion of Super-Heroes, I ditched the Aquababe for teen hottie Element Lad. He had a bag of character background angst, and curly blonde hair, and a really cool super power: the power to manipulate and change elements. That would make him even more powerful than Superman, IMHO, because he could just turn Superman into kryptonite. That is the sort of thing fangirls think about.

I gleefully shared my comics with my high school friends. I took them to drama club and we read them backstage. I recall one memorable day when we all sat around reading the first issue of *Dazzler*. The book was ghastly, but we dove into it and did live readings, attracted to the idea that a superhero might also want to be an entertainer. Comics got passed around every class. It was subversive fun. We figured out a dozen ways to read them without being caught. Everyone from the quarterback to the cheerleader to the uber-nerd wanted a comic.

One day, my history teacher caught us and scornfully read *The Defenders* aloud in an attempt to shame us with its awful prose. A futile exercise considering the awful prose we had to listen to every time the principal read the daily announcements. No one was deterred from the comics.

I joined clubs and Amateur Press Associations (Apas). In the days before the Internet, fans could only communicate by mail, and APAs were gathering points for that mail. Usually limited to around 50 members, each member created their own zine, sent copies to a central mailer, and the copies were stapled, collated, and shipped to all 50 fans. Fandom wasn't for anyone who had access to a computer, it was of necessity limited to people with intense dedication to obscure subject matter. It took hours, weeks, months to track down favorite comics, and the price on back issues skyrocketed. If you missed an important storyline, you either had to find someone who would trust you to read their own precious copies, or you had to pay through the nose to some comic store run by some guy who spent most of his time scorning you for being a girl and trying to talk you out of whatever it is you wanted to buy. While fans in fan clubs delighted in having girls around, fans running comic shops did not. Apparently our girl cooties devalued our cash.

Perhaps the comic shop of my teen years made a deliberate GIRLS GET OUT decision when he displayed the comics next to the *Playboy*.

After years of loving comics, buying every one I could find, spending countless hours drawing them, joining clubs, going to portfolio reviews and entering contests, the closer I got to pro-dom, the more resistance I encountered, and it was resistance I did not understand at all.

"Girls Don't Read Comics."

I'd read comics for years, I drew comics, I wanted to make comics professionally. Every girl I knew to whom I gave a comic read it with joy. But, for the most part, the people in comics did not really want little girls in comics.

They didn't want to think of them. They didn't want them around.

I got a Marvel Comics company calendar with the names and birth dates of many Marvel employees. There were a number of women on that calendar. So why was I hearing that girls didn't read comics? Surely, *some* girl at Marvel read comics.

And someone at DC sure knew girls read comics. Because one of those APAs I belonged to, *Interlac*, the Legion of Super-Heroes APA, got passed around the DC offices, and spotted by *Legion of Super-Heroes* artist Keith Giffen. He called me up and asked if I'd like to audition to draw the *Legion*.

Hot diggity. My very favorite comic, featuring my very favorite biggest crush superhero!

Alas... too late.

I'd already agreed to sign on with a small press publisher. The letter of agreement I signed wasn't binding, but I still felt I had to honor it. So instead of going right to the big leagues, I spent years toiling for lousy pay at exploitative small press publishers.

And no Element Lad.

But all was not lost. My uber-crush on Element Lad was so well-known, it became a kind of industry joke. My very first job for DC Comics was a pin-up of Element Lad in an issue of *Who's Who*. For nearly 18 years, whenever DC ran a solo story or needed a pin-up of E-Lad, DC Comics came to me for the job. Other comic book artists from Curt Swan to Dave Cockrum sent me sketches of Element Lad bringing me flowers and candy.

My Element Lad uber-crush gave me my big break in comics. From my first scribblings in an APAzine, to my first mainstream comics gig!

So strange, the bizarre mixed messages from the comics world: a little gig here and there, the fun of having the pros you like and respect include you in the comics universe by giving you a connection to the focus of your girly crush... and then the reality that it was an industry that didn't really like or respect girls very much, that deeply resented our presence to the extent that store owners felt comfortable enough telling us our business wasn't welcome, and respected male pros acted like our only purpose in the industry was as potential girlfriend material.

The meme wasn't merely that "Girls Don't Read Comics," it was also that "Girls Could Not Read Comics."

One pro after another pontificated that women weren't visual, that only men could understand the storytelling process. Wasn't that why men were all the greatest designers, greatest cartoonists, greatest film directors?

Men read and enjoy porn. This proves that they are visual, while women reject porn. This proves that they are not visual. Therefore, the dominance of the visual in comics repels women, in the same way porn repels women.

I'm not making this up. I wish I were.

For years, I spent most of my waking hours thinking about, reading and drawing comics. When I became a comics pro, there wasn't a single day at a comics show or an encounter with almost any male pro that didn't devolve into a moratorium on why I should not be there, why I should not do what I wanted to do, or why I should not read comics, or draw them. Even women bought into this mess. To this day, some women bloggers will go on at tedious length about why women don't (or shouldn't) read superheroes.

When boys escape from reality into fiction, comics responds. When girls do, comics recoils.

I dug through the trash to raise money for comics, spent countless hours and days plowing through every dusty box of old papers in every flea market in the county to find comics, and spent 40 hours or more a week after school drawing comics, only to be told "Girls Don't Read Comics."

When I tell young women cartoonists tales of my early days in the biz, they look at me as if I came from the moon. They never experience discrimination, no one avoids them because they're girls, no one tells them they have some sort of visual processing handicap that is somehow estrogen related, no editor tries to crawl up their skirt.

Therefore discrimination against women in comics doesn't exist. I'm really glad it doesn't exist for them, because there are better things to do in life than deal with dumb crap like old farts who didn't want icky girls in the clubhouse.

This icky girl went on to a very nice comics career. I doubt I'd have stuck it out, or even read comics in the first place, if a couple of the characters in them weren't awesomely cute.

So, thanks Aquaman. Our love is true.

Except for the part where I dumped you for Element Lad. But it was great while it lasted. Swim on, little goldfish!

Most superhero tales are just soap operas where people beat each other up. Everything that made Chris Claremont's run on the classic *Uncanny X-Men* tales popular could have given *All My Children* five seasons of hanky material. I don't know a single female comics fan that didn't have an enormous crush on Nightwing, half the readers of the classic *Teen Titans* were swooning teen girls, and even though I think Morpheus is the worst boyfriend ever, Neil Gaiman's *Sandman* was half goth sex appeal.

Get a clue, publishers.

Go ahead, think we're silly girls going pitty pat over fictional characters. Snarl at the *Twilight* fans invading San Diego Comic-Con. Sneer at the manga. Sell to the guy drooling over Dark Phoenix, but recoil from the girl sighing over Gambit.

Something is taking over your industry.

Girls. With big crushes.

Editors' Bios & Acknowledgements

Lynne M. Thomas is the Curator of Rare Books and Special Collections at Northern Illinois University in DeKalb, IL, where she is responsible for popular culture special collections that include the literary papers of over 50 SF/F authors. She is the co-author of *Special Collections 2.0*, with Beth Whittaker (Libraries Unlimited, 2009), as well as academic articles about cross-dressing in dime novels and using libraries to survive the zombie apocalypse. She is perhaps best known as the co-editor of the Hugo Award-winning *Chicks Dig Time Lords* (2010) with Tara O'Shea, and *Whedonistas* (2011) with Deborah Stanish; both books were published by Mad Norwegian Press. Along with the Geek Girl Chronicles book series, Lynne is the editor of *Apex Magazine*, an online professional prose and poetry magazine of science fiction, fantasy, horror and mash-ups of all three. For more about Lynne and her shenanigans, please visit lynnemthomas.com.

Sigrid Ellis is a writer of fiction, non-fiction, and comics; an editor; a parent of two homeschooled children; and an air traffic controller. She lives in Saint Paul, Minnesota, with her partner, their kids, her partner's other partner, and a host of pets both vertebrate and invertebrate. Her work can be found in the online speculative fiction magazine *Strange Horizons* and in Mad Norwegian's *Whedonistas: A Celebration of the Worlds of Joss Whedon by the Women Who Love Them*.

Acknowledgements: Books are the work of many hands, anthologies more so than most. In addition to our friends and family, the editors would like to extend particular thanks to Alisa Bendis, Amanda Conner, Terry Moore, Greg Rucka and Louise Simonson for their time and conversation. We would also like to thank Sean Ausmus, Elizabeth Bear, Michelle Billingsley, Paul Cornell, Kelly Sue DeConnick, Neil Gaiman, Lorraine Garland, Ellen Kushner, Michael Lee, Carla Speed McNeil, Robyn Moore, Tara O'Shea, and Steven A. Torres-Roman for all of their help.

Credits

Publisher / Editor-in-Chief
Lars Pearson

Design Manager / Senior Editor
Christa Dickson

Associate Editor (Chicks Dig Comics)
Damian Taylor

Associate Editor (Mad Norwegian Press)
Joshua Wilson

The publisher wishes to thank...
A very special thank you to Lynne and Sigrid for the time, talent and sweat that they poured into making this book happen – I was always rested comfortably in the knowledge that exactly the right editors had been hired for the job. Thanks are also due to Christa Dickson (my favorite chick who digs comics); Katy Shuttleworth, for providing a cover that knocked it out of the park; and Damian Taylor, whom I suspect smothered all manner of brushfires without my even knowing about it. A very personal and heartfelt thank you goes to Amanda Conner, Colleen Doran, Jimmy Palmiotti, and Mark Waid, who were all immensely supportive of all of my various endeavors back when I was just a little Norwegian (or so it felt at times) at *Wizard* magazine. Thanks to all of the writers who contributed to this book, as well as to Jeremy Bement, Alisa Bendis, Shawne Kleckner, George Krstic, Shoshana Magnet, Cameron and Steph McCoy, Terry Moore, Tara O'Shea, Greg Rucka, Louise Simonson, Robert Smith?, Josh Wilson and that nice lady who sends me newspaper articles.

1150 46th Street
Des Moines, Iowa 50311
madnorwegian@gmail.com
www.madnorwegian.com

And please join the Chicks Dig Comics and Mad Norwegian Press groups on Facebook!